ARCHITECTURE

D0896180

SAN FRANCISCO
THE GUIDE

SALLY B. WOODBRIDGE
JOHN M. WOODBRIDGE FAIA

Design and Illustration   Alexandra Wills

American Institute of Architects/ San Francisco Chapter
101 Productions/ San Francisco

Printed and bound in
the United States of America.

Distributed to the book trade
in the United States
by Charles Scribner's Sons, New York.

Published by 101 Productions
834 Mission Street
San Francisco, California 94103

Library of Congress Cataloging in Publication Data

Woodbridge, Sally Byrne.
  Architecture--San Francisco.

  Includes index.
    1. Architecture--California--San Francisco--
Guide-books.   2. San Francisco (Calif.)--
Buildings--Guide-books.   3. San Francisco
(Calif.)--Description and travel--Guide-books.
I. Woodbridge, John Marshall.
II. Title.
NA735.S35W63   1982   917.94'610453
ISBN 0-89286-204-1   82-14291

Contents

Introduction

Guidebooks do not normally have "themes." Nor should they if they are to serve a broad spectrum of users. But authors inevitably have a point of view. To pretend complete objectivity is both misleading and dull. Our aim in this guide is to list buildings worth looking at. Whether great or small, historic or mundane, known or unknown, we consider them worth looking at both because they are interesting, and occasionally because they are examples of what not to do. Past guides, our own included, have tended to concentrate on famous buildings, famous architects, and what is in fashion. This guide attempts to take a broader look and to help the user assess what is of value to the city as a place to experience, to inhabit, to enjoy.

This concern has led us to discover and present a range of buildings that were not designed for connoisseurs—or for publication—but that do express in interesting and sometimes curious ways the avant-garde ideas of the times. We have also discovered a host of forgotten architects and builders who contributed importantly to the city's architectural heritage.

The fortunate tide of restoration and repainting that has swept the city these past few years makes the exploring of it more rewarding than ever. Our reawakened interest in architectural ornament can be well fed by the wealth of decorative detail that enlivens otherwise very mundane buildings, now lovingly gussied up. It is astonishing to see how many of the current devices of "post-Modernism" were used by some forgotten house designer of 50 to 100 years ago.

Visitors to San Francisco often remark on its sparkling Mediterranean look, the result of sunlight reflecting off the patchwork of low, pastel-colored buildings marching over the hills, their bay windows looking out to the views that seem to be at the end of every street.

Compared to Mediterranean cities, even to eastern cities, San Francisco is young. But its 130-odd years of urban development are nearly all well represented and so present a wide range of architectural history. Although there are fewer architectural landmarks than in Chicago, Boston, or New York, there is an impressive number of good buildings that live well together and repay repeated inspection. In spite of its terrain—even because of it—this is a great city for walking and browsing, and this is what we recommend. Although we believe that all the high spots are included, we think they should be seen in context, because that is what cities are all about.

To look backward from present-day San Francisco—"everybody's favorite city"—to the barren fog-swept headlands that greeted Juan Bautista de Anza and his little band of Spanish settlers in the spring of 1776 requires an enormous leap of the imagination. Only a trip to the still-wild sections of the Point Reyes peninsula can suggest why the Indians shunned the San Francisco peninsula and the Spaniards considered it a hardship post. The scenic topography that seems so glamorous to us was an obstacle exacerbated by the scarcity of water and the almost total absence of tree cover to give shelter from the biting winds.

For nearly 60 years after the Presidio and the mission were established there was hardly any other settlement. About 1835, when William A. Richardson, an Englishman, built his house on what is now Portsmouth Square, the village that was to become the city began. By 1846, when the Treaty of Guadalupe Hidalgo made California part of the United States, the village of Yerba Buena had attracted about 500 North Americans. In 1847, Jasper O'Farrell surveyed the land north and south of Market Street and platted two gridiron plans that extended as far west as Hyde Street and, prophetically, out into the Bay to the east. In the wake of the Gold Rush, the grid was imposed over the hills with more enthusiasm for real estate development than logic. The panoramic views could hardly have been appreciated since the heights were inaccessible to horse and wagon.

Scarcely discouraged by numerous fires and a few warning earthquakes, development pushed more or less evenly westward through the remainder of the century. By 1906, the area bounded by Divisadero on the west, the Bay on the north and east, and 30th Street to the south was well settled, largely with the closely packed two- and three-story wooden houses that are such a distinguishing feature of the city today. Nob Hill and Pacific Heights

Introduction

and the grand boulevards of Van Ness and Dolores were the choice sites for grand mansions. The flatter lands—the Western Addition and most of the Mission district—were built up speculatively by builders using more or less standard plans with an almost endlessly inventive array of facades.

By 1906 the structure of downtown had evolved through a series of disastrous fires to something very similar to that of today. Shopping was concentrated near Union Square, finance and business along Montgomery Street. Most business buildings had four to eight stories. Typically the frames combined heavy timbers and cast-iron columns; the walls were brick sometimes clad with stone but more often with iron cast in varying degrees of elaboration that imitated stone. Such structures had none of the resistance to earthquakes that either the residential wooden balloon frame or the new steel frame offered. Nor were they fireproof, which proved an equal drawback since the real disaster of 1906 was not the earthquake, but the fire. For what the quake did was rupture most of the water and gas lines, causing fires to ignite everywhere at the same time that it crippled the firefighters. By the time the fire was finally contained by dynamiting Van Ness Avenue, it had destroyed all of downtown and most of the close-in residential areas.

Even though the great Chicago architect Daniel Hudson Burnham had providentially provided the city with a new plan in 1904 embodying all precepts of the City Beautiful Movement, the disaster of 1906 was more of a trauma than a turning point in the city's development. The drive to rebuild was just as impetuous and greed inspired as the gold fever that produced it. Things were put back pretty much as they had been with few significant differences. Since the value of the fireproofed steel frame had been proven by the survival of the new skyscrapers, the post-fire business buildings used this structural system to increase their size and height.

The area around downtown became a zone of low- to mid-rise apartments. Many were built in haste to rehouse the homeless; many more were built to house the crowds expected for the Panama-Pacific International Exposition of 1915 that was to celebrate the Panama Canal's completion and the city's rebirth. Single-family houses dominated the streetcar suburbs and the older enclaves of Russian and Telegraph hills.

Implemented by improved transportation, the growing population pushed the city south and west in the post-fire decades. After 1918, when streetcar service through the Twin Peaks tunnel became available to those residing in the Sunset area, development pushed farther west over the sand dunes. While there were exclusive planned developments such as Forest Hill and St. Francis Wood, most of the housing in the Sunset and the Richmond districts was built for those of more modest means. Because of cheap land and low construction costs, builders could build and sell for less, thereby serving the growing demand for suburban living fed by the now-affordable automobile. The flat terrain was carpeted with boxy bungalows. Their stuccoed facades were as varied as their 19th-century counterparts but derived from current Hollywood images based on Mediterranean prototypes and contemporary styles like the Moderne.

Little major construction took place during the Depression. In fact, the skyline remained virtually unchanged from 1930 to 1960. World War II brought all non-defense building to a halt but produced major social upheavals that changed the character of some of the city's older residential and commercial areas. One such was the Western Addition, where large numbers of black defense workers occupied what was already an area in transition, causing further decline of its housing and commercial stock. Serious overcrowding was typical of the poor parts of the city. Because of the flight to the rural suburbia of Marin County and the San Francisco Peninsula, Victorian houses in Pacific Heights were selling for under $15,000.

The 1950s brought urban renewal—or at least the planning for it. So-called blighted areas were treated like cancers to be cut out of the body of the city and replaced with healthy tissue that would bring back urban vitality. Redevelopment areas— the Golden Gateway, the Western Addition, Diamond Heights, and Yerba Buena—were approved,

Introduction

cleared, and left like bombed-out wastelands, which have taken interminable amounts of time to refill. No one worried about historic preservation; too few worried about human relocation. In both categories the devastation was pretty complete.

In the 1960s and 1970s we built what the 1950s had planned. The 1960s saw the beginning of the boom in high-rise office building, which has continued with minor interruptions to the present. This boom has transformed the downtown skyline and brought vast numbers of new office workers in and out of the city each day. At the same time, the resident population of the city has declined, becoming both richer and poorer and much less family based. Recently the high cost of land and new construction has abetted an already flourishing trend toward rehabilitating older buildings, so that today a trip around older residential areas—30 years ago a sobering experience—is a voyage of discovery.

For the visitor with limited time to explore, downtown and the hills immediately around it show San Francisco's image and origins best. Here the juxtaposition of hills and water, high and low rise, mansions and shacks, along with the compactness of it all combine to make a kind of urbanity that exists nowhere else in this country. The cityscape resulting from this combination is so rich and varied that it would be wise not to take this guide as the sum total of architectural interest. The rhythms of bay-windowed fronts and rectilinear backs of white wooden row houses marching over the hills are more satisfying than most high-rise facades. Seen from the surrounding hills, the Baroque and Gothic church towers of North Beach provide vertical accents as effective as some of the great churches of Europe. The city is full of happy accidents, where minor buildings fill major posts in the cityscape. So we urge you to walk, even at the pain of your leg muscles, to enjoy the surprises offered by this improbable conjunction of man and nature: the green of Angel Island seen at the end of a street, the cascade of little wooden houses tumbling down Telegraph Hill into the skyscraper canyon of lower Montgomery Street, or the fog making ethereal and translucent those all too solid towers.

ACKNOWLEDGMENTS

The authors wish to thank the following individuals for their assistance in compiling information for this guide:

Gerald Adams
Ann Bloomfield
Sara Holmes Boutelle
Gray Brechin
Michael Corbett
Randolph Delehanty
Gary Goss
Dennis Keating
Jeremy Kotas
Johnathan Malone
Edward Michael
Dan Solomon
Chris Yip

The authors wish to thank the following people for editorial and production assistance:

David Keitel
Judith Kopec
Ira Saletan
John Wilson
Carolyn Kizer Woodbridge
Diana Woodbridge
Pamela Woodbridge

Introduction

HOW TO USE THIS GUIDE

This guide is organized geographically in a spiral starting at Union Square and spinning counterclockwise out through the Financial District, North Beach, and so on through 18 sections. Each has its own map. In the inner city, the sections are designed to be of more or less walkable scale, with about 60 entries in each. In the outer areas there are often fewer entries spread much farther apart. When there is a likely movement pattern, the entries are numbered in that order, but otherwise the entries are numbered starting in the upper left corner. North is always up, and the maps have been kept as close to the same scale as possible except in the outlying sections that cover larger areas at a smaller scale. Each number on a map is as close to the location of a group of buildings as possible.

San Francisco streets are numbered from east to west and from south to north, north of Market; and from north to south, south of Market. There are 100 numbers in each block (not including alleys). Even numbers are generally on the north side of east-west streets, but the north-south streets vary, reversing north and south of Market. While we have tried to show and label all the streets necessary to get around, a good city map will be helpful, especially in the outlying areas. Alas, we have found no map without errors in this hilly city where streets that look as though they continue in defiance of the terrain sometimes do and sometimes do not.

San Francisco's public transit system covers the city remarkably well, if on somewhat erratic schedules. A none-too-clear bus and trolley map is in the front of the yellow pages; or you can call 673-MUNI for information. BART runs along Market and Mission, then southwest to Daly City. BART maps are very clear. The Muni trolleys run along Market and then far out west of Twin Peaks to provide good coverage of the Sunset. Busses run in all directions. Cable cars run on California and on Powell to Mason or Hyde. But walking, particularly for architectural sightseers, is the best way to see the city.

Weather has an enormous effect on sightseeing. San Francisco weather puzzles even natives. At the risk of being proven wrong as often as not, here are some suggestions. The fog in summer tends to blanket the city in the late afternoon and burn off in the mid-morning, although it often lingers all day in the westernmost areas. The most fog-free areas are the Mission district and the eastern edge of the city away from the Golden Gate. Winter weather is either clear all over or overcast all over. The hills and the water's edges can be very windy and cold even on a summer day. It is almost never what anyone other than a San Franciscan would call hot. Although the fog can be damp, it virtually never rains between May and October. It does rain a lot in the winter, especially from January to March.

All of the buildings listed in this guide are visible from a public thoroughfare. In no way does the listing of any building imply that anyone has the right to trespass on private property or that it is open to visitors. Houses, museums and monuments that are open to the public are so indicated in the listings. Their hours should be checked by phone.

We would have liked to illustrate every building, but with the number of entries in this guide that was clearly impossible. Instead of emphasizing the familiar, we have opted to show unusual examples or buildings which might be difficult to describe. The most common architectural styles are illustrated or explained in the glossary in the back of the book.

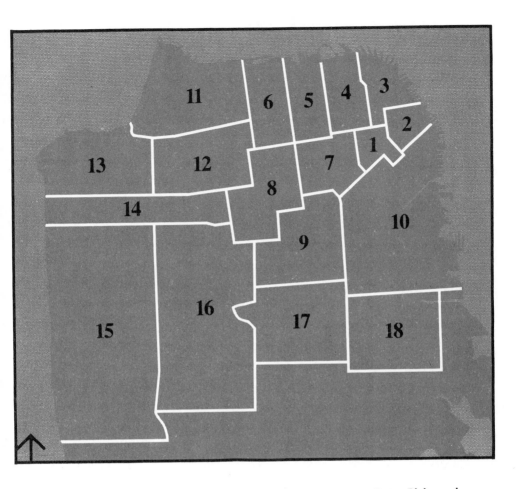

1 Union Square

2 Financial District

✓ 3 Chinatown
Telegraph Hill
North Beach

4 Nob Hill
Russian Hill

5 Pacific Heights
Inner Marina

6 Pacific Heights
Outer Marina

7 Civic Center
Western Addition I

8 Haight Ashbury
Western Addition II

9 West Mission

10 South of Market
East Mission
Potrero Hill

11 Presidio

12 Inner Richmond
Presidio Heights

13 Outer Richmond

14 Golden Gate Park

15 Outer Sunset

16 Twin Peaks West
Inner Sunset

17 Outer Mission
Diamond Heights

18 Bernal Heights
Bayview

1
Union
Square

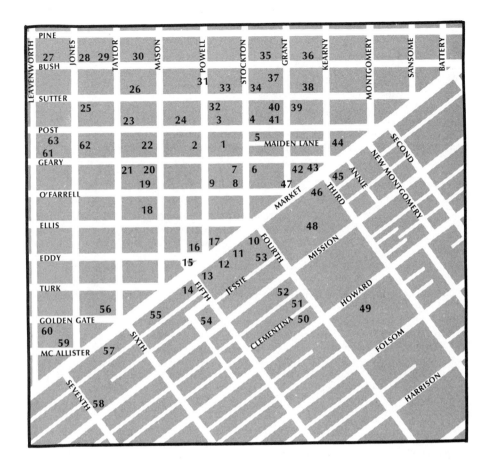

U nion Square (1) has been the heart of San Francisco's shopping and hotel district since well before the 1906 earthquake leveled its first commercial buildings. Laid out in 1850 during the mayoralty of John W. Geary, the informal grassy plot, then the heart of a residential district, acquired its name in the 1860s when pro-Union rallies were held there. Its civic status was further assured by the erection of the monument to Admiral Dewey's 1898 victory over the Spanish at Manila Bay. The 90-foot high column was designed in 1901 by Robert Aitken, sculptor, and Newton Tharp, architect. It survived both the 1906 disaster and the 1942 transformation of the square into the first-ever under-park garage designed by Timothy Pflueger in cooperation with the city park department. Built in wartime, the concrete structure was meant to double as a bomb shelter. Covering it, minimal but effective landscaping has room for a wide cross-section of urban population and for seasonal floral displays that contribute to the square's festiveness.

Around the square and on the adjacent blocks is one of the most compact and varied retail cores in the country, remarkably unaffected by the post- World War II flight of shopping to the suburbs.

The buildings on the square are a generally undistinguished but agreeable hodgepodge covering the period from 1906 on. What unity it had in the past in terms of height and scale has not survived the square's recent development.

The west side is defined by a single building, the St. Francis Hotel; it is also the oldest building on the perimeter of the square, with part of its structure antedating the earthquake. The four dark-gray rusticated wings are perfect in scale and dignity for downtown's major square, even though they are now overshadowed by the towers behind them.

3

1 Union Square

The north side has the most complicated recent history. Until 1980, there stood at the northwest corner a fitting mate for the St. Francis, the Fitzhugh Building. The Planning Commission chose its 140-foot height as a limit for the square. The economics of the time seemed also to dictate this height as reasonable for the future. The Qantas Building next door to the Fitzhugh adhered to the limit, but the same architects were unable to persuade the Hyatt Hotel to build a 140-foot pavilion on the square in front of their tower. Instead they settled for a triangle of commercial space on Post Street that matched the lower height of Bullock and Jones. Just short of a decade later, a long battle to save the Fitzhugh Building was lost; the Saks Building that replaced it did not match either height.

All this suggests that the framing of an urban square in the manner of Paris's Place Vendome is still best done the way it was done there: by building all the facades first.

On the square's east side the signs are more important than the architecture. A great loss is the old City of Paris's Eiffel Tower sign at the southwest corner. Bisecting this side is a narrow pedestrian street that was once a notorious "red light" alley lined with prostitutes' cribs; it is now a decorous shopping mall euphemistically called Maiden Lane.

The heavily remodeled south side of the square retains a relatively uniform height. I. Magnin and Company, the most architecturally distinguished building, anchors the southwest corner along with Johnson/Burgee's new Neiman-Marcus store on the site of the old City of Paris. Powell Street, where the cable car reigns, is introduced by two worthy buildings—that is, if you raise your eyes above their ground floors. The more commanding one is G.A. Lansburgh's 1908 Elkan Gunst Building, 301 Geary.

This brief review of Union Square's development suggests that commercial vitality, not architecture, is its most significant aspect. Indeed, the economic advantage of being "on the Square" has furnished the impetus to change its character over the years, even in the face of considerable opposition.

2 St. Francis Hotel
1904-07, 1913, Bliss & Faville
Hotel Tower
1972, William Pereira
301-45 Powell St.

Gutted in the 1906 fire, the hotel was restored and enlarged by the architects who built it. In 1913, an addition on the Post Street end altered its symmetrical E shape. Typical of the Renaissance revival then in vogue is the Italian palazzo treatment concentrated in the upper stories capped by an ornate cornice, and in the ground floor arcade. Wide, rusticated bands running up the midsection tie the top and bottom together. The elegance of the ground floor arcade extends across the sidewalk to the light standards, presumably designed by Bliss & Faville, and the boxed trees.

3 Saks Fifth Avenue
1981, Hellmuth, Obata & Kassabaum
364-84 Post St.

When the Fitzhugh Building stood on this site there was a nice counterpoint be-tween the elaborate decoration of the older facades and the planar severity of the new ones. With the completion of Saks, the melody is gone.

Qantas Building
1972, Skidmore, Owings & Merrill
350 Post St.

Designed as a background building between its two ornate Classical neighbors, Qantas now looms blandly over the new Saks.

Bullock & Jones store
1923, Reid Bros.
370 Post St.

Hyatt on Union Square
1972, Skidmore, Owings & Merrill
345 Stockton St.

A well-mannered design that put commercial space back on the square while creating a plaza that is mostly unshaded. A special delight is the fountain set into the plaza steps. Designed by Ruth Asawa, the bronze reliefs on the drum were cast from "baker's clay," a flour, salt, and

3. North side of Union Square

6. Neiman-Marcus, dome from City of Paris

water dough modeled by family members, neighbors, and scores of schoolchildren into scenes of San Francisco.

4 Joseph Frederick's & Co.
1910, D.H. Burnham & Co.
Willis Polk, designer
278-99 Post St.

A good example of a neo-Classical commercial building in which the "architecture" was designed to ride above the changing shop front.

Gumps
1861
Rem. 1908, Clinton Day
246-68 Post St.

Originally dating from 1861, but remodeled extensively after the fire. No one who has heard of it needs to be told to visit this store, where good taste costs more and more, but is made to seem worth every penny.

5 Helga Howie Boutique (formerly V.C. Morris)
1949, Frank Lloyd Wright
140 Maiden Lane

This store has preserved the spatial magic that anticipated the Guggenheim Museum's celebrated interior. One of the city's internationally famous architectural masterworks.

6 Neiman-Marcus
1982, Johnson/Burgee
SE corner Stockton and Geary sts.

Replacing a beloved landmark, the 1896/1908 City of Paris store by Clinton Day and Bakewell & Brown, this design preserves the latter's great stained-glass rotunda, modeled on turn-of-the- century Parisian department stores, but not in its original central position. Though many remain unconvinced, the architects and owners held that the old building could not be made to work as a modern department store because the rotunda in the middle left too little usable space per floor. In any case, the comfortably open ground floor arcade and the diversified facade have been replaced by a stylish packing crate that may deliver more for commerce than for architecture.

7. I. Magnin

7 I. Magnin
1946, Timothy Pflueger
233 Geary St.

This elegant skin, hung on a 1905 office building frame, was made flush to keep off the pigeons who, as Union Square's most numerous residents, should after all influence its architecture. The design was so successful with shoppers and so discouraging to pigeons that it was echoed in the Seattle store.

8 Macy's
1928, Lewis Hobart
101 Stockton St.

Rising above a marble-clad base, the conventionally composed pier-and-spandrel walls that retain their windows have the kind of eye appeal that is sadly lacking in the blank modern additions to the store on Union Square.

9 Commercial Building
1933
200-16 Powell St.

A sculptural jewel box, now somewhat mutilated, that is a Moderne remodeling of a shop in the previous decade's stylish mode of Spanish Mediterranean.

Market Street
Our first look at Market Street takes in the retail area, which, having risen with confidence after 1906, declined in the Depression and post- World War II suburbanization of living and shopping. After generous injections of cash the area is once more on the rise. The architecture of the blocks between Fourth and Fifth and Stockton and Powell streets has the kind of authority a great street deserves.

10 The Pacific Building
1907, C.F. Whittlesey
801-23 Market St.
The West Bank Building
1908, C.F. Whittlesey
800-30 Market St.

The Pacific Building's form and decorative detail recall Chicago's Carson Pirie Scott Store, despite the loss of its cornice and original ground floor, now being restored. Particularly arresting is the color scheme of green tile and cream terracotta over a red tile base, which the architect employed "because the climate of our city is decidedly gray." Across the street, the West Bank Building, also originally by Whittlesey, has nothing left but the form to link it to the original Sullivanesque design. Whittlesey worked for Sullivan in Chicago before coming west.

11 Commercial Building
1908, Lewis Hobart
825-33 Market St.

A respectable companion to the buildings on either side of it, Hobart's design observes the cornice line of its neighbors with a row of projecting balconies. As usual, ground floor remodelings have left the older architecture above with nothing to stand on.

12 The Emporium
1896, Joseph Moore
1908, Albert Pissis
835-65 Market St.

Only the facade survives from Moore's original pre-fire building, which housed stores, offices, and the California Supreme Court. Using a strategy we now associate with historic preservation, Pissis kept the existing facade and designed the department store behind it. The rotunda has been recently restored and the gray sandstone facade repainted in a color scheme reminiscent of Georgian London.

13 Lincoln Realty Building
1908, D.H. Burnham & Co./Willis Polk
9-41 Fifth St.

Of the two buildings that anchor the south side of this important Market Street intersection, this one is the most compromised by ground floor alterations and signs, largely from 1944.

14 Hale Bros. Department Store
1912, Reid Bros.
901-19 Market St.

A commercial palace in the best Renaissance-Baroque tradition, this building, last occupied by J.C. Penney, is unaltered except for the removal of the ground floor belt cornice and the elegant glass and metal canopy that projected over the main entranceway. In the coming restoration we hope these losses will be regained.

16. Bank of America/17. James Flood Building

15 Hallidie Plaza
Lawrence Halprin & Assoc.
Powell St. BART Station
1973, Skidmore, Owings & Merrill

One of the city's oldest transportation modes, the cable car, meets the newest one, the Bay Area Rapid Transit, at this important juncture of Powell and Fifth streets with Market. This was always an important transportation node. The San Francisco-San Mateo Interurban line, 1903-49, ended near Fifth and Market; the network of the Market Street Railway Company's lines served the area from all over, at one time requiring four tracks on the street. In the 1970s, the city took advantage of the construction of BART to change the street pattern by extending Fifth across Market to connect with the north grid and by closing the end of Eddy to vehicles. A sunken plaza, named for cable car inventor Andrew S. Hallidie, was created to give access to the station. The idea was to woo a sophisticated public to Market Street by creating two pleasant, protected outdoor rooms, using costly and durable materials, where civic entertainment would take place. For the

most part, fine and civil buildings strengthen the space. However, its social use does not yet conform to the visions of planners, architects, and members of the business community. Instead of the measured trend of urbanites parading the latest taste, the area resounds to the harangues of evangelists and the wild beat of street musicians while people sleep on the benches. Except for tourists waiting for the cable car, the milling crowd doesn't appear to have much disposable income. Distressing as this situation is to those who had hoped to gain a safe precinct for people of means, this is a place where center- city public life is revealed in all its complexity. If Market Street's present gentrification trend continues, this hurly-burly scene may vanish along with those who produce it. See it while it lasts!

16 Bank of America
1920, Bliss & Faville
1 Powell St. at Hallidie Plaza

A handsome neo-Renaissance palace designed fittingly for the Bank of Italy (now Bank of America). Bliss & Faville's competition-winning design testifies to their admiration for McKim, Mead & White's University Club in New York. The architects economized by cladding the building's base in granite and the rest in the less expensive terra-cotta. The entrance sculpture is by John Portonavo; the interior is also worth seeing for its decorative detail, particularly on the ceiling.

17 James Flood Building
1904, Albert Pissis
870-98 Market St.

Virtually complete in 1906, the Flood Building was considerably damaged by the fire. The rounded corner element is boldly articulated, but in a different way from Whittlesey's buildings at the other end of the block. The engaged colonnade is a leitmotif picked up in the Emporium across the street and in the former Hale Brothers Store. Though the elegant ground floor entrance now wears a dull mask, the building still gives, in the architect's words,"a touch of grandeur to Market Street."

In front of 856 Market Street stands the Albert S. Samuels Clock, created in 1915

1 Union Square

by Samuels and Joseph Mayer and now sadly inoperative thanks to repeated vandalizing. Until 1943 it stood in front of the Samuels Jewelry shop in the Lincoln Building across the street.

18 San Francisco Hilton Hotel
1964, William Tabler
1971, John Carl Warnecke
201 Mason St.

The 1964 hotel looks like an L.A. import; the 1971 aluminum-clad tower rises discreetly above its lackluster base and has dominated the skyline in this part of town for over a decade. Plans are now underway in Warnecke's office for a major addition that will put the Hilton in possession of the whole block and increase its capacity to about 2,000 rooms.

19 Downtown Center Garage
1954, George A. Applegarth
325 Mason St.

A double spiral ramp at the corner provides a well-placed climax for this straightforward, uncluttered structure, one of the last works of a well-known Beaux-Arts architect.

20 Geary Theatre
1909, Bliss & Faville
415 Geary St.
Curran Theatre
1922, Alfred H. Jacobs
445 Geary St.

The city's two leading theaters reveal the versatility of the Classical language of architecture. The facades have the same format, but the proportions and ornamental detail are sufficiently different to make each one a distinctive composition.

21 Clift Hotel
1913, MacDonald & Applegarth
1926, Schultze & Weaver
491-99 Geary St.

One of the most lavish of the many hotels built nearby in anticipation of the incoming crowds for the 1915 Panama-Pacific International Exposition. The client was a lawyer, Frederick Clift, for whom there was a "stone bungalow" suite on a upper floor. (Photographs of the original interiors are in a case on the mezzanine.) In 1926, Schultze & Weaver, architects for

the Hunter-Dulin Building (2:9), the Waldorf Astoria and Sherry Netherlands hotels in New York, and the Biltmore in Los Angeles, designed a 240-room addition. The exterior treatment remained the same; the heavy cornice is now gone. G.A. Lansburgh designed two of the present interiors, the Parisian Room and the Redwood Room. The latter was done in 1935 in collaboration with Anthony Heinsbergen, another prominent theater designer, and is one of downtown's most elegant public rooms in the Moderne style. Across the street is the Bellvue Hotel of 1908 (S.H. Woodruff). Except for the Chateauesque fireplace in the lobby, the interior does not match the the-atricality of the exterior.

22 Native Sons Building
1911, Righetti & Headman/E.H. Hildebrand
414-30 Mason St.

Yet another version of the Renaissance-Baroque palazzo, the favorite model for pre-World War I downtown business blocks. This one is worth scrutinizing for its finely textured brick walls, graceful top floor loggia, and decorative detail, including panels by Jo Moro on the mezzanine.

San Francisco Water Department
1922, Willis Polk & Co.
425 Mason St.

A similar composition to the one across the street, but comparatively restrained in the use of materials and decorative detail. However, note that the ground floor facade drips with stony water, which even runs over the keystone above the entrance arch. Inside the business office are murals by Maynard Dixon. The original client for the building was the Spring Valley Water Company, owned by William Bourn, Willis Polk's best patron. His fine house, also by Polk, is 5:27 at 2550 Webster Street.

23 Bohemian Club
1934, Lewis Hobart
625 Taylor St.
Olympic Club
1912, Paff & Baur
524 Post St.
Two of the city's distinguished club buildings. While the latter rests firmly in the Ecole des Beaux-Arts academic Classical tradition, the former conveys the same exclusiveness with a touch of the Moderne. The bronze and terra-cotta plaques are by Carlo Taliabua, Haig Pattigan, and Jo Moro, prominent local artist-members of this colorful institution.

The following group of four buildings was designed by some of San Francisco's most prominent practitioners during the first quarter of the 20th century. Because of their range of size and building type they are interesting to compare both with each other and with other examples of these architects' work.

24 First Congregational Church
1913, Reid Bros.
491 Post St.
Medico-Dental Building
1925, George Kelham/William G. Merchant
490 Post St.
Elks Club
1924, Meyer & Johnson
450-60 Post St.
Chamberlain Building
1925, Arthur Brown, Jr.
442-44 Post St.
Two massive imposing fronts followed by a sliver of a largely glazed facade that wears a filligreed fire escape.

25 Belgravia Apartments
1916, Frederick H. Meyer
795 Sutter St.

26 Metropolitan Club
1916, 1922, Bliss & Faville
640 Sutter St.
Originally the Women's Athletic Club, the design invites comparison with Hobart's later Bohemian Club, entry 23.

YWCA
1918, Lewis Hobart
620 Sutter St.

27 Apartments
1914, 1912
1086, 1060 Bush St.
Two that stand out from the rest in the block, but in fact form part of the great collection of post- fire apartment buildings that were built in a hurry on the south slopes of Nob Hill.

28 Apartments
1909, Frederick H. Meyer
980 Bush St.
Apartments
1914, Grace Jewett
972 Bush St.
Two substantial Renaissance Revival apartment buildings, the latter by one of the very few women architects in practice at this time.

29 The Galleria
1981, Kaplan, McLaughlin & Diaz
NW corner Taylor and Bush sts.
A large, well-designed contemporary building that does not overwhelm its neighbors; beside the building at 828 Taylor, 1914, you can glimpse a garden retreat tucked away inside the block.

30 Dennis T. Sullivan Memorial Fire Chief's Home
1922
870 Bush St.
This building owes its existence to the fact that the fire chief at the time of the 1906 earthquake, Dennis T. Sullivan, was killed when the firehouse in which he lived shook apart. The memorial fund commemorating this tragedy was used to build a new home designed to resemble a firehouse. The architect, alas, is unknown.

31 The Family Club
1909, C.A. Meussdorffer
545 Powell St.
Town house
1911, C.A. Meussdorffer
535 Powell St.
Chesterfield Apartments
1911
560 Powell St.

Academy of Art College
(originally Elks Building)
1909, A.A. Cantin
540 Powell St.
Built within two years of each other, these four buildings exhibit a wild variety of styles. The two by Meussdorffer illustrate his skill and confidence in rendering two period styles; the town house is a rare survivor in downtown. Both buildings have outstanding ornamental detail. Cantin's Elks Building improbably combines Classic and Mission Revival.

32 Sir Francis Drake Hotel
1928, Weeks & Day
432-62 Powell St.
Gothic motifs are freely used here to accentuate the hotel's stepped-back form, made fashionable by New York's 1918 zoning law for tall buildings. The glazed void below the crown is the 1947 remodeling of a penthouse apartment that preceded the Starlight Roof, a bar with a great city view.

33 Medical-Dental Office Building
1929, Miller & Pflueger
450 Sutter St.
One of the city's most admired office towers, its undulating wall inspired that of the Bank of America Building, entry 16. The skyscraper's low budget dictated the use of terra-cotta instead of stone, and the minimal lobby. Though the smooth continuous piers give the structure a vertical emphasis, the woven beveled spandrels and corners create the appearance of a skin or wrapper that was prophetic of today's notions of how to dress tall buildings.

34 Sutter-Stockton Garage
1960, John Lord King
1977, Sokoloff, Hamilton & Bennett
330 Sutter St.
The garage , whose base is lined with shops, is next to the Stockton Street tunnel entrance, a Classical triumphal arch adapted for vehicular traffic. The 1914 tunnel was part of the municipal improvement program instigated by City Engineer Michael O'Shaughnessy to handle traffic flow to the Panama-Pacific International Exposition.

33. Medical-Dental building, 450 Sutter

35 Notre Dame des Victoires
1913, Louis Brouchoud
564 Bush St.
This church occupies the site of the city's first French church; it is more significant as a center of San Francisco's influential French colony than as architecture.

San Francisco Environmental Center
1916, W. Garden Mitchell
1982, Storek & Storek
530 Bush St.
An exemplary project that involved both historic preservation, in the conversion of a 1916 steam generating plant into office and retail space, and energy-conscious design, next door in a ten-story office building that was the first to use both active and passive solar energy systems. The array of solar collectors is integrated with the building envelope on the upper floors.

36 S.F. Fire Station No.2
1909, Newton J. Tharp
466 Bush St.
Appropriately the city's first fireproof structure erected after the 1906 disaster, this fine example of civic monumentality also perfectly expresses its function: housing motorized equipment downstairs and human beings upstairs. A formal gateway to Chinatown was created here in 1976.

37 Pacific Telephone & Telegraph
(formerly Home Telephone Co.)
1908, Ernest Coxhead
333 Grant Ave.
A facade composed of boldly scaled Classical elements in projected and recessed forms. Coxhead's skill at manipulating the Classical vocabulary is nowhere better shown than in the entrance composition, where an elegant portal with a swan-necked pediment is fused with an arch tied at the top by an outsized keystone to the belt cornice above. Don't miss the capitals of the giant columns.

37. Pacific Telephone & Telegraph

38 Goldberg Bowen Building
1909, Meyers & Ward
250-54 Sutter St.
Bemiss Building
1908
266-70 Sutter St.
Two commercial buildings that invite comparison. Bemiss's elegant, almost Miesian steel frame capped by a fringed metal valance accommodates what may have been the largest sheets of glass then available. The Goldberg Bowen Building's architects chose to gussy up the brick frame with piers that erupt in floral bouquets at the cornice. The more restrained base retains the sockets for electric bulbs that once framed the display windows with light.

39 The White House
1908, Albert Pissis
255 Sutter St.
In 1968 an uncommon preservation strategy converted what was once one of the city's two major French department stores into a parking garage with shops on the ground floor. Unfortunately it is not well maintained. This store was the home of the Raphael Weill Company, which started here in the dry goods business in 1885.

40 Sutter's Corner
1907
301-3 Sutter St.
An improbable relic from the post-quake downtown that makes much of its small scale, like a music box with a fancy lid.

41 Shreve Building
1905, William Curlett
201 Grant Ave.
Hastings Building
1908, Meyer & O'Brien
180 Post St.
Phoenix Building
1908, George A. Applegarth
220-8 Grant Ave.
Head Building
1909, William Curlett & Sons
201-9 Post St.

Rochat Cordes Building
1909, Albert Pissis
126-30 Post St.

Five solidly respectable buildings, the first four of which compose a gateway to the heart of the shopping district to the west. The Shreve Building is both the most intact and the most luxurious in terms of materials, being sheathed with Colusa limestone. While the Hastings Building, also well preserved, has the most elaborate ornamentation, the Phoenix makes a simple but eloquent statement with its square windows set like transparencies in delicate floriate frames. The Podesta Baldocchi florist shop, a city landmark of its kind, is a paradisiacal experience.

42 Grant-Geary Center
1912, William Mooser
1917, Frederick H. Meyer
1929, Bliss & Fairweather
1983, Storek & Storek
50 Grant Ave.

A much worked-over building that is remarkably coherent. The latest remodeling will preserve the exterior and enhance the energy-conservation potential of the structure with the addition of passive and active solar systems. Storek & Storek used the same approach in entry 35 on Bush Street.

43 Citizens Savings
1902, 1906, William Curlett
Add. 1964, Clark & Beuttler
704 Market St.

Charles W. Moore and Alan Morgan, designers of the corner addition, echoed the form of the highly decorated older building in a way that is clearly contemporary. The structure turns the corner by making a major element of the stair tower.

44 Chronicle Building
1889, Burnham & Root
1962, Hagman & Meyer
690 Market St.

The original design, now covered with sheet metal, was one of two local buildings by this famous Chicago firm of the first skyscraper era.

43. Citizens Savings

44. Original Chronicle Building

Lotta's Fountain
1875, Wyneken & Townsend
Kearny and Geary sts. at Market St.
Lotta Crabtree, the most highly paid American actress of her day, spent most of her professional life touring, but she retired in 1891 to San Francisco. Her $4 million fortune went to charity; the best-known gift is this fountain, which had its shaft lengthened in 1915 by eight feet to better match the Market Street light standards.

45 Hearst Building
1909, Kirby, Petit & Green
691-99 Market St.
Of the three newspaper buildings once on this intersection, this is the only one still in use by the original client. (It replaced a romantic composition by A.C. Schweinfurth, destroyed in the 1906 fire.) *Splendid Survivors'* text notes that the existing building is a reduced version of the New York firm's design, which had an impressive crown topped by a colossal clock tower. Certainly the large-scale, colorful cresting above the cornice suggests a wedding cake—too bad the funds ran out. The entrance also shows off terra-cotta's capacity for exuberance.

46 Central Tower
(formerly Call Building)
1938, Albert Roller
703 Market St.
Though acceptable Moderne, this remodeling is a pale echo of the Reid Brothers' 1898 neo-Baroque design. With its domed tower bristling with oeil- deboeuf dormers and domelets, the original Call Building was no doubt designed to outclass the older Chronicle Building. If the plans had been fulfilled, all three of the buildings would have had flamboyant towers to signal their competitive power. With the passing of the *Call* and the merging of the *Chronicle* and the *Examiner*, it is fitting that the buildings too have been altered beyond recognition.

47. Wells Fargo & Security Pacific banks

47 Wells Fargo Bank
1910, Clinton Day
744 Market St.
Security Pacific National Bank
1910, Bliss & Faville
1 Grant Ave.
Phelan Building
1908, William Curlett
760-84 Market St.
Humboldt Bank Building
1906, Meyer & O'Brien
783-85 Market St.
A vintage Market Street intersection framed by buildings erected within four years of each other. One day they will be contoured by the gateway to the long-awaited Yerba Buena Center complex. The two smaller buildings illustrate the versatility of Beaux-Arts Classicism as well as the enduring power of the Pantheon as a prototype for religious and financial temples. The Wells Fargo has a rich, sculptural facade and an equally opulent gold and white interior. Across the street, the Phelan Building, built by a famous mayor and U.S. senator, is a fine traditional rendering of the steel-framed flatiron structure sheathed in terra-cotta. The Humboldt Bank Building is a smaller and less flamboyant version of the 1898 Call Building.

48 Yerba Buena Center/Gardens
1968/87, Zeidler Roberts Partnership/
Willis & Assoc.
Lawrence Halprin/Omi-Lang Assoc.,
landscape architects
Market St. to Folsom St.,
Third St. to Fourth St.
Jessie Street Substation
1905, 1907, 1909, Willis Polk
222- 26 Jessie St.

49. *George R. Moscone Convention Center, Photo: Peter Henricks*

St. Patrick's Church
1872
Interior rem. 1907, Shea & Lofquist
756 Mission St.
Aronson Building
1903, Hemenway & Miller
700 Mission St.

**49 George R. Moscone
Convention Center**
1981, Hellmuth, Obata & Kassabaum
T.Y. Lin, structural engineer
Howard St. to Folsom St.,
Third St. to Fourth St.

50 Clementina Towers
1966, John Bolles & Assoc.
10 Clementina St.

51 Woolf House
1979, Robert Herman & Assoc.
SW corner Howard and Fourth sts.
Spanning three blocks that have long
been an urban wasteland, this 25-acre
parcel is the lodestone of an 86-acre redevelopment area. In the late 1960s a design team headed by Kenzo Tange, with
Gerald McCue, John Bolles, and Lawrence Halprin, prepared a plan for a convention facility interlocked with office
and hotel structures. Lyman Ju was se-

lected as master developer. In spite of the
Redevelopment Agency's entrepreneurial
efforts, the plan was mired in endless
lawsuits over housing for the area's displaced citizens, largely single, elderly
people who had occupied the many residential hotels. Though the replacement
housing problem was never solved, some
projects were built. The most praisewor-
thy example is Woolf House, named for
George Woolf, a neighborhood hero and
leader of the Tenants and Owners Development Corporation, which battled the
Redevelopment Agency over housing. Although Woolf House appears traditional
because of its bay windows, the plan is
innovative in that the 112 apartments are
rotated 45 degrees to gain a proper orientation and to integrate with balconies and
bay-window views of the street. In the
late 1970s, an urban design team headed
by John Kriken of Skidmore, Owings &
Merrill, with former Planning Director
Alan Jacobs and Tom Aidala as consultants, worked with the agency to develop
alternative schemes for the central blocks
that, among other things, introduced
housing, devised an open landscape
spine through the blocks' center, and preserved two landmark buildings: St. Patrick's Church and the Jessie Street

1 Union Square

Substation. In 1980, after a competition among several developers who submitted proposals to the city, Canadian developers Olympia & York were selected. Their scheme, designed by the Toronto-based Zeidler Roberts Partnership with local architects Beverly Willis & Associates, will take shape over the next four years. It is conceived as follows: On Market Street the Grant Avenue Concourse will provide access to the first of three blocks with interior garden squares. This one is planned as a market square that, because of its adjacency to St. Patrick's, will recall medieval European town centers. Also facing the square is the rehabilitated Jessie Street Substation, a richly ornamented neo- Classical structure by Willis Polk that is a perfect background building. The Sullivanesque Aronson Building that occupies the northwest corner will become a mercantile center. The new buildings on the block will include an office tower on Market, a 700-room Meridien Hotel on Third Street designed by Architects Associated, and two residential buildings with retail space. New structures combining residential, cultural, recreational, and entertainment uses will frame Festival Plaza, the second mid-block garden square.

Moscone Center, the largely underground convention hall occupying the last block, opened in the fall of 1981. The exhibition hall, which is the size of six football fields, is spanned by eight pairs of arches that not only brace the hall but are designed to support the future rooftop garden and a pair of small buildings. The only distinctive part of the structure visible from the outside is the lobby. Its four large tubular steel trusses are supported at one end by cantilevered arch abutments and at the other end by giant X-braced members. The glass walls and space-frame roof compose a large, airy pavilion with a festive circulation sequence via escalators and granite staircases to the lower level.

52 Yerba Buena West Building
1982, Herzka & Knowles
Fourth St. bet. Mission and Howard sts.

New development continues in the area adjacent to the center blocks. Among the projects in various stages of building at this writing are

Condominiums
1980, Kaplan, McLaughlin & Diaz
Third and Folsom sts.
Hotel
1983, Architects Associated
SW corner Third and Stevenson sts.

53 S.F. Community College
1979, Caudill Rowlett Scott/ROMA
NW corner Fourth and Mission sts.
The Apparel Mart
1981, Whisler-Patri
22 Fourth St.

A good example of a large building discreetly inserted into a mid-block site with minimal impact on the old Pacific Building next door on Market to which it connects.

The Victorian Hotel
c 1915, William Curlett
54 Fourth St.

A better name would be Exposition Hotel, recalling that it was built to capture the family tourist trade to the Civic Center and the grounds of the 1915 Panama-Pacific International Exposition, now the Marina. Located conveniently near major transportation lines such as the San Francisco-San Mateo Interurban Line and the Market Street lines, the hotel plan featured suites on the front for the family and corresponding rooms on the back for servants. The hotels that once occupied the South of Market area in great numbers depended on the trade generated by the Southern Pacific Railroad Station that formerly stood at Third and Townsend. From there train passengers were served by the Market Street Railroad Company, which had a trolley turnaround by the station, itself a splendid monument to California's own Mission Revival style. The station, the trolleys, and most of the hotels have disappeared.

54 The Old U.S. Mint

1869-74, Alfred B. Mullet

Fifth and Mission sts.

When built, the Tuscan-Doric temple style was a bit *retarditaire* compared to Mullet's Second Empire buildings of the same period in Washington and St. Louis. But it was considered to be one of the best appointed mints in the world. Resplendent after a long and complicated restoration by Walter Sondheimer, the Old Mint Museum, a National Landmark opened in 1976, is well worth a visit.

55 Hale Bros. Department Store

1902, 1907, Reid Bros.

979-89 Market St.

Despite a 1930s ground floor remodeling, the building invites comparison with the later Hale Brothers Store, entry 14.

56 Fox Warfield Theatre

1921, G.A. Lansburgh

982-98 Market St.

Golden Gate Theatre

1922, G.A. Lansburgh

42 Golden Gate Ave.

Two combination theater-office buildings designed by the prominent local theater architect who also designed the hall of the Opera House. The Market Street theater district, formerly in these blocks from Fifth to Eighth streets, is experiencing a comeback with the restoration of the Golden Gate Theatre in 1980 and a proposed rehabilitation of the Warfield Building that will retain the theater. Next door to the Golden Gate Theatre at No.50 Golden Gate is an apartment house with remarkable grotesque heads on its facade.

57 Eastern Outfitting Co. Building

1909, George A. Applegarth

1019 Market St.

A remarkable bay-window wall set in one section of a monumental Classical colonnade—too bad it is not a series.

58 U.S. Post Office & District Court of Appeals Building

1902-05, John Knox Taylor

1931 George Kelham

Seventh and Mission sts.

A powerful expression of the Federal authority in neo-Baroque that looks as though it was designed with the Washington D.C. Mall, not San Francisco's Mission Street, in mind. Grand interiors, too.

59 Hibernia Bank

1892, 1905, 1907, Albert Pissis

1 Jones St.

The city's oldest Classic Revival bank, with its colonnade splayed to fit the triangular site and articulated like a folded-out Roman temple. The domed rotunda looks very like a composition Pissis might have refined from his student days at the Ecole des Beaux-Arts in Paris. Don't miss the interior.

60 St. Boniface

1900, Brother Wewer

133 Golden Gate Ave.

57. Eastern Outfitting Company Building

59. Hibernia Bank

61 Alcazar Theatre
1917, T. Patterson Ross
650 Geary St.
A convincing Islamic design and a great surprise on the street. Alas, it is slated for demolition, but the facade may be saved.

62 Gaylord Apartments
c 1925, H.C. Baumann
620 Jones St.
One of Baumann's most important commissions and most elaborate renditions of the Spanish neo-Churrigueresque—for others see 4:35 and 8:50. Baumann drew up the ornament full scale for his crew of Italian craftsmen to execute in plaster, wrought iron, terra-cotta, etc. Ah, those were the days!

63 Hotel Bedford
c 1925
781 Post St.

61. Alcazar Theatre

2 Financial District

1 Palace Hotel, 633 Market
2 Bldgs, New Montgomery
3 PT&T bldg, 134 New Montgomery
4 Aetna bldg, Market; Mechanics' Inst, Post
5 Crocker Northern Hdqtrs, 1 Montgomery
6 Wells Fargo bldg, 2 Montgomery
7 Hobart bldg, 582 Market
8 Office bldg, 595 Market
9 Hunter-Dulin bldg, 111 Sutter
10 French Bank & Hallidie bldgs, Sutter
11 Office bldg, 130 Montgomery
12 Mills bldg & tower, 220 Montgomery
13 Russ bldg, 235 Montgomery
14 Calif Commercial Union, 315 Montgomery
15 Security Pacific Bank, 300 Montgomery
16 B of A World Hdqtrs, 555 California
17 International bldg, 601 California
18 Hartford bldg, 636-50 California
19 Kohl bldg, 400 Montgomery
20 Office bldg, 456 Montgomery
21 Bank of America, 552 Montgomery
22 Transamerica bldg, 600 Montgomery
23 Office bldgs, 695 Mongomery, 343
   Sansome
24 Old Federal Reserve Bank, 400 Sansome
25 Bank of California, 400 California
26 California First Bank, 350 California
27 Insurance Exchange & Merchants Exchange
   Great Western Bank
   433, 465 & 425 California
28 Dollar bldgs, 301, 341 California
29 Royal Globe Insurance Co , 201 Sansome
30 Pacific Coast Stock Exchange, 301 Pine
31 Hong Kong Bank & Adam Grant bldg,
   Sansome
32 Standard Oil bldg, 200 Bush
33 Standard Oil bldg, 225 Bush
34 Crown Zellerbach bldg, 1 Bush
35 One Sansome bldg, Old London Paris Bank
36 Flatiron bldg, 540 Market
37 Standard Oil of Calif., 555 Market
38 Golden Gate University, 540 Mission
39 Transbay Transit Terminal, 425 Mission
40 Shell & Heineman bldgs, 100, 130 Bush
41 Shaklee bldg, 444 Market
42 Industrial Indemnity & Hibernia Bank
   255 & 201 California
43 Tadich Grill, 240 California
44 Daon bldg, 353 Sacramento
45 Embarcadero Center
46 Alcoa bldg, 1 Maritime Plaza
47 Three bldgs, 100, 50, 1 California
48 Itel bldg, 101 California
49 Bechtel/Metropolitan Life complex
50 Pacific Gateway, Mission
51 PG&E, Matson bldg
52 SF Federal Reserve Bank, 100 block Market
53 Southern Pacific bldg, 1 Market
54 Rincon Annex Post Office, 99 Mission
55 Audiffred bldg, 1 Mission
56 Justin Herman Park & Plaza, end of Market
57 Ferry bldg complex, Market & Embarcadero
58 YMCA, 166 Embarcadero

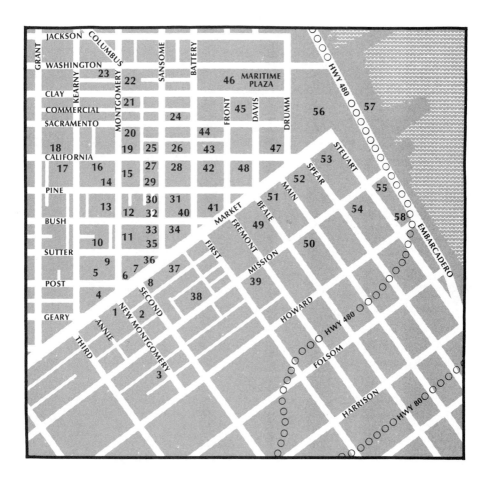

Most of what is now the densest part of the city was once water. The shoreline was roughly at Montgomery Street; the east-west streets ended in wharves. To the south the great diagonal of Market Street was laid out parallel to the road from the Bay to Mission Dolores, and to the north was the original settlement of Yerba Buena around Portsmouth Square, a collection of humble buildings that achieved city status overnight with the discovery of gold. By 1850, a financial district, fed by the Gold Rush, had grown up around Montgomery and Washington streets. The location was convenient both to the Customs House and the gambling houses around Portsmouth Square, and the commercial wharves that extended out into the Bay. These became streets lined with buildings set on the hulks of abandoned ships. During 1850 two devastating fires drove the bankers to remove themselves from crime-infested Sidneytown—at the base of Telegraph Hill—whose denizens had set the fires, and to shift from wooden to more fireproof brick buildings. The more permanent structures were built on choice sites to the south that the fire had cleared. The Customs House also moved to a brick building at Montgomery and California. Other factors contributing to the move south were the improvement of the central wharves of Clay and Sacramento and the cutting through of Commercial Street from the Long Wharf to Kearny. Finally, since in 1850 income from the city's booming service industries surpassed that from gold, the ties to gold revenues from Portmouth Square were loosened.

From 1850 to 1875, banks set the trend for the southward shift along Montgomery toward Market, influencing the relocation of legal services, real estate interests, and stock and insurance brokers. After 1888 the district began to expand vertically, encouraged by the use of the steel frame, which was considered more earthquake resistant. Buildings over ten stories rose on the fringes of the district and on California Street. Even the 1906 disaster did not permanently dislodge the banks from Montgomery and California streets; the intersection is still the district's heart.

Until recently the triangle these two streets make with Market defined one of the country's most compact clusters of skyscrapers. The forest of towers was dense but not overwhelming. Lulled into complacency by the relatively small building sites north of Market and a slow development cycle, the planners retained a permissive high- rise zoning code that allowed a floor-area ratio (FAR) of 25:1 on a corner site (see the Wells Fargo Building entry 6) . A belated reform of downtown codes that lowered the FAR and included the then- popular set of bonuses for plazas failed to halt the march of the giants. In the 1970s, the public finally awoke to "Mahattanization," responding with anti-high-rise initiatives of inspired futility. By now the old scale is gone and the once dramatic contrasts of sun and shadow in the interior blocks are eclipsed. The district's boundaries have pushed out, muscling in on Chinatown, North Beach, and Jackson Square and creating a larger and more ominous forest of towers on the much larger blocks south of Market. Now, a combination of limits on tower-plan dimensions, more restricted height zones, and a fairly stringent project-by-project review has half-closed the door—some would say too late to rescue the once-vivid skyline. Still, it is a more dramatic urban area than most, thanks largely to the surrounding water. At the edges unforgettable contrasts still exist, as when Montgomery Street bursts through its canyon into pre-fire Jackson Square and Telegraph Hill or Nob Hill.

1 Sheraton Palace Hotel

1909, Trowbridge & Livingston
633-65 Market St.

The airy opulence of the landmark Garden Court in this large block recaptures the spirit of William Ralston's first Palace Hotel of 1873, long the West Coast's finest. The warm brick exterior, stitched like a tapestry with terra-cotta ornamental motifs and crowned with a fancy cornice, dignifies the whole block. The city gained one of its most important architects when the New York firm Trowbridge & Livingston sent George Kelham out to supervise the project, and he, like Willis Polk before him, stayed to form his own practice.

2 Buildings

New Montgomery St.

The story of New Montgomery Street is worth recalling in these times when the South of Market blocks are regularly extruding the office towers that the scarcity of land and the high cost of construction have forced out of the north of Market district. A similar condition in the late l9th century inspired William C. Ralston and fellow capitalist Ashbury Harpending

1. Sheraton Palace Hotel

to set up the New Montgomery Real Estate Company, launching a drive to the profitable south-waterfront area where the Pacific Mail Steamship Company had its docks. Rincon Hills, the premier residential suburb, stood in the way, but having already been eroded by industrial development, its days appeared to be numbered. Still, two stubborn millionaires, John Parrott and Milton Catham, stopped the street's progress at Howard by refusing to give up their mansions and property. Although stymied, Ralston and Harpending continued their scheme to make the short spur street the equal of its namesake. But the times were not propitious. The lots, with expensive improvements in lighting, paving, etc., did not sell when offered in 1869. Ralston's response to the bad news was to up the ante by announcing the construction of the world's finest hotel, the Palace, at the head of the street. The hotel's success did not come in time to save Ralston's financial empire, which collapsed with the closing of the Bank of California on August 26, 1875. Ralston drowned mysteriously that afternoon while taking his usual Bay swim.

The street lived on, never matching the projected image of its founders, but managing to accommodate some substantial buildings long before adjoining streets did. Today, future developments once again promise to "up the ante." One project with Kaplan,McLaughlin & Diaz as architects will be the 1 New Montgomery Place Building, a 660,000-square-foot office and residential complex. Hoffman's Grill, 619 Market, a long-favored San Francisco restaurant that opened in 1891 and has been at its present location since 1913, will be reconstructed within the new complex. Notable buildings along the street are

Sharon Building
1912, George Kelham
39-63 New Montgomery St.
A right-angle building that is not much more than a facade on the main street; the ground floor has a colorful old restaurant, the House of Shields.

Call Building
1914, Reid Bros.
74 New Montgomery St.
Originally built for the newspaper industry, the building is anchored at each end by a well- composed and richly detailed neo-Classical pavilion. Its demeanor seems more fitting for the Crocker Bank, which now occupies it, than for its last occupant, the strident *Call Bulletin*.

Rialto Building
1902, Meyer & O'Brien
1910, Bliss & Faville
116 New Montgomery St.
A pre-fire structure rebuilt according to the original design, which broke the mass of the building in two parts by inserting a light well at the front.

3 Pacific Telephone & Telegraph Co.
1925, Miller & Pflueger/A.A. Cantin
134-40 New Montgomery St.
Eliel Saarinen's second-prize design for the Chicago Tribune Tower competition was the main inspiration for this influential skyscraper. Though the building appears as a stepped-back block from New Montgomery Street, it is a notched ell from the southwest, contributing a welcome variety to the skyline. The eclectic yet original system of ornamental detail is well integrated into the building's form. The black marble Moderne lobby is embellished with a stenciled *chinoise* ceiling and elaborate elevator doors.

4 Aetna Life & Casualty Building
1969, Welton Beckett & Assoc.
600 Market St.
One of several office towers of this vintage, with a strong vertical emphasis and slender form caused by the cramped site. The granite-clad piers stand on heavy feet and define a singularly grim arcade on the ground floor. The sunken plaza with its spikey barred fence is protected from the weather but not so well used as the street level. There is a connection to the Montgomery Street BART station, designed by Skidmore, Owings & Merrill.

Mechanics' Institute
1909, Albert Pissis
57-65 Post St.
The various functions housed in this building are well expressed on the facade. The Institute's libraries occupy the arcaded floor and offices are on the top floors. A mural by Arthur Matthew embellishes the marble elevator lobby. The Mechanics' Institute was one of the state's first educational institutions; it occupied this site in another building from 1866 to its destruction in 1906.

5. Crocker Northern Headquarters

5 Crocker Northern Headquarters
1983, Skidmore, Owings & Merrill
1 Montgomery St.
A thoroughly distinguished design, commendable for its sensitivity to both urban planning and preservation issues. When complete, the three-part complex will include the original neo-Classical banking hall of Willis Polk's 1908 First National Bank Building, a barrel-vaulted galleria, and a 38-story office tower. The subtle play of light on the plaid pattern of polished and thermal-finished granite and the reflective colored-glass windows change the tower's visual image during the day. The office building surmounting the old banking hall roof will be demolished and replaced with a rooftop garden.

6 Wells Fargo Building
1966, John Graham
2-44 Montgomery St.
Another vertically striped tower, this time with gleaming aluminum piers, by a Seattle firm. On the sidewalk in front of the bank is the Native Sons Monument of 1897 by Douglas Tilden, moved here from Golden Gate Park in 1977 as part of the Market Street Beautification Project.

7 Hobart Building
1914, Willis Polk
582-92 Market St.
An idiosyncratic design rumored to be a favorite of its author. The Hobart's eccentricity has become increasingly apparent with age, particularly when compared with its immediate neighbors.
Though the building is shaped to address its polygonal site, the demolition of Clinton Day's Union Trust Building for the Wells Fargo banking hall exposed a bare flank, so that the Hobart tower seems now to be peering over its shoulder in embarrassment. The ground floor has been grossly remodeled. Just down the block at 562-66 and 567-80 Market are two more Willis Polk buildings that make textured backdrops for the street.

8 Office building
1979, Skidmore, Owings & Merrill
595 Market St.
A large speculative office tower that attempts to respect the different grids north and south of Market while achieving maximum floor area under the new restrictions designed to discourage bulky tower construction.

9 Hunter-Dulin Building
1926, Schultze & Weaver
111 Sutter St.

A stylistic combination of Romanesque and Chateauesque, with the building's shaft a clear expression of the structural frame and the chateau on top more staid than picturesque. The array of visible decorative motifs ranges from medallions with wistful young women shouldering Classical garlands, and a belt cornice with squat eagles and ox heads, to the neo-Norman arched entrance and the pseudo-Medieval lobby. Such a free-wheeling approach to historicism typified this firm's work.

10 French Bank Building
1902, Hemenway & Miller
Rem. 1907-13, E.A. Bozio
108-10 Sutter St.

Originally a skeletal Chicago School building, the facade was gussied up for the French Bank after the 1906 fire. The banded ground floor columns borrowed from the Mannerists are mysteriously embellished with shields bearing caducei, the physician's symbol.

Hallidie Building
1917, Willis Polk
130-50 Sutter St.

Credited as the first glass-curtain wall and more curtainlike in its unbroken transparency, bracketed away from the structural frame, than almost anything since. The Hallidie Building responded to a demand for offices with maximum glazed areas that resulted in a number of window-walled facades; for an example, see the Bemiss Building at 266 Sutter. Much of the design's appeal lies in the delicacy of the glazed grid, hung curtainlike from an intricate High Victorian cast-iron cornice resembling a window valance. Even the fire escapes, which look like pull cords, contribute to the fantasy. Commissioned by the Regents of the University of California, the building is named after the inventor of the cable car, Andrew S. Hallidie. It was renovated in 1979 by Kaplan, McLauglin & Diaz and painted in U.C.'s blue and gold.

10. Hallidie Building

12. Mills Building

11 130 Montgomery St.
1930, O'Brien Bros./Wilbur D. Peugh

Moderne styling for a narrow office building with a generously fenestrated shaft. The ground floor is devoted to an entrance composition that combines a simulated corbeled arch crowned by a monumental keystone, and a scored lintel apparently held in place by figures carved on the end blocks, one of which sits incongruously on the alarm box. The whole facade is a sophisticated play on forms from several historical sources. The 1972 interior by Michel A. Marx & Associates is one of the few contemporary bank interiors that complements its older facade.

12 Mills Building
1891, Burnham & Root
1908, 1914, 1918, D.H. Burnham &
Co./Willis Polk
Mills Tower
1931, George Kelham
220 Montgomery St.

The only surviving pre-fire skyscraper
that clearly reflects the great Chicago
School tradition from which it sprang—
the wall composition recalls Adler & Sullivan's Auditorium Building of 1888.
Damaged but structurally intact after the
1906 earthquake and fire, the building
was restored and enlarged twice by Willis
Polk, who headed the local D.H. Burnham & Company office. Lewis Hobart's
tower respects the original design. The
multiple-arched entranceway with its fine
white marble detail leads to a relatively
plain lobby ornamented only by a graceful branching stairway with unusual foliated balusters and handsome newels.

13 Russ Building
1927, George Kelham
235 Montgomery St.

For many years the city's largest and tallest office building, its Gothicized tower
marked the center of the financial district
until the 1970s, when it was dwarfed by a
forest of new towers. The Gothic ornament is more perfunctory than inventive,
but the lobby has a handsome inlaid marble tile floor. Around the corner at 441
Pine Street is the skillful 1978 remodeling
by Wudke, Watson & Davis of a 1906
brick commercial structure to house a
McDonald's.

14 California Commercial Union
1923, George Kelham and Kenneth
MacDonald
315 Montgomery St.

A composition that employs the rhetoric
of the High Renaissance at the top and
bottom. Note the touch of local color in
the medallions on either side of the entrance, one of which shows a California
bear shambling over the city skyline.

15 Security Pacific Bank
1922, George Kelham
Rem. 1941, The Capitol Co.
300 Montgomery St.

This building has three important facades. The 1941 remodeling transformed
a textured brick wall into a smooth skin
with a restrained, woven pier-and-spandrel effect; the cornice was also stripped
to conform to the tasteful modern Classicism of the forties. The ground floor remains intact, contributing an impressive
colonnade to the street. The Security Pacific banking hall, strikingly refurbished
by Baldwin- Clarke in 1978, is a modified
Roman basilica interior with a double
row of *faux marbre* Corinthian columns
supporting a handsome white and gold
coffered ceiling. The lobby inside the
300 Montgomery Street entrance is 1941-
style Moderne with fine marble walls and
lighting fixtures.

16 Bank of America
World Headquarters
1969, Wurster, Bernardi & Emmons/
Skidmore, Owings & Merrill
Pietro Belluschi, consultant
555 California St.

The world's largest bank set out to build
the city's most important office building
and succeeded, although at the expense
of its surroundings. The tower's faceted
form was partly inspired by Pflueger's
450 Sutter Building; the height (52 stories), bulk, and dark red color made the
building's appearance ominous when it
stood new and alone. Even with more
company it still dominates the skyline,
but at sunset it becomes eerily transparent. The shaded north plaza, windswept like the steppes, has a polished
black granite sculpture by Masayuki
Nagare dubbed "the Banker's Heart" by
an irate citizen. An opulent three-level
banking hall fronts on Montgomery
Street.

17 International Building
1960, Anshen & Allen
601 California St.

The architects made a real effort to give
this small tower a more delicate scale
and a richer form—appropriate to its location on the edge of Chinatown—than

the typical office building of its time. The dark metal forms at the corners are the air conditioning risers. The building enjoys an enviable location next to St. Mary's Square, a garage-top park by John J. Gould (1955), relandscaped in 1960 by Eckbo, Roysten & Williams.

18 Hartford Insurance Building
1965, Skidmore, Owings & Merrill
636-50 California St.
Briefly the city's tallest and most controversial building because of its proximity to Chinatown, this 33-story tower clad in precast concrete panels has now faded into the background of the new giants.

19 Kohl Building
1904, Percy & Polk
1907, Willis Polk
400 Montgomery St.
Less damaged than most of the pre-fire "fireproof" buildings, the Kohl was restored by Polk after the fire only to suffer the usual ground floor depredations. The entrance portico is still a fine composition, with winged grotesques and an unusual openwork frieze in the tympanum. Don't miss the florid top floors or the white marble lobby, mostly original. The 1972 Banco di Roma is by Skidmore, Owings & Merrill.

20 456 Montgomery Building
1983, Roger Owen Boyer Assoc./MLT Assoc.
This 24-story-tower will be set back from the street and incorporate the temple-form facades of Albert Pissis' 1908 Anton Borel and Company Bank and Howard & Galloway's 1908 bank for Sutro and Company. The latter, meticulously detailed in granite, bronze, and green marble, is the more distinguished and costly design. Across the street at 500 Montgomery is the American Asian Bank of 1918 by Wilde & Schiller, another temple testifying to the popularity of this form for shrines dedicated to the rituals of finance. In the short block before Commercial Street, State Landmark plaque No. 819 recalls the Hudson's Bay Company headquarters located here in 1841, when this was the waterfront. In fact, Commercial Street, from Montgomery

19. Kohl Building

down toward the Bay, was the Central or Long Wharf, begun in 1848 and extended in 1850 when it was the major pier of the city. Another state plaque, No. 87 at 608-10 Commercial, marks the site of the first U.S. branch mint in California, which opened in 1854. In 1875, the U.S. Subtreasury Building replaced the mint. It was gutted in 1906 and rebuilt as the one-story structure now on the site. Although the buildings in the blocks around Commercial and Leidesdorff have the scale of the Gold Rush city, they are all post-fire. Most house restaurants for the office-worker lunch trade including, for example, the old PG&E Station J (1914) by Frederick Meyer on Commercial Street between Montgomery and Sansome.

21 Bank of America
(old Bank of Italy)
1908, Shea & Lofquist
552 Montgomery St.
A rich facade that, like some other buildings in the financial district, employs an interesting economy of means: expensive granite cladding for the ground floor and

2 Financial District

less expensive terra-cotta that mimics granite for the upper floors. The program for the exterior decorative detail, though complicated, is far surpassed by the white marble interior that, despite some alterations, is a real jewel box. Captain John Montgomery is thought to have landed at this spot in 1846 to claim the city for the United States.

22 Transamerica Building
1971, William Pereira & Assoc.
600 Montgomery St.

The butt of many jokes when it first appeared, this pyramidal tower has settled into the affections of many San Franciscans. Its pointed top is now a valuable anchor for the eye amidst all those unmemorable others. It is still hard to forgive the heedless destruction of the Montgomery Block, among the Gold Rush city's most historic buildings, or the way the current structure rests spiderlike on the ground, ignoring its context. Next door is the 1971 Redwood Park by Tom Galli. Abutting the park is a 1980 building by William Pereira.

23 695 Montgomery Street
1984, Kaplan, McLaughlin & Diaz

One of the first mixed office- and residential-use towers to be built in compliance with San Francisco's latest policy toward downtown development.

343 Sansome Street
c 1930, Hyman & Appleton

A 1908 building totally restyled in Moderne; similar decorative motifs reoccur in concrete on the building next door.

24 Federal Reserve Bank
of San Francisco
1924, George Kelham
400 Sansome St.

A design in transition from the academic Beaux- Arts on the ground level to Le Style Moderne on the upper part— as you can see by comparing the Ionic capitals of the freestanding columns with those of the giant pilasters above. The lobby, with murals by Jules Guerin, and the banking hall are worth seeing. The bank operation will soon move to its new headquarters on Market Street.

25. Bank of California & Tower

25 Bank of California
1907, Bliss & Faville
Bank of California Tower
1967, Anshen & Allen
400 California St.

The banking temple par excellence, with a beautifully detailed Corinthian order forming the colonnade. Inside, the banking hall is a great cage with a coffered ceiling. Next door, the 1967 tower's fretted floor spandrels pick up the rhythm of the fluted columns, while over the ground floor a copper cornice stamped with a curvilinear pattern holds its own against the Classical riches of its neighbor. Amazingly enough, the alley sides of both these buildings are finished with the same care as the facades.

26 California First Bank Building
1977, Skidmore, Owings & Merrill
350 California St.

A sculptural, contemporary version of the classic skyscraper, divided into a two-part base, shaft, and capital with the corners visually strengthened by paired columns. The panels of precast bosses represent an effort to overcome the typical blankness of the contemporary office tower; the expanses of glass permit a view into the dramatic banking hall. But somehow the eye is more engaged by the Corinthian colonnade across the street. At the top of the rear property wall, walrus heads wreathed in rope peer over what look to be icebergs. Forlorn relics, they solemnly represent the Alaska Commercial Building that formerly occupied the site.

27 Insurance Exchange Building
1913, Willis Polk
433 California St.
Merchants Exchange Building
1903, D.H. Burnham & Co./Willis
Polk
465 California St.
Two buildings with similar wall composition and surface treatment. The Merchants Exchange (rebuilt after the fire) served as a local model for later buildings in the financial district; for example, the Matson and PG&E buildings on Market Street. An interior skylit arcade leads to the exchange hall, now the Charter Bank of London. Attributed to Julia Morgan, the high airy space, designed to recall a Roman basilica, is lavishly detailed and bathed in natural light that shows off the seascape paintings by William Coulter. The now nearly invisible lookout tower on the roof once had a practical purpose. From there news of ships coming into the harbor was received and transmitted to the merchants assembled below in the great hall.

Great Western Savings Building
1968, John Carl Warnecke
425 California St.

28 J. Harold Dollar Building
1920, George Kelham
341 California St.
Robert Dollar Building
1919, Charles McCall
301-33 California St.
The two Dollar buildings were headquarters for the Robert Dollar Steamship Lines.

29 Royal Globe Insurance Company
1907, Howells & Stokes
201 Sansome St.
An exemplary Edwardian building with the right color scheme of red and white. The entrance composition and ornamental detail of the base and attic sections provide a visual feast. All surface materials were brought from the east, where the company had a similar building.

30 Pacific Coast Stock Exchange
1915, J. Milton Dyer
1930, Miller & Pflueger
Trading room at 301 Pine St.
Office tower at 155 Sansome St.
A ponderous, mausoleumlike block, this is a 1930 remodeling of a temple-front structure that had housed the U.S. Treasury. The monumental pylons in front have cast-stone sculptures by Ralph Stackpole. The trading hall interior is worth seeing for the ceiling, a curvilinear grill made of thin metal strips laid endwise on a frame. This ingenious way of making a lightweight ceiling beneath the air plenum with an apparently changing depth of field was also used by the same architects in Oakland's famed Paramount Theatre. The tower next door has a restrained Moderne entranceway; it houses the Stock Exchange Club (open only to members) on an upper floor that has one of the few remaining intact interiors by this accomplished firm.

31 Hong Kong Bank Building
1965, Hertzka & Knowles
160-80 Sansome St.
Adam Grant Building
1908, c 1910, Howard & Galloway
114 Sansome St.

32 Standard Oil Building
1912, 1916, Benjamin C. McDougall
200 Bush St.

33 Standard Oil Building
1922, George Kelham
225 Bush St.
A heavily corbeled cornice appears to support a temple loggia topped with a red tile roof 20-odd stories up in the air at 225 Bush. In the intervening stories are the offices for Standard Oil's second San Francisco building. The first, across the street at 200 Bush Street, is richly detailed outside and, on the ground floor, was sensitively remodeled by Bull, Field, Volkman & Stockwell for California Federal Savings in 1976.

34. Crown Zellerbach Building

34 Crown Zellerbach Building
1959, Hertzka & Knowles/ Skidmore, Owings & Merrill
1 Bush St.

The first of the city's glass curtain-walled towers in the first and best of the tower-plaza settings. Expensive walls like those of the tower, where the air-conditioning console is set in to permit the glass to extend unbroken from the floor to above the ceiling, will never be done again. The same goes for the elegant but extravagant placement of the elevators and stairs in their own mosaic-clad tower outside the office block. The playful form of the round bank is an integral part of the plaza composition.

35 One Sansome Building
(orig. London Paris National Bank)
1910, Albert Pissis
1921, George Kelham
1984, Pereira & Assoc.

Once a banking temple of the kind that called forth Louis Sullivan's scorning *Kindergarden Chats*, this is now to be an atrium for a new office tower rising behind that will preserve, by incorporation into ground floor public areas, sections of the cornice and other decorative features of the 1912 Holbrook Building, by Mac-Donald & Applegarth, which once occupied the site.

36 Flatiron Building
1913, Havens & Toepke
540-48 Market St.

37 Standard Oil of California
1964, 1975, Hertzka & Knowles
555-75 Market St.

Two towers with different heights and orientations but identical designs share a lushly landscaped plaza and garden by Osmundson & Staley that the public may now only look at.

Ecker Street cuts through the block to Jessie, where several modest brick warehouses have been rehabilitated to house restaurants, etc. One Ecker is a 1972 remodeling by Arthur Gensler. At the end of the slot is a fine view back toward Market and the financial district's collage of towers.

38 Golden Gate University
1978, William D. Podesto
T.Y. Lin International, structural engineer
540-52 Mission St.

39 Transbay Transit Terminal
1939, Timothy Pflueger
Arthur Brown, Jr., and John J. Donovan, consulting architects
425 Mission St.

Designed to handle the Key System trains, which ran across the Bay Bridge from 1939 until 1958, this is now a bus terminal. The stripped functionalist expression encloses a well-designed circulation system. The construction of this terminal signaled the demise of the Ferry Building as the prime gateway to the city.

40. Shell Building

41. Shaklee Building

40 Shell Building
1929, George Kelham
100 Bush St.
A slender stepped tower clad in rusticated beige terra-cotta; the ornament makes good use of the shell form as, for example, in the elegant shell worked into the gilt metal transom. High above the street, projecting shell forms conceal light fixtures that can suffuse the building's crown with golden light. The lobby carries out the general theme.

Heineman Building
1910, MacDonald & Applegarth
130 Bush St.
Mechanic's Monument
1894-95, Douglas Tilden, sculptor
Willis Polk, architect
Mechanic's Plaza, gore of Battery St.
and Market St. at Bush St.
Polk designed the granite base of this truly heroic sculpture by Tilden, a deaf mute who was an internationally known artist and a native son. James Donahue gave the monument in memory of his father Peter Donahue, who in 1850 started the state's first ironworks and machine shop, established the first gas company for street lighting in the city in 1852, and later initiated the city's first streetcar line. Imbedded in the sidewalks at this intersection are three bronze plaques that mark the old shoreline of Yerba Buena Cove.

41 Shaklee Building
1982, Skidmore, Owings & Merrill
444 Market St.
The rolled-back Market Street facade and finely scaled flush aluminum skin make this one of the more ingratiating of the recent crop of skyscrapers. It is connected by a hyphen to the 1908 Postal Telegraph Building by Lewis Hobart at 22 Battery Street.

42 Industrial Indemnity
(formerly John Hancock Building)
1959, Skidmore, Owings & Merrill
255 California St.

Illustrating the jump in scale of office towers in the last couple of decades, this one was and is still·remarkable for its deference in scale and wall composition to its neighbors, particularly Lewis Hobart's 1910-17 Newhall Building at 260 California Street. Executive offices are on the second floor under the arched vaults, facing a garden terrace designed by Lawrence Halprin.

Hibernia Bank Building
1978, Arthur Gensler & Assoc.
201 California St.

43 Tadich Grill
1909, Crim & Scott
240-42 California St.

The restaurant—in business in San Francisco since 1865—moved here from the site of the Transamerica pyramid; the interior itself is a landmark. The facade also deserves notice for the simple elegance of its terra-cotta frame.

44 Daon Building
1983, Skidmore, Owings & Merrill
353 Sacramento St.

45 Embarcadero Center
1967-81, John C. Portman, Jr.
Bounded by Clay, Battery, Sacramento, Drumm, California, and Market sts. and the M. Justin Herman Plaza

An 8 1/2-acre portion of the 51-acre Golden Gateway Redevelopment Center fostered by M. Justin Herman, San Francisco's entrepreneurial Redevelopment Agency director from 1959 until his death in 1971. The project, called a "city within a city," has grown incrementally over the past 14 years, paralleling the Manhattanization of the financial district. Often scorned in its early stages as a merely formal gesture at multilevel urbanity, its present daytime population now fills its many levels to capacity. Designed as a city in the sky linked by footbridges, the complex of four towers plus the Hyatt Regency Hotel is excep-

tional for its successful integration of shopping—on the first three levels of each block-sized podium—and office towers, whose coverage is limited to one-third of the site. The towers, clad in rough-finished, precast concrete, are composed of slablike elements stepped to create 10 to 14 corner offices per floor instead of the usual 4. Their slender profiles are increasingly welcome as the skyline fills up. The city's requirement that 1 percent of development money be spent for art has endowed the Center with a number of works of art, including sculptures by Willi Gutmann, Michael Biggers, Nicolas Schoffer, Anne Van Kleeck, Louise Nevelson, Barbara Shawcroft, and Robert Russin; and tapestries by Francoise Grossen, Lia Cook, and Olga de Amaral. Circulation is baffling, but directories in each building give the locations of shops, restaurants, and works of art, and the whole complex seethes with pedestrian life during the day.

The Center is introduced on Market Street by the Hyatt Regency Hotel, completed in 1973, one of Portman's most successful atrium hotels. The great interior space has a monumental spherical sculpture of aluminum tubing by Charles Perry titled *Eclipse.* Seen from the Embarcadero Freeway, the staggered floors of the hotel recall an old- fashioned typewriter keyboard and contribute a lively form to the skyline. But this liveliness is strangely absent from the main entranceway on the other side of the building, which neither addresses the importance of its gateway corner nor hints at the spatial riches of the interior.

46 Alcoa Building
1964, Skidmore, Owings & Merrill
Sasaki Walker & Assoc., landscape architect
1 Maritime Plaza

The major office tower in the Golden Gateway Redevelopment Project, for which SOM did a master plan in 1957. Alcoa was the first design to use the seismic X-bracing as part of its structural aesthetic. The idea was used again in Chicago's Hancock Building, designed in the firm's

46. Alcoa Building

Chicago office. The formal plan for the garden squares on top of the garages was intended to create the effect of an outdoor sculpture museum. Major pieces are by Marino Marini, Henry Moore, Charles Perry, and Jan Peter Stern; the fountain is by Robert Woodward. Now that the Embarcadero Center towers are built, the rooftop plazas have become convincing as pedestrian precincts in the sky. However, the street level is a grim reminder of what happens when an area is abandoned to auto traffic.

47 100 California St.
l959, Welton Becket & Assoc.
Union Bank Building
1972, Welton Becket & Assoc.
50 California St.
Mutual Benefit Life Building
1969, Welton Becket & Assoc.
1 California St.
Of these three works by the same firm, only the first looks as though it was designed for San Francisco. (By the way, the metal bolts on the piers were added later for seismic safety.) The other two look like the Los Angeles imports that they are.

48 Itel Building
1982, Johnson/Burgee
101 California St.
Philip Johnson's first project in San Francisco for his Houston patron Gerald Heins, this colossal round tower will have as dramatic an impact on the skyline as its sloping, glazed atrium will have on California Street.

**49 Bechtel/Metropolitan
Life complex**
1973, Skidmore, Owings & Merrill
1 Metro Plaza

425, 333 Market St.
1978, Gin Wong & Assoc.

45 Fremont St.
1978, Skidmore, Owings & Merrill

50 Beale St.
1967, Skidmore, Owings & Merrill

5 Fremont Center
1984, Skidmore, Owings & Merrill
A blockful of buildings that were conceived for more or less the same client over a period of time. The complex's hodgepodginess is exceeded only by its civic stinginess, which is hard to understand since the principal client, one of the world's largest engineering firms, was building this headquarters in its hometown. The only building of any distinction is 45 Fremont, which has a handsome taut skin of painted aluminum.

50 Pacific Gateway
1983, Primiani-Weaver
Mission St. bet. Beale and Main sts.
Embarcadero BART Station
1972, Tallie B. Maule/Hertzka & Knowles

51 Pacific Gas & Electric Co.
1925, Bakewell & Brown
77 Beale St.
An engaged colonnade with a giant order topped by freestanding urns forms the climax of this imposing facade. Clad in terra-cotta cast to mimic granite, the decorative detail, like that in the Matson Building, is exceptional. The sculptural group over the entrance by Edgar Walter

is particularly fine. In 1949 the building was enlarged in the style of the original by Weihe, Frick & Kruse; in 1971 an office tower was added in the rear by Hertzka & Knowles.

Matson Building
1921, Bliss & Faville
215 Market St.

Clad in polychromed terra-cotta, the Matson Building was designed, like the Southern Pacific Building to the east and the PG&E building next door, to evoke the princely age of commerce embodied in the Renaissance palace. Now these structures recall the days when large office buildings lined the streets at uniform heights and spoke the same civilized language. The Matson was once the mainland headquarters for Hawaii's Big Five corporations; it is now occupied by PG&E.

52. SF Federal Reserve Bank

52 San Francisco Federal Reserve Bank
1982, Skidmore, Owings & Merrill
100 block Market St. bet. Main and Spear sts.

A monumental loggia along Market and a reticent but granite-clad stepped facade distinguish this functionally complicated building. It houses everything from executive offices to a very large money-counting and warehousing operation with its attendant security systems.

53 Southern Pacific Building
1916, Bliss & Faville
1 Market St.

A vast Reniassance palace built to house one of the city's first major corporate

headquarters. Behind it rise two towers designed in 1976 by Welton Becket & Associates that connect to the older building by means of a skylit galleria. Just out of the main circulation area is the Orient Express Restaurant, designed by Dan Solomon & Associates in 1979. Although undeniably busy, the galleria hardly qualifies as a public space in terms of gracious amenity. The rear of the complex on Mission Street contains the restaurant Franks for the Memory, by Richard Fernau (1980), a monument of high whimsy with surreal touches.

54 Rincon Annex Post Office
1940, Gilbert Stanley Underwood
99 Mission St.

The Public Works Administration employed a minimal Classicism that is now called PWA Moderne; the style is well represented in this building with its symmetrical massing and a colonnade reduced to barely projecting piers capped by a narrow lintel. Inside are a set of WPA murals, which are to be preserved if and when the site is redeveloped.

55 Audiffred Building
1889
1-21 Mission St.

Built by Hippolyte Audiffred to recall his native France, the building survived the 1906 fire only to be gutted by another fire in 1980. It is now being rehabilitated by William E. Cullen.

56 Justin Herman Park & Plaza
1971, Mario Ciampi/Lawrence Halprin & Assoc./John Bolles
Foot of Market St.

Part of the Market Street Beautification Project, a combination of poor orientation and weak spatial organization makes this a relatively uninviting public area; it does come to life with crafts markets and an occasional pageant. In the corner near the freeway is a fountain by Armand Vaillancourt that, when installed, aroused heated controversy mostly for its apparent emulation of the hated freeway structure beyond, as a kind of stockpile for the unused freeway parts. Actually a more plausible explanation for its form is that it was originally conceived in steel, not cast concrete. The plaza's other sculpture is an equestrian statue of Juan Bautista de Anza by Julian Martinez, given to the city by the governor of Sonora, Mexico.

57 Ferry Building Complex
1988, I.M. Pei & Partners/Gensler & Assoc.
SWA Group, landscape architects
Market St. at the Embarcadero
Ferry Building
1895-1903, A. Page Brown
Edward R.A. Pyle, State Dept. of Engineering
Pier One/World Trade Center
Embarcadero Promenade
1982, MLTW/Turnbull Assoc.

Before the bridges and the infamous freeway this was the transportation hub of the city, where 170 ferries docked every day disgorging their passengers for an easy walk to downtown offices or to the trolley line up Market. The completion of the Bay bridges, the Key System, and the Transbay Terminal diverted much of the traffic to rail, bus, and auto. When the ferries stopped in 1958, the building was converted to offices. A mezzanine floor intercepted the great skylit galleries that ran the length of the building. By the time the freeway was built in the late 1950s, the building was a dingy shadow of its former self. In 1978, in accordance with a master plan by Rockrise Odermatt Mountjoy Associates for the northeast waterfront, the Port Commission requested proposals to reactivate the dormant facility. Continental Development Corporation, winners of the competition, commissioned I.M. Pei & Partners for the task, which, in addition to the restoration of the Ferry Building and the Argriculture Building , entailed the reshaping of the shoreline and creation of a World Trade Center on Pier One. The current scheme is to integrate the buildings with the site through bay-side promenades and sequences of glass-roofed shopping ar-

57. Ferry Building

cades. The Ferry Building galleries will be restored and the portico opened up to permit a view of the water as well as access to the ferry landing and an outdoor market. The latter will attempt to recapture the colorful atmosphere of the old produce market that used to occupy the Golden Gateway area. The Agriculture Building will house a Food Hall where all manner of "food experiences" will abound. But before the larger project is complete, the public will be able to simply enjoy the waterfront on William Turnbull and Donlyn Lyndon's Embarcadero Promenade, which will stretch from Mission to Folsom Street.

58 YMCA
1924, Carl Werner
166 Embarcadero
Formerly a prominent landmark; now hiding behind the freeway and peering over it.

3
Chinatown
Telegraph Hill
North Beach

1 Cogswell College, 600 Stockton
2 Sing Fat Co, 717 California
  Sing Chong Co, 601 Grant
  Old St. Mary's Chruch, California & Grant
  St. Mary's Square
3 Chinatown Housing, Stockton & Sacramento
4 D. Cameron house, 920 Sacramento
5 Chinatown YWCA, 940 Powell
  YWCA Clay St Ctr, 965 Clay
6 Chinatown Library, 1135 Powell
7 Moon residence, 940 Washington
  Commodore Stockton School Annex
8 Chinese Presbyterian Church, 925 Stockton
  St. Mary's Mission, 930 Stockton
9 Six Companies, 843 Stockton
10 Chinatown YWCA, 855 Sacramento
11 Chinese Baptist Church, 15 Waverly
12 Nam Kue School, 765 Sacramento
  Yeong Wo Benevolent Assn
  Chamber of Commerce, 728 Sacramento
13 Bldgs, 745, 736, 801 Grant
14 Bank of Canton, 743 Washington
15 Portsmouth Square
  Chinese Cultural & Trade Ctr
16 Old Transamerica bldg, 4 Columbus
17 Pacific Lumber Co, Washington & Sansome
18 US Customs House, 555 Battery
19 Golden Gateway town houses
20 Musto PLaza, 350 Pacific
21 Jackson Square & bldgs, 400 block Jackson
  700 block Montgomery, 530 Washington
22 Columbus Tower, Columbus & Kearny
23 City Lights Book Store & Vesuvio's
24 St. Francis of Assisi, 610 Vallejo
25 Fugazi Hall, 678 Green
26 Washington Square, SS Peter & Paul Church
27 Bldg, 1736 Stockton
28 Union Court, 418 Union
29 Houses, end of Union & Alta
30 Kahn house, 66 Calhoun
31 Houses, 60 Alta, 1308 Montgomery
  Apts, 1360 Montgomery
32 Garfield School, 420 Filbert
33 Apts, 290 Lombard, 1725 Kearny
34 House, 275 Telegraph Hill
35 Coit Tower & Filbert Steps
36 House, 298 Chestnut
37 Francisco Middle School, Francisco & Powell
38 San Remo Restaurant, 2237 Mason
39 Condos, Vandewater & Francisco
40 Office bldgs, 333, 327 Bay
41 Northpoint Apts
  200, 300 blocks North Point
42 Pier 39
43 City bldgs, 100 block Bay
44 Office Park, 50 Chestnut
45 Telegraph Landing, 1 Chestnut
46 Condos, 101 Lombard
47 HOK offices, 1 Lombard
48 Levi Plaza
49 The Ice Houses, 1265 Battery, 151 Union

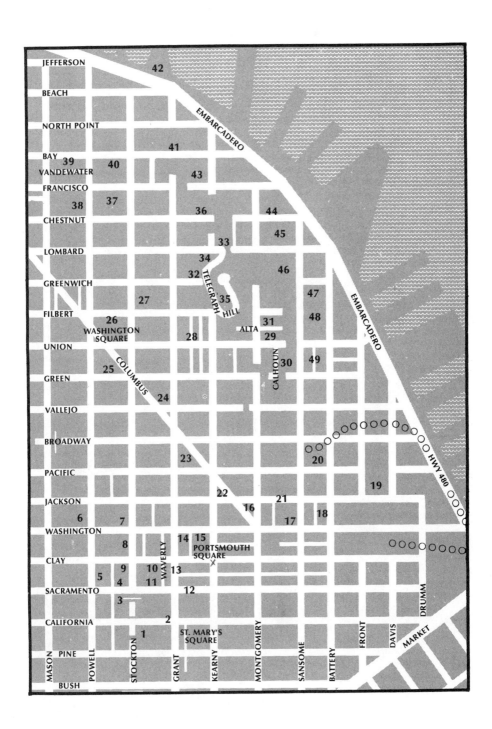

3 Chinatown/Telegraph Hill/North Beach

Since 1880 the boundaries of Chinatown have been California to Broadway and Kearny to Stockton Street. But the street now called Grant Avenue is linked to the beginnings of the tiny port settlement called Yerba Buena. In 1835 the street was called the Calle de la Fundacion. Its first resident, the Englishman William Richardson, drew a map showing the location of his tent store at the intersection of the Calle and Clay Street, which ran down to the Bay at what is now Montgomery Street. By 1837 he had built an adobe house called La Casa Grande; its location is marked by a plaque at 823 Grant. More history of Yerba Buena is given below in the entry for Portsmouth Square, I5.

The first Chinese came, almost entirely from the province of Canton (Kwangtung), for the Gold Rush. Their numbers were sufficient to establish the *hui-kuan*, or district associations, whose memberships were based on common origin of place or family. The buildings these associations eventually built as their headquarters are Chinatown's most distinctive building type.

3 Chinatown/Telegraph Hill/North Beach

By 1852 the Chinese had settled around the intersection of Dupont—as the Calle was renamed in that year—and Sacramento, replacing the original French residents there. The combination of discrimination at the mines and the mines' diminishing returns brought the Chinese back to the city, where by 1860 they composed 5 percent of the population. During this decade, light industries such as the manufacturing of clothing, footwear, and cigars were taken over by the Chinese, whose frugality and dedication to work did not endear them to the predominantly white male population. Building materials such as iron, pre-cut granite, and even prefabricated cast-iron buildings shaped like Quonset huts were also imported from China. Strange as it seems, it was less expensive to import stone because of the poor quality of local stone and the lack of interest in developing quarries in this country. St. Mary's Church, entry 2, still has its original Chinese granite foundations.

The story of the Chinese contribution to the building of the transcontinental railroad, completed in 1869, has been told elsewhere. The history of the anti-Chinese movement and the growing violence and discrimination against them in the depression years following the national financial panic of 1873 have also been well documented. The Chinese Exclusion Act of 1882 was extended indefinitely in 1902; it was finally eased in 1952. Despite this inhuman treatment the Chinese persevered. In fact, Chinatown became the most densely populated part of San Francisco when the Chinese population doubled to 10 percent of the city by 1890.

When, like the rest of the central city, Chinatown was razed by the 1906 fire, a group of merchants saw an opportunity to revamp the squalid, vice-ridden image propagated by the district's gambling, opium, and prostitution dens. (The alleys notorious for such pursuits, Waverly, Ross, and Spofford, were linked to the equally infamous Barbary Coast nearby.) Whereas the pre-fire Chinatown had been built largely of prefabricated wooden buildings of no architectural pretension or style, the post-fire "city within a city" was reconstructed of lasting materials such as brick. The district was also imprinted architecturally with Oriental stage-set trappings designed lure tourists up from the downtown shopping area to a world-famous Oriental bazaar. The scheme worked. From the gateway formed by the Sing Chong and Sing Fat buildings at the intersection of Grant and California Street, to Jackson where the market section begins, Grant Avenue, officially so named in 1908, is now punctuated with Orientalized buildings, new and old. Much of the new building is out of scale and sadly lacking in the naive theatricality of the old. The exotic herbal and grocery shops are vanishing too, along with the colorful street furniture, lanterns, neon signs, etc. that added so much to the visual festivity. The bustle of commercial life continues on the densely populated streets. Their vitality, never truly reflected in the architecture, is expressed—at least to those of us on the outside—in the street life, the displays of exotic foodstuffs, and the festivals that punctuate the year.

A note about the association buildings, mentioned above: According to architectural historian Christopher Yip, the mainland prototype of the local association building was one in which the hierarchy of elements was expressed by increasing the size and number of courtyards moving back along the main axis of the complex. Because this form was impossible in a dense urban location, the typical 19th-century commercial building was adapted to its symbolic needs by stacking the elements vertically. This arrangement resulted in the temple occupying the top floor, which became the most important part of the facade. Tourists will note a number of these buildings, in which a protected balcony runs the length of the top floor, the curving eave supports ritual bells at the corners, and other ritual trappings are displayed.

1. Cogswell College

2. Old St. Mary's Church

1 Cogswell College
(formerly Metropolitan Life Insurance Co.)
1909, LeBrun & Sons
1913, Miller & Colmesnil
1929, Miller & Pflueger
Landscape architect for court,
Thomas Church
600 Stockton St.
Monumental Roman-Renaissance grandeur in gleaming terra-cotta. The building is occupied by Cogswell College, a vocational college.

2 Sing Chong Building
1908, T. Patterson Ross
601-15 Grant Ave.
Sing Fat Building
1908, T. Patterson Ross
717-19 California St.
Old St. Mary's Church
1853-54
1907-09, Craine & England
1969, Welsh & Carey
Grant Ave. and California St.
St. Mary's Square
1960, Ekbo, Royston & Williams
Statue of Sun Yat-Sen by Beniamino Bufano
California St. at Grant Ave.
The Sing Chong and Sing Fat buildings heralded Chinatown's post-fire architectural image. The pagodalike corner towers and other Orientalizing detail give distinction to what are otherwise standard brick commercial blocks. The owners sited their buildings at the south end of Grant to establish the location as the new center of the Oriental bazaar that Chinatown was to become.
Old St. Mary's preceded the new Chinatown by half a century. Although it too burned in 1906, the granite foundations, imported from China, and the brick and iron walls, imported from the eastern United States, survived. The church was soon restored, was remodeled and enlarged in the 1920s, burned again in 1969, and was again restored. St. Mary's academic Gothic Revival form was complemented in 1964 by the addition of a rectory, the Paulist Center of the West,

3 Chinatown/Telegraph Hill/North Beach

600 California Street, designed by Skidmore, Owings & Merrill. Inside this restrained and respectful brick block, the Paulist Fathers have a small chapel with stained glass and stations of the cross by Mark Adams.

3 Mei Lun Yuen Chinatown Housing
1982, Architects Associated
Stockton and Sacramento sts.
A well-planned, mixed-use development with 185 units of public housing. The project was years in the making and is the result of much community participation and patient effort on the part of the architects to make the most of a low budget and a difficult site.

4 Donaldina Cameron House
1907, Julia Morgan
Rem. 1940s
Add. 1972, E. Sue
920 Sacramento St.
In 1873, the Presbyterian Church set up a foreign mission to serve San Francisco's Chinese. After the original hall burned in 1906, a new one was built on the present site and officially named for its famous director in 1942. The architect was rightly favored by many eleemosynary institutions; she knew how to design practical buildings that had dignity and presence.

5 Chinatown Women's YWCA Residence Hall
1932, Julia Morgan
940-50 Powell St.
YWCA Clay St. Center
1931, Julia Morgan
965 Clay St.
Two facilities designed concurrently by Morgan, for some years the official YWCA architect for the western region. The former, a severe, elongated Tuscan villa, is now for senior citizens; the latter, an active social center, is more stylistically adventuresome; it has an urbane yet residential scale and plan.

6 Chinatown Public Library
1920, G.A. Lansburgh
1135 Powell St.
Designed with the Beaux-Arts rather than the Chinatown image in mind—the inside is worth a look.

7. Methodist Church

7 Commodore Stockton School Annex
1924, Angus McSweeney
Rem. 1974-75, Bruce, Wendell & Beebe
Washington St. at Stone St.
A handsome blend of Mediterranean and Oriental images.

Gum Moon Residence
1912, Julia Morgan
940 Washington St.
The Protestant missions in Chinatown were largely devoted to rescuing Chinese girls from prostitution. They were run by women of impeccable reputation and enormous energy. Their favorite architect, Julia Morgan, was of the same stripe. This understated Florentine villa was the residence for the original Methodist Church next door, also designed by Morgan, which burned in 1906 and was replaced by the present building, designed in 1911 by Clarence Ward.

8 Chinese Presbyterian Church
1916, Julia Morgan
925 Stockton St.
Another work by Morgan for the Presbyterians, this time a Palladian rather than a Tuscan villa. Across the street at 930 Stockton is St. Mary's Chinese Mission, a simple yet substantial Classical design built after 1906 and added to in 1920 by Charles E. Gottschalk.

9 Chinese Consolidated Benevolent Association of the United States (Six Companies)
1908
843 Stockton St.
The six *hui-kuan* banded together in the 1860s to battle legal and extralegal discrimination against their members. The building of this long-lived and powerful institution is a strong expression of the association type.
The blocks between Stockton and Grant and Sacramento and Jackson are laced with alleys once notorious for gambling and other vices that contributed to Chinatown's lurid past. Spofford and Ross were particularly infamous. Today's sewing factories do not favor the street with similar colorful signs and symbols. At 36 Spofford is a modest building designed by Charles M. Rousseau and built in 1907 for the Chee Kung Tong, the Chinese Freemasons, which was for six years a major center of Sun Yat-Sen's revolutionary movement. Following the 1906 disaster, Waverly Place was lined with three- and four-story association buildings, many of which persist today. At its Washington Street end are two fine examples. Another particularly colorful example is the Sue Hing Benevolent Association of 1911 at 125-29 Waverly. The top floor has metal lotus-shaped lanterns, incense pots, shrines, and placard stands. A particularly narrow example of the association-building type is the Bo On Tong building of 1908, at 808-10 Clay Street.

10 YMCA Chinatown Branch
1926, Meyer & Johnson
855 Sacramento St.

11 Chinese Baptist Church
1887, G.H. Moore
Rebuilt 1908, G.E. Burlingame
15 Waverly Pl. at Sacramento St.
A composition in two kinds of brick, particularly arresting when the setting sun highlights the projecting header bricks.

12 Nam Kue School
1925, Charles E. Rogers
765 Sacramento St.
A more traditionally styled Chinese institutional building with a forecourt, the school was established to instruct Chinatown youth in Chinese culture.

Yeong Wo Benevolent Association
1908
746 Sacramento St.
Here the unusually wide frontage may be the reason for abandoning the association-building type in favor of a more conventional expression of mixed commercial and institutional use.

Chinese Chamber of Commerce
1912
728-30 Sacramento St.
A good example of the more typical association-building type. Although the Chinese began settling on Commercial Street in the 1850s, the streetscape still retains the 19th-century character of pre-Orientalized Chinatown. At the northwest corner of Commercial and Kearny is a small fiesty brick block with exuberant Art Nouveau decorative detail. No. 746- 48 is another curious building, a residence by Righetti & Kuhl, 1907, with a strange Art Nouveau window.

13 Building
c 1915
745 Grant Ave.
A fancy rendition of the association-building type. Across the street at 736-38 Grant is the *Chinese World* (newspaper) building of 1907.

12. Nam Kue School

16. Old Transamerica Building

Soo Yuen Benevolent Association
1907-19, Salfield & Kohlberg
801-7 Grant Ave.
An unusual interpretation of the associa-tion- building type that wraps around the corner lot in an imaginative way with a tripartite facade and graceful balcony.

14 Bank of Canton
(formerly Chinese Telephone Ex-change)
1909
743 Washington St.
The site of San Francisco's first news-paper, the *California Star*, published by Sam Brannan, it later became the home of the country's only Chinese telephone exchange. Outmoded by the 1950s, the exchange was closed and the building purchased and remodeled on the interior by the Bank of Canton.

15 Portsmouth Square/Chinese Cultural and Trade Center with Holiday Inn
1971, Clement Chen/John Carl Warnecke & Assoc.
750 Kearny St.
The site of the old Spanish Colonial plaza of Yerba Buena, renamed San Francisco in 1847. By 1844, the first official build-ing, a customs house, was built at the northwest corner of the plaza. In 1846, Captain Montgomery raised the Ameri-can flag here and named the plaza Ports-mouth Square after his U.S. Navy sloop. At the time of the Gold Rush, the square acquired the set of hotels and gambling houses that, along with the customs house, were vital to the town's economy. As the city center moved southward and the mining industry ceased to provide the city its economic base, the Square de-clined in civic importance, finally be-coming a community park. In 1963, a split-level park with garage below, de-signed by Royston, Hanamoto & Mayes, reshaped the square but fortunately did not drive away the Chinese, who use it heavily. Various monuments, including one to Robert Louis Stevenson designed by Bruce Porter and Willis Polk in 1897, were reinstalled. A plaque giving the his-tory of the square is at the stair from the upper to the lower level.
The Holiday Inn building, which houses the Chinese Cultural and Trade Center, is a brutally scaled building with a pedes-trian bridge to the park. The center gets its name from a token level of community space beneath the high-rise motel.

16 Old Transamerica Building
1911, Salfield & Kohlberg
4 Columbus Ave. at Montgomery St.
A wedding-cake building that reveals terra-cotta's ability to rival stone in the rendering of decorative detail. The bank, originally the Fugazi Banca Popolare, be-gan in 1859 as John Fugazi's travel agency with banking on the side.

17 Pacific Lumber Co.
1982, Environmental Planning & Research
Washington and Sansome sts.

18 U.S. Customs House
1906-11, Eames & Young
555 Battery St.
While most of the post-fire buildings in the downtown area used stone sparingly, usually in combination with other, less expensive materials such as terra-cotta, the federal goverment built for the ages, as is shown by the Customs House. Decorative detail incorporating patriotic symbols of authority— chiefly the American eagle—enriches the exterior. The interior has generous public spaces, a handsome stairway, and other fine detail.

19 Golden Gateway
Redevelopment Project
Battery St. to the Embarcadero bet. Broadway and Clay St.
Urban renewal plan 1957, Skidmore, Owings & Merrill
Design and development competition 1959, won by Wurster Bernardi & Emmons/DeMars Reay
Phase I residential development, 1961-63:
Master plan, garages, point towers, and town houses along Jackson, WBE/DeMars & Reay
Town houses along Washington St., Anshen & Allen
Landscape architect, Sasaki Walker Assoc.
Phase II Residential development, 1981-82, Fisher/Friedman
This first major downtown housing development, a Redevelopment Agency project, replaced the city's colorful produce market with slab towers and a neat, suburban village of town houses. In 1981-82, the final increments of the project, designed by Fisher/Friedman in a cutout cardboard-model mode veneered with brick, were completed. The ground floors of both phases of the project have commercial space; parking is below grade. Although the interior courts are well scaled and landscaped, the project suffers from discrepancies of scale and shifts

21. Golden Era Building

of style that promise to accelerate its period-piece aspects.

20 Musto Plaza
1970, Bull, Field, Volkmann & Stockwell
350 Pacific Ave.
One of the area's first rehabilitations of an older warehouse structure for office use, it also provides an off-street landscaped plaza. The architects' offices are in the building.

21 Jackson Square
Jackson St. bet. Montgomery and Sansome sts. and adjacent to Montgomery St., Hotaling Pl., and Washington St.
The city's first official Historic District and the only group of downtown business buildings to survive the 1906 earthquake and fire. It has long been the center for wholesale showrooms for interior decorating firms. For a detailed history of the district see the *Jackson Square Report*, San Francisco Department of City Planning, 1971.

Building
400-1 Jackson St.
A post-1906 rebuilding of a c 1882 office structure.

Ghirardelli Building
1853
415-31 Jackson St.
Tobacco and coffee warehouse
1861
435-41 Jackson St.
Jackson Hotaling Annex East
c 1860
443-45 Jackson St.
Hotaling Building
1866
451-61 Jackson St.
Hotaling Annex West
c 1860
463-73 Jackson St.
The last three buildings housed A.P. Hotaling's wholesale liquor business. The main building, 451-61, has the only surviving example of an elaborate, prefabricated, cast-iron facade assembled on brick bearing walls. The Classical-Italian Renaissance styling of the window and wall detail link the building symbolically to the palaces of the merchant princes of the Renaissance.

Building
432 Jackson St.
Rebuilt after 1906 from rubble of other buildings.

Solari Building, East-Larco's Building
1866
470 Jackson St.
Bank of Lucas Turner & Co.
1853-54
498 Jackson St., cor. Montgomery St.
Golden Era Building
(now Knoll Showroom)
1852
Rem. 1950s, Francis Knoll
732 Montgomery St.
The *Golden Era* was an early literary magazine. Mark Twain and Bret Harte were among its famous contributors.

Genella Building-Belli Annex
728-30 Montgomery St.
Belli Building-Langerman's Building
1851
722-24 Montgomery St.
Burr Building
1859-60
530 Washington St.
Nearby along corresponding blocks of Pacific Avenue was the so-called Barbary Coast, the city's major vice center, which alternately prospered and declined until the post-World War II era when it definitely lost its luster. The buildings are all post-l906, but were rebuilt at the former scale. Notable buildings are 450 Pacific, once a well-known brothel, remodeled in 1972 for the *Saturday Review* by Bull, Field, Volkmann & Stockwell, and, at 555 Pacific, a 1907 dancehall. Running through the middle of the block between Washington and Jackson and Sansome and Battery is One Jackson Place, two 1907 warehouses with a passage through to a back courtyard. In 1964 they were remodeled by Lloyd Flood for Alex Tellis into downtown's first conversion of an older building into an interior shopping mall.

22 Columbus Tower
1905, Salfield & Kohlberg
Rem. 1959, Henrik Bull
Columbus Ave. and Kearny St.

23 City Lights Book Store and Vesuvio's
c 1910
235-53 Columbus Ave.
Two social landmarks of the Beat Generation era, the first was the country's first all-paperback bookstore as well as a principal hangout for the literati, which included Allen Ginsberg, Jack Kerouac, Kenneth Rexroth, the owner Lawrence Ferlinghetti, and many others. Across the alley, Vesuvio's was an extension of this memorable scene. Though most of the other gathering places have passed on, a few, such as the Caffe Trieste and the Spaghetti Factory on upper Grant Avenue, survive in name at least.

3 Chinatown/Telegraph Hill/North Beach

T he term North Beach refers to the area west of Telegraph Hill that once was a sand beach, the shoreline of which has been extended about four blocks by fill. It is now terminated by the sea wall constructed between 1881 and 1913. At the foot of Powell was Harry Meiggs's 2,000-foot wharf and amusement park, the location of Abe Warner's famous Spider Palace where the cobwebs were so thick they were said to support human weight. Besides bathhouses and other facilities for swimming and healthful recreation, the area was also home to a number of prominent citizens before the 1860s when Rincon replaced it as the zone of "better residence." A number of industries took advantage of the waterside location, mostly breweries, of which there were ten by 1876. The old Malting House on Francisco between Mason and Powell streets is a lone survivor. It is slated for conversion at some future date into a mixed-use housing and commerical development to be designed by Backen, Arrigoni & Ross. North Beach has long been the local equivalent of New York's Greenwich Village. Over the years its ethnic complexion has changed from Italian to partly Chinese.

24 St. Francis of Assisi
1860, 1918
610 Vallejo St.
The exterior fabric of this church, including the towers, survived the 1906 fire and was incorporated into the present structure. This was the city's first parish church and was founded by the French community. Stylistically it is related to Old St. Mary's, but its Gothic Revival styling is simpler.

25 Fugazi Hall
1912, Italo Fanolini
678 Green St.
John Fugazi, donor of Fugazi Hall, was also the founder of the Transamerica Company, see entry 16. He competed with two other Italian bankers, A.P. Giannini and Andrea Sbarbaro, but eventually all three combined to create the giant Bank of America. Fugazi had the hall constructed as a cultural and community center given in perpetuity to the Italian community. Today, in addition to a museum, it houses a variety of community enterprises.

26 Washington Square
Columbus Ave. to Stockton St.,
Union St. to Filbert St.
Originally a rectangular plot leveled in the 1860s, the square became a promenade after Montgomery Avenue, renamed Columbus in 1909, was cut

through in the 1870s. Several monuments dot the square, including Lillie Coit's monument to the Volunteer Fire Department, sculpted by Haig Pattigan and installed in 1933, and the 1879 statue of Ben Franklin given to the city by H.G. Cogswell. The square was relandscaped in the 1960s by Lawrence Halprin & Associates, and Douglas Baylis.

SS Peter & Paul Church
1922-24, Charles Fantoni
1939, John A. Poporato
666 Filbert St.
This Italianesque Gothic Revival church anchors the square, claiming it as the traditional center of the Italian community. More or less venerable enterprises of Italian origin are located around its edges. SS Peter and Paul's original design, perhaps derived from the cathedral at Orvieto, called for a large mosaic for the central facade. This scheme was abandoned in 1939 when Poporato assumed the commission to finish the church.

27 Building
(formerly Telegraph Hill
Neighborhood Association)
1908-09, Bernard Maybeck
Adds. 1913, 1928
Rebuilt 1940s, John Kelly
1736 Stockton St.
A historic neighborhood center founded by Alice Griffith, a pioneering social

26. SS Peter & Paul Church

27. Former Telegraph Hill Neighborhood Assn.

30. Kahn house

worker, the building was designed in an informal, pseudo-Swiss chalet style and has an attractive courtyard. Converted to apartments and commercial space in the

1960s, the complex received an addition, designed by AGORA, in the 1980s.

28 Union Court
1974, Peters & Clayberg
418-20 Union St.
An attractive rehabilitation project. Nearby are Varennes and Sonoma streets, two of the block-through alley-ways characteristic of the hill. These are lined with simple flat-front buildings, flush with the sidewalk, that recall similar, but older, streetscapes in eastern cities.

29 Houses
1860s
1309, 1313-15 Montgomery St.

c 1870
25, 29 Alta St.

1852
31 Alta St.

1850s
287-89 Union St.

1860s
293 Union St.

Although most of Telegraph Hill's buildings are post-l906, two clusters of houses on the eastern flank of the hill reveal what it looked like in its earliest period of development. The simple wood-frame buildings of almost miniature scale resemble the prefabs shipped from New England to this Yankee outpost. Though few have escaped alterations, they have a time-bound quality that is inseparable from their physical setting. At the end of Union Street there is a spectacular view of the Bay, Levi Plaza, and the Embarcadero.

30 Kahn house
1939, Richard Neutra
66 Calhoun Terr.
A rare northern California example of the European International style by its southern California master, whose most famous work in the idiom is the decade-earlier Lovell Health house in Los Angeles. For another local example of Neutra's work see 6:3.

31 House
1936, William W. Wurster
60 Alta St.
A stuccoed box with a lid, designed for Helen Forbes, the artist of the murals at the Mothers' House in the San Francisco Zoo. Her mural of sea gulls is visible just beneath the roof.

House
c 1860
Rem. c 1970, Audrey Emmons
1308 Montgomery St.
Apartment house
1937, J.S. Malloch, builder
1360 Montgomery St.
One of the city's most exemplary Moderne designs. At the end of Montgomery Street is Julius' Castle, a city landmark on the hill since 1922.

32 Garfield School
1981, Esherick, Homsey, Dodge & Davis
420 Filbert St.
A successful work of environmental design with post-Modern details like the rusticated entrance arch, translated from the previous school. Through its informal massing, plan, choice of color and materials, the building escapes being an institutional blockbuster in this sensitive location.

33 Apartment houses
1940, H.C. Baumann
290 Lombard St.
Bay-Hill Apartments
1950, Hill & Kruse
1725 Kearny St.
An opportunity to contrast two phases of Modern design. 290 Lombard is from the early phase, cubistic with Art Deco ornament, while the Bay-Hill Apartments designed by Henry Hill, a leading architect of the fifties, exemplify the fully developed, post-war Modern aesthetic. Even the unfortunate paint job does not obscure the geometry of the boxlike form, closed on one side and opened up on the other through alternating bands of solids and voids.

31. Apts, 1360 Montgomery

28. Varennes Street

34 Gardner Dailey house
1942, Gardner Dailey
275 Telegraph Hill Blvd.
Designed for himself by one of the Bay Area's most prominent architects of the Modern period, whose work influenced the evolution of a regional expression. This smooth but tasteful box all but vanishes into the streetscape and blends in with its neighbors, which also reflect the beginnings of Modernism. The apartment house at 301 Telegraph Hill Boulevard, 1928, offers an instructive comparison. The architecture wisely does not compete with the splendid view across the street.

32. Garfield School

35 Coit Tower

1934, Arthur Brown, Jr.
End of Telegraph Hill Blvd.

Given to the city by Lillie Coit in memory of her husband, this most familiar landmark occupies the site of the first West Coast telegraph, which originated at Point Lobos and terminated at Point Loma, as the hill was then called. The semaphore telegraph station, built in 1849, communicated the arrival of ships at the Golden Gate; its importance caused the hill's name to be changed. By 1853 the station had been replaced by an electromagnetic line. The next landmark was a castlelike observatory. Built in 1882 and served by a cable car line from 1884 to 1895, it burned in 1903. In 1929, Lillie Coit, a heroine with a penchant for fire-fighting, died, leaving a bequest for beautification with which a monument was commissioned from Arthur Brown, Jr., principal architect of the Civic Center. The result, popularly decoded as a stylized hose nozzle, may also be interpreted as a declassified column because of its fluted shaft and missing capital. The recently restored interior features WPA murals by several artists; it is well worth a visit.

Filbert Steps
Darrell Place
Napier Lane

Below Pioneer Park where Coit Tower stands, Filbert becomes a flight of steps. At 351 is a pair of flats by Gardner Dailey, 1942, that exemplify early Bay Area Modernism in their cubistic form, with balconies angled to the view. The hillside is well landscaped and maintained by the Telegraph Hill Dwellers Association. Below Montgomery the landscaping has been for some years the personal effort of Grace Marchant, whose contribution is commemorated with a plaque. The hill's other cluster of houses from the 1860s and 1870s is here at 228 and 224 Filbert and across the way on the two pedestrian lanes, Darrell Place and Napier Lane. At the end of Darrell is a 1958 studio house by George Rockrise, better seen from below. Though the dates are somewhat uncertain, the houses, as of this writing, are dated as follows: No.10, 1875; No. 15, 1884; No.16, 1872; No.2l, 1885; No.22, 1876; and No.32-34, 1890 but remodeled. A flight of wooden steps leads down the precipitous hillside. Its scarred flank bears witness to the many quarrying operations that chipped away at its rounded base over the years. Among other uses the quarried rock provided fill for the Embarcadero.

36 House

1929
298 Chestnut St.

Although a Mediterranean villa seems logical in this setting, this is the only one.

37 Francisco Middle School

1926, J. Francis Ward
Reconst. 1974-79, Bales & Burns
Francisco St. bet. Stockton and Powell sts.

The popularity of the Spanish-Mediterranean Revival style in the 1920s is attested to by its adoption as the official school style for the decade.

38 San Remo Restaurant
c 1915
Rem. 1978, Monte Bell
2237 Mason St.

39 Building
(formerly T.Y. Lin office)
1974, Jerry Weisbach
15 Vandewater St.
Condominiums
1981, Donald McDonald
33 Vandewater St.
Two other projects by McDonald are at
444 and 460 Francisco St.

39. Condominiums, 55 Vandewater

Condominiums
1981, Daniel Solomon & Assoc.
55 Vandewater St.
This short street has become a showcase
for contemporary design. It also boasts
two architects' offices, Daniel Solomon &
Associates and Batey/Mack, at No. 84.

40 Trinity Properties
1979, Esherick, Homsey, Dodge &
Davis
333 Bay St.
Headquarters for a major local real estate
developer, chiefly in rental housing. The
handsome interior is by the Los Angeles
interior designer Deborah Sussman.
EHDD has designed several projects for
Mr. Sangiacomo. Just down the street at
Stockton and Bay is one that exemplifies
the contemporary, bay-windowed shingle
style of the 1970s.

T.Y. Lin Offices
1977, Sandy & Babcock
327 Bay St.
Among the significant projects of this
world-famous engineer is the Moscone
Convention Center, 1:49.

41 Northpoint Apartments
1967, Wurster, Bernardi & Emmons
2211 Stockton St., 200 and 300
blocks North Point St.
Behind the wall-like facade along North
Point are well-designed courtyards that
make this project an environmental delight for the residents.

42 Pier 39
1981
A triumph of commodity fetishism in
which the circulation is calculated to take
the visitor past all doors with enough
change of scene to hide the lack of
choice. The architecture has all the appeal of a computer program.

43 City buildings
c 1925
111 Bay St.

44 Francisco Bay Office Park
1974-75, Robinson & Mills
50 Chestnut St.
A tasteful, well-scaled and -sited office
park.

45 Telegraph Landing
1979, Bull, Field, Volkmann &
Stockwell
1 Chestnut St.
The first condominium project at this end
of the Embarcadero, the units are varied
in plan and carefully oriented to give privacy and select views of the Bay or the
interior court.

46 Condominiums
1982, Treffinger, Walz & MacLeod
101 Lombard St.

48. Levi Plaza

47 Warehouse
c 1900
Rem. 1980, Hellmuth, Obata &
Kassabaum
1 Lombard St.
An extensive interior remodeling of one
of the fine warehouse buildings in the
north Embarcadero district. The architects
have their offices on the top floors.

48 Levi Plaza
1982, HOK/Howard Friedman/Gen-
sler & Assoc.
Lawrence Halprin, landscape
architect
Battery St. to Sansome St., Union St.
to Greenwich St.
A benchmark in corporate headquarters
design, this low-rise complex of brick
buildings is scenographically composed
to enhance the view of Telegraph Hill
and even incorporate it as borrowed scenery. The well-orchestrated site plan in-
terlocks the buildings with the
landscaped plaza and provides a sweep-
ing surburban park across Battery that is
the most luxuriously appointed corporate
front yard in town. The fountains are the
latest in the line of Sierra mountainscape
tour de forces designed by Lawrence

Halprin. Also commendable is the rehabilitation of two older warehouse
buildings, the Italian Swiss Colony Building (1903, Hemenway & Miller) and the
Cargo West Building of 1879 at Battery
and Union.

49 The Ice Houses No.l & No. 2
1914
Rem. 1970, Wurster Bernardi &
Emmons
1265 Battery St., 151 Union St.
The first of many conversions of old
warehouses to new uses that have enlivened the area with often inventive designs melding the old and the new. A
walk down Battery Street, the verge of the
original waterfront, will reveal many
more.

4
Nob Hill
Russian
Hill

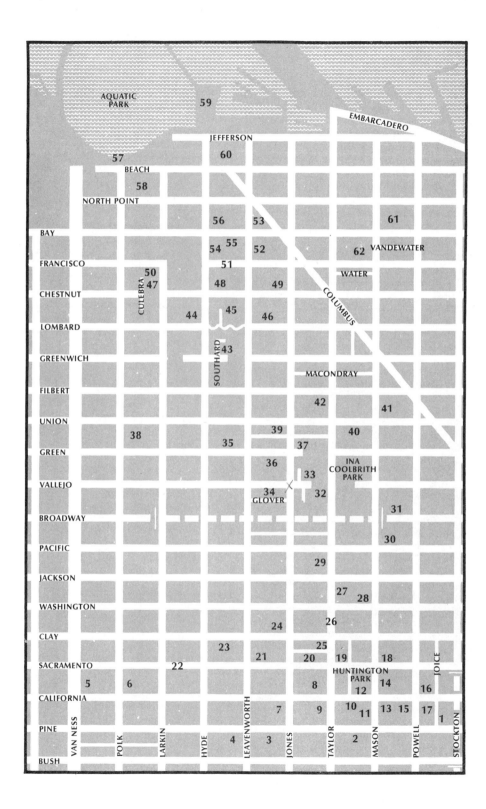

AQUATIC PARK

59

EMBARCADERO

JEFFERSON

57   60

BEACH

58

NORTH POINT

56   53   61

BAY

54 55   52   62 VANDEWATER

FRANCISCO   51

50   WATER

CULEBRA 47   48   49

CHESTNUT

44   45   46   COLUMBUS

LOMBARD

SOUTHARD 43

GREENWICH

MACONDRAY

FILBERT   42

41

UNION

38   39   40

35   37

GREEN   36

33   INA COOLBRITH PARK

VALLEJO   34   32

GLOVER   31

BROADWAY   30

PACIFIC   29

JACKSON   27 28

WASHINGTON   26

24

CLAY

23   25

21   20 19 18   JOICE

SACRAMENTO   22

HUNTINGTON PARK

5   6   8   14   16

CALIFORNIA   12

7   9   10 11 13 15 17   1

PINE   4   3   2

BUSH

VAN NESS   POLK   LARKIN   HYDE   LEAVENWORTH   JONES   TAYLOR   MASON   POWELL   STOCKTON

51

4 Nob Hill/Russian Hill

Only a few people ventured to live on the knoblike hill that rose up sharply behind the burgeoning city of the 1850s and 1860s. Rincon Hill was the prime residential neighborhood and remained so until Andrew Hallidie invented the cable car, which ran first up Clay Street in 1873 and then up California Street in 1878. Thereafter the hill was called Nob—no one really knows why. The ostentation of the first hill climbers—the Big Four who controlled the all-powerful railroads, the Comstock Bonanza kings, and other assorted millionaires—was expressed in a stand of mansions redolent of instant wealth, which, along with their setting, have been forever stamped on the national memory.

The powerful were not spared by the 1906 fire; all the instant palaces were leveled except for James C. Flood's brownstone mansion, entry 12, and the Fairmont Hotel, entry 14, still under construction when the disaster struck. The hill's first owners have been perpetuated in the hotel names (the Mark Hopkins, the Fairmont, and the Stanford Court) and various shards of the pre-fire scene. One such remnant is the impressive Sierra granite wall, contributed by the engineers of the Central Pacific Railroad in the mid-1870s, that surrounds the block on which the mansions of Mark Hopkins and Leland Stanford stood. Elegance did not depart the hilltop with the nabobs, following the fire. The hotels, town houses, and Grace Cathedral preside over one of the city's truly urbane areas. Still, the hill is much larger than its illustrious center; the overall population is mixed both ethnically and economically, as the reader who follows this tour will see.

1. Joice Street Steps

1 Joice Street Steps
One of the charming byways that contribute to San Francisco's Old World image. No. 50, designed by John Kelley in 1949, is a good example of post-war Bay Region Modernism.

2 Apartment houses
1915, Rousseau & Rousseau
900-8 Pine St.

1911, Sitler Bros., builders
901-23 Pine St.

1911, Rousseau & Rousseau
930 Pine

1912, Joseph Cahen
950 Pine St.

1974, Beverly Willis & Assoc.
955 Nob Hill Ct.

1912, James F. Dunn
961 Pine St.

1910, J.A. Poporato
972-76 Pine St.

1909-11, Cunningham & Politeo
985-95 Pine St.

4 Nob Hill/Russian Hill

2. Apts, 901-23 Pine

One of the city's most homogeneous stands of apartment houses occupies the downtown slopes of Nob Hill. Since most of them were built within a few years after the 1906 fire, they convey the fashionable streetscape of that time. Although their names may be unfamiliar today, the architects of these buildings were among the post-fire decades' most active practitioners. The viewer will note thematic variations on styles that are difficult to classify. The basic vocabulary of decorative detail is Classical, but there is also a liberal sprinkling of the curvaceous floriate forms associated with Art Nouveau. A few contemporary designs have been pieced into the old fabric. A walk up and down Pine, Bush, and the cross streets in this district will be particularly rewarding to those for whom architectural sightseeing is a typological game.

3 Apartments
1909, C.O. Smith
1111 Pine St.

1968, Whisler/Patri
1144 Pine St.

1912, Charles J. Rousseau
1145 Pine St.

1913, F.S. Holland
1155 Pine St.

1913, Rousseau & Rousseau
1163 Pine St.

4 Marie Antoinette Apartments
1909
1201 Pine St.
French flats
1919, James F. Dunn
1250 Pine St.
The entrance composition of the first building is truly eye-catching; the second is one of the half dozen or so often-flamboyant exercises in French Art Nouveau that Dunn built in various parts of the city. For others see entry 20 and 8:12.

5 Bank of America
Auto Center Branch
1969, Smith, Barker & Hanssen
1640 Van Ness Ave.
An early drive-in city bank. Its most interesting elevation is around the corner on California Street.

6 Royal Theatre
1925, Miller & Pflueger
1529 Polk St.
One of several exotic theaters designed by this firm in the 1920s and 1930s, but not so exotic as the Alhambra down the street, entry 38.

7 Cathedral Apartments
1930, Weeks & Day
1201 California St.
This firm designed two of the largest apartment buildings on the top of Nob Hill, see also entry 18, as well as two of the major hotels, entries 10 and 13. Although the work is more competent than exciting, its consistency and restraint are qualities that help knit this otherwise not-very- coherent assemblage of buildings together.

8 Grace Cathedral
1911-28, Lewis P. Hobart
Completed 1964, Weihe, Frick & Kruse
California St. bet. Taylor and Jones sts.
Cathedral House
1911, Austin Whittlesey
1055 Taylor St.

10. Morsehead Apts/ 11. Town houses

Diocesan House
c 1912, Austin Whittlesey
1051 Taylor St.
Cathedral School
1965, Rockrise & Watson
1275 Sacramento St.

This complex of buildings occupies the site of the Charles Crocker mansion. After the mansion was destroyed in 1906, the family gave the property to the Episcopal diocese, which commissioned the English architect George Bodley to design a structure that was built and supervised by Lewis Hobart's office from 1910, when the cornerstone was laid, to 1928, when construction ceased for lack of funds. The structure could not be executed in stone for seismic reasons. Although Gothic in reinforced concrete was highly aberrant to purists, the quality of the bush-hammered concrete surface is now much admired. On its completion in 1964, replicas of Ghiberti's bronze doors from the Cathedral Baptistry in Florence, Italy, were installed at the new east end. The stained glass in the west end is by the Charles Connick Studios in Boston, while that in the east end is by Gabriel

Loire of France and the Willet Studios in Philadelphia. Tours of the interior are given several times a week.

Cathedral House was originally designed as the Church Divinity School of the Pacific, but is now used for offices, as is the Diocesan House next door. Both buildings are well scaled to buffer the street edge and help define an entrance court. The new Cathedral School is neatly shoehorned into its restricted site and its rooftop playground is an architectural feature.

9 Masonic Memorial Temple
1958, Albert Roller
1111 California St.
A gleaming white monumental mass that, if it does nothing else, anchors one corner of the hilltop.

10 Huntington Hotel
1924, Weeks & Day
1075 California St.
Nob Hill Center Garage
1956, Anshen & Allen
1045 California St.
Town house
1911, George Schasty
1021 California St.
Morsehead Apartments
1915, Houghton Sawyer
1001 California St.

Though quite different in style and scale, these four buildings hang together very well. The hotel epitomizes discretion and taste, and the garage is, for the times, remarkably deferential to its old neighbors. Schasty's town house is a welcome transplant from New York, while Sawyer's apartment house, also reminiscent of Paris, turns the corner gracefully by means of its baroque cornice and balconies.

11 Town houses
1917, Willis Polk
831-49 Mason St.
An urbane row that continues the spirit of the previous entries.

12 Pacific Union Club

(orig. James Flood mansion)
1886, Augustus Laver
1908-12, Willis Polk/ D. H. Burnham & Co.
1934, George Kelham
1000 California St.

Because it was built of Connecticut brownstone and not wood, Flood's mansion survived the 1906 fire that devastated the more ostentatious homes of his neighbors. When the gutted shell was to be restored as the new home of the Pacific Union Club, William Bourn, Willis Polk's great patron who was on the building committee, got him the commission. Polk's sensitive remodeling, which consisted in adding wings, suppressing the tower over the entrance, and fenestrating and topping the third floor with a balustrade, improved the proportions and changed the architectural character from that of a dry, tightly drawn 19th-century town house to more free-flowing, neo-Classical 20th-century manor house. The interiors, accessible only to members and their male guests, are the quintessential image of a gentleman's club. The bronze fence surrounding the property is the city's finest; Flood allegedly employed one man just to polish it.

West of the club is Huntington Park where stood the David Colton house, later purchased by Collis P. Huntington, who gave the land to the city after l906. This oasis features a replica of the Tartarughe Fountain in Rome minus the tortoises. To sit in the park on a sunny day is to feel on top of the world.

13 Mark Hopkins Hotel

1925, Weeks & Day
999 California St.

The city's most flamboyant Stick-style palace occupied this site before the fire. Built by Mark Hopkins, the most aescetic of the Big Four, the pinnacled pile was really for his wife, who inherited it when Hopkins died in 1878. In 1893, she gave it to the San Francisco Art Association (now the Art Institute), which occupied it until it burned in 1906, subsequently selling it to purchase the Institute's present site on Russian Hill. The hotel is in the abbreviated Gothic Revival style of the 1920s and is notable for its site plan, which incorporates a drive-in entrance court, and for the 1936 rooftop lounge designed by Timothy Pflueger, the Top of the Mark, long the most famous cocktail lounge in town and ancestor of all hotel-top restaurants.

14 Fairmont Hotel

1906, Reid Bros.
Rest. 1907, Julia Morgan
Tower add. 1962, Mario Gaidano
950 Mason St.

James G. Fair, a Comstock silver king, owned the property; his daughter Tessie Fair Oelrichs built the hotel, which was on the verge of opening when the 1906 disaster struck. Julia Morgan restored and completed the interior, but Dorothy Draper is rumored to have designed the lobby appointments, including the wonderful carpet. The Fairmont and the Pacific Union Club are the two most complementary structures on the hill, the one huge and light, the other compact and dark. Despite the much larger size and neo-Baroque grandeur of the hotel, its scale does not diminish the importance of the former mansion. Inquire at the hotel desk for the location of the Reid Brothers rendering of the hotel with terraced gardens that were never built. Ride the elevator in Gaidano's 1962 tower for an unforgettable view of the city.

12. Pacific Union Club/ 14. Fairmont Hotel

15 Stanford Court
1911, Creighton Withers
Rem. 1972, Curtis & Davis
905 California St.
The California Street Cable Car line was started by Leland Stanford as a tidy investment that could also, if he wished, transport him to his door. After 1906 a luxury apartment house with an inner court replaced his palace. It was converted at great expense to a luxury hotel, but somehow the low-ceilinged court does not convey a sense of grandeur.

16 University Club
1912, Bliss & Faville
800 Powell St.
Apartments
c 1915
830-50 Powell St.
Francesca Apartments
1923, MacDonald & Couchot
850 Powell St.
The University Club was designed in the Italian Renaissance palace style that was once fashionable for city clubs. It is a very dry exercise compared with similar buildings by this firm: see 1:26. The apartment houses that line the rest of the block continue the general decorum of the hilltop above.

17 Arcona Apartments
1912, C.A. Meussdorffer
851 California St.
A standard U-plan building tarted up with pseudo-Tudor detail.

18 Brocklebank Apartments
1926, Weeks & Day
1000 Mason St.
Park Lane Apartments
1924, Edward E. Young
1100 Sacramento St.
The drive-in court of the Brocklebank echoes that of the Mark Hopkins on the other side of the Fairmont and provides a protected circulation zone along this side of the hill.
The Park Lane Apartments provide a counterbalancing mass for the Brocklebank, with rather minimal Moderne detail.

19 The Nob Hill
1958
1190 Sacramento St.
An unusually slender apartment tower that preserves the scale of the hilltop far better than its more recent neighbors.

20 Apartments
1916, Arthur Laib
1230, 1242 Sacramento St.
Parisian influence is very strong in these two finely detailed apartment houses in a particularly choice block. The incongruous tiled roof on No. 1242 is perhaps a later remodeling.

The Chambord Apartments
1921, James F. Dunn
1298 Sacramento St.
Often remarked on for its kinship with the work of Antonio Gaudi, this apartment building owes its swelling forms to an unusual floor plan in which oval living rooms are stacked in the corners of the building and expressed in the bowed-out balconies. The plasterwork Art Nouveau cartouches that adorned the balconies were stripped away years ago, but Dunn's other work, such as entry 4, 5:30, and 8:12, will permit the viewer to fill in the blanks.

21 Apartments
c 1911, Charles McCall
1202-6 Leavenworth St.
Apartments
1908-09, James F. Dunn
1201-19 Leavenworth St.
McCall's design for this brown-shingled apartment house was for years attributed to Julia Morgan because of its resemblance to Morgan's rural-suburban residential buildings in Berkeley. Across the street is an example of Dunn's pre-Francophile style in a Classic Revival apartment house that rambles on and on up the block.

20. Apts, 1230, 1242 Sacramento

23. Apts, 1425-29 Clay

22 Coronado Apartments
1911
1590 Sacramento St.
Apartments
c 1910
1601 Sacramento St.
Apartments
c 1910
1451 Larkin St.
Apartments
1907
1560 Larkin St.

Apartment houses listed here and in the following entries were built, with a few exceptions, during the post-fire decade. They have an engaging diversity of style within the two broad and enduring categories of Classical and Medieval: some have a more or less symmetrical composition and use a Classical vocabulary of ornament, and others are composed asymmetrically or picturesquely and use decorative motifs associated with Gothic. Yet there are no hard and fast rules; some designs are a rich stew of both. The last two buildings listed above are good examples of the two stylistic types.

23 Apartments
1907, G.H. Osterbeck, builder
1425-29 Clay St.
Apartments
1909
1417-27 Clay St.

24 Clayerest Apartments
1912-13, E.L. Marlsbury
1357 Clay St.
House
1908, McCall & Wythe
1329 Clay St.
Clay-Jones Apartments
1929, Albert H. Larsen
1250 Jones St.
Comstock Apartments
1960, Hammarberg & Herman
1333 Jones St.
Apartments
1913, Henry C. Smith
1342 Jones St.
Apartments
1908, W.G. Hind
1350 Jones St.

A diverse group. The first listing, the Clayerest, exemplifies a building type that is found throughout the older neigh-

26. Apts, 1255-57 Taylor

31. Nuestra Senora de Guadalupe

borhoods and is sometimes called Edwardian to distinguish it from Victorian styles. Its characteristics are rounded bays—although slanted bays are sometimes used for variety—Classical porticos, and substantial cornices with dentil courses and modillions. The house at 1329 Clay is a good example of Elizabethan Revival style, one of a variety of medieval styles that became popular in the late 19th century and crossed over into the 20th. The thirty years that separate the Clay-Jones from the Comstock reveal significant changes in scale and massing. Though the Comstock is a relatively thin slab, its dehumanized base with auto access and two levels of parking breaks the continuity of the street in ways that the previous generation of giants such as the Clay-Jones did not.

25 Apartments
1908, Bakewell & Brown
1135-41 Taylor St. at Pleasant St.
A restrained shingled block designed as a home and studio for the artist Emil Pissis. Oddly enough, the most formal elevation is up the hill on the side street. These treelined blocks of Taylor offer a pleasant interlude that reminds us that street- tree planting is a relatively recent phenomenon in San Francisco.

26 Apartments
1914, Austin Whittlesey
1224-32 Taylor St.

1911, U.E. Evans
1250 Taylor St.

1980, Kurtzman & Kodama
1234 Taylor St.

1915, Falch & Knoll
1255-57 Taylor St.

Apartments
1909, Charles Whittlesey
1230-38 Washington St.

1910, Henry C. Smith
1240-54 Washington St. (1315 Taylor)
No. 1224-32 is strongly influenced by contemporary Parisian apartment design.

Charles Whittlesey favored the Pueblo Revival style, as can be seen in 1240 Washington, which also fronts on Taylor. For his other work in this vein see entry 33. Next door at No. 1230 is a vigorous example of the Craftsman style.

27 Row of flats
1910, Arthur J. Laib
1314-30 Taylor St.
Clearly a more modest budget dictated this row of Mission Revival flats than Laib's other work on Sacramento, entry 20.

Hillgate Manor
1923, Henry Gutterson
1360-90 Taylor St.
An agreeable way of planning a moderate-sized apartment building that gives the occupants the amenity of a garden court and the passersby a visual treat. This type of building in the city appears to have been a rare commission for Gutterson— more's the pity. For other work by this prominent architect of the 1920s and 1930s, see St. Francis Wood, 16:22; the Camp Fire Girls building, 12:30; and Arden Wood, 16:24.

28 Cable Car Barn and Museum
c 1910
1200 Mason St.
This is the last cable car powerhouse in operation in the world and worth a visit both for the machinery and for the museum collection, which includes the original Clay Street cable car. Hallidie was an English-born inventor and engineer who came to San Francisco during the Gold Rush era and produced the West Coast's first wire cable, the first step in the invention of the cable car. Both a building, 2:10, and a plaza, 1:15, are named for him.

29 Apartments
1929, Albert H. Larsen
1425 Taylor St.
This neo-Churrigueresque apartment house is almost interchangeable with some in the same style that were built by H.C. Baumann, a competitor in the field of apartment house design, see entry 35.

30 Public housing for the elderly
1980, John Bolles
True Sunshine Episcopal Church
1970, John Bolles
1430 Mason St.
Monolithic terraced housing with a reasonable scale for this densely packed area; the chapel and playground provide streetside amenities.

31 Nuestra Senora de Guadalupe
1906, 1912, Shea & Lofquist
908 Broadway
Once the parish church for the city's Latin quarter, this lovely landmark would fit just as well in the landscape of Spain or Portugal. The interior is a bit of the Old World.

32 House
1909, Houghton Sawyer
1629 Taylor St.
A Tudor Revival house in gray stucco, freely planned to take advantage of the hillside site.

4 Nob Hill/Russian Hill

Though the Russian sailors' cemetery for which the hill is named may be mythical, the name is secure. Both historically and architecturally this is one of the city's richest areas, worth exploring at leisure. The 1000 block of Vallejo marks the hill's 360-foot summit and a peak architectural experience as well. While those who wished to lord it over downtown lived on Nob Hill, a bohemian aristocracy inhabited the more rustic slopes of Russian Hill, where the Livermore family had a farm and orchard and where lived such writers as Ina Coolbrith, Bret Harte,and Charles Warren Stoddard, known collectively as the Golden Gate Trinity. Coolbrith, state poet laureate, lived at Taylor and Vallejo, where there is now a tiny park named for her. Helen Hunt Jackson also lived and died on the hill's eastern brow. Perhaps because it was so sparsely built and because there were wells, a few enclaves escaped the 1906 fire. The largest of these is bounded by Green, Taylor, Broadway, and Jones; it still has a woodsy look. Tucked in here and there on its slopes are some very early, nearly invisible houses. Out of respect for the occupants' privacy we list only the visible ones, a considerable treasure trove.

33 1000 block Vallejo St.,
Russian Hill Pl.,
Florence St. &
Ina Coolbrith Park

Willis Polk designed the double access ramp in 1914 when the Livermore family commissioned him to design the houses at 1, 3, 5, and 7 Russian Hill Place, built in 1916. The plan of the block is scenographic, with the ramps converging on a central access to the heart of the block, while the flanking side streets, Russian Hill Place and Florence Street, are lined with houses that define a keyhole view and shield the block's interior. Polk's Russian Hill Place houses make two important contributions: on the Jones Street side they form a subtly articulated wall closing off the street and on the upper side they become cottages lining a brick-paved country lane. Polk's use of over-scaled Classical detail is particularly effective here. No. 1085 Vallejo by Charles McCall and Nos.35, 37, and 39 Florence Street by Charles Whittlesey (c 1920) depart from Polk's variations on the Spanish Mediterranean theme. Whittlesey's are Pueblo Revival, but they perform the same functions as Polk's designs in regard to the street.

Until very recently the interior of the block was quite open. The new condominiums by Esherick, Homsey, Dodge & Davis, designed with great respect for their famous setting, occupy the sites of two famous brown-shingle houses that were demolished for a fortunately never-realized high-rise scheme. Still recalling the early context of the hill are the Marshall houses at 1034 and 1036, two of three gable-roofed, brown- shingled reminders of New England farmhouses. They were built by a parishioner of Joseph Worcester, pastor of the Swedenborgian Church, 6:38, whose rustic cottage once stood at at the end of the row. The old Livermore house behind the fence at 1045 dates from 1860. Willis Polk remodeled it c 1891. Another famous architect who lived in the house in the late 1930s was William W. Wurster, who also did some remodeling to the interior. The gem of the hilltop is the Polk-Williams house at 1013-19. Willis Polk designed it for his family, which, at the time it was built in 1892, included his father, mother, brother, and wife. The client for this double house was a painter, Mrs. Virgil Williams, whose husband had founded the California Institute of Design. According to Richard Longstreth, an authority on Polk, he apparently waived the commission in exchange for the eastern frontage for his own use. The shingled facade does not divide neatly in two parts, but rather suggests a street row in a medieval village. The old saw about the house with the Queen Anne front and the Mary Ann behind fits well here. The back tumbles down the hillside, taking advantage of the slope to add layers of space. Polk's studio was on a lower rear level. The interior of the Polk house is a remarkable sequence of vertically organized spaces.

Below the parapet at the end of the block is a 1958 house by Anshen & Allen, with a 1970s addition by Claude Oakland. At the head of the Vallejo Street steps leading down to Mason is Ina Coolbrith Park.

34 Condominiums
1982, Daniel Solomon & Assoc.
15-17 Glover St.
An ingenious use of a narrow site.

35 Apartments
c 1925, H.C. Baumann
1101 Green St.
One of Baumann's neo-Churrigueresque apartment blocks with a well-detailed lobby. Fortunate are those who live on the upper floors!

House
c 1980, Kirby Fitzpatrick
1110 Green St.
The houses across the street from this contemporary town house are not so remarkable as the mighty retaining wall that supports their site.

33. Houses, 1,3,5,7 Russian Hill Place

34. Condominiums, 15-17 Glover
Photo: Henry Bowles

36 Houses
1907
1088 Green St. (former firehouse)

1966, Joseph Esherick
1085 Green St.

1857, adds. 1880s
1067 Green St.
(Feusier Octagon)

1866
Rem. 1916, Julia Morgan
1055 Green St.

1880s
1045 Green St.

1880s
1039-43 Green St.

Except for 1085 this is a rare group of survivors of the l906 fire; the flats, No. l039-43, were moved here after the fire. The Feusier Octagon, like the octagonal house occupied by the Colonial Dames,

5:10, was inspired by Orson Fowler's tract on healthful living, *A Home for All.* The added mansard roof made it fashionable in the 1880s. This rather miscellaneous collection of houses established a homogeneous domestic scale for the block.

37 House
1880s(?)
982 Green St.
This is probably another 1906 survivor.

38 Alhambra Theatre
1930, Miller & Pflueger
Polk St. bet. Union and Green sts.
Moorish was but one of several exotic styles early movie palaces employed; this is San Francisco's only example.

39 Macondray Lane
A walk down this two-block pedestrian street on the steep north face of Russian Hill should make you want to move right in—unless both your soul and your feet are flat. Macondray Terrace, the contemporary condominiums by Hood Miller Associates (1981), deserve the highest praise for sensitive siting, planning, use of materials, and compatibility with a difficult site.

40 Houses
1910-12, John A. Porporato
858, 864, 873 Union

1912, Charles Fantoni
811 Union St.

1917, Paul DeMartini
887 Union St.

1907, Righetti & Kulh
901 Union St.

1907, 1917, John A. Porporato
919, 920 Union St.

1909, 1907, John A. Porporato
927, 953, 988 Union St.

1922, Louis Traverso
940 Union St.

1917, Rousseau & Rousseau
962 Union St.

41 1800 block Mason St.
1909-11, Paul J. DeMartini and Louis Traverso
(except for 1834-38 by Biglietto & Trevia)
Italian architect-builders had lucrative practices in this neighborhood after the 1906 fire. These blocks are representative of the kind of multiunit buildings that were considered simply adequate for the neighborhood population of the time but today represent an almost priceless investment.

42 Hancock School
1910, Newton Tharp
Filbert and Taylor sts.

43 Southard Place
1981, Daniel Solomon & Assoc.
Southard Pl. and Greenwich Terr.
Another well-designed condominium complex by a leading firm in the field. For others see 6:38 and 13:10.

44 Fannie Osborne Stevenson house
1900, Willis Polk, with later additions
1100 Lombard St.
Additions have made a hodgepodge of this house, but the client, widow of Robert Louis Stevenson, and the architect, a staunch member of San Francisco's Bohemia, validate its claim to importance.

Condominiums
1980, Treffinger Walz MacLeod
1141 Chestnut St.
Condominiums
1979, Sandy & Babcock
2320-2 Hyde St.
Hyde-Greenwich Condominiums
1980, Bull; Field, Volkmann & Stockwell
A series of contemporary condominiums by some of the most accomplished practitioners in the field.

Lombard Street wiggle
This may be San Francisco's most famous street, as can be attested to by the number of photographers stationed at the top or bottom of the block on any given day. The gardens in the median strip are communal.

36. Feusier Octagon

48. House, 998 Chestnut

49. SF Art Institute

45 House
1938, Gardner Dailey
65 Montclair Terr.
An example of Gardner Dailey's adaptation of the European International style.

House
1956, Henry Hill
66 Montclair Terr.
The influence of Eric Mendelsohn on Hill's work is clear in this ribbonlike wall that balloons out into a cantilevered semicircular bay, giving dramatic accent to an otherwise simple house. The entrance off Montclair opens onto a sheltered court.

46 Wright house
1907, Willis Polk
950 Lombard St.

47 Houses
1963, Joseph Esherick & Assoc.
120-2, 126-28 Culebra Terr.
Esherick's own house plus rental units, neatly tucked into a tight site on a very steep hillside.

48 House
1948, John Funk
998 Chestnut St.
Almost a textbook illustration of the International- style compositional approach to designing a building as a series of overlapping horizontal and vertical planes. The cubistic geometry shows off to advantage on this spectacular site. The 1954 duplex by Funk at No. 19-21 Sharp Street was pure geometry on a very private site until an insensitive upper floor was added.

49 San Francisco Art Institute
1926, Bakewell & Brown
Adds. 1970, Paffard Keatinge Clay
800 Chestnut St.
Two versions of exposed concrete, each highly successful in its own way. The older building is a stripped-down but gracious Mediterranean Revival building cast as a monastery complete with cloister. The contemporary addition is in Le Corbusian *beton brut* with rooftop elements treated as sculpture and walls articulated with the master's work in mind.

House
1927, B.F. Wayne
805-7 Chestnut St.
A very sensitive site plan for this house, which combines traditional Mediterranean Revival elements with nontraditional materials such as industrial steel sash windows.

50 Walters house
1951, Wurster, Bernardi & Emmons
2475 Larkin St.
This large town house is handled with a splendid disregard for formality. Its casual exterior covers an interior of great dignity and spatial interest, organized to take maximum advantage of the view.

51 Houses and apartments
c 1940, James Hjul, engineer
800 Francisco St. (Moderne apartments)

1890s
Rem. Joseph Esherick
807 Francisco St.

Before 1854, R.C. Ruskin
Rem. several times
825 Francisco St.

1912, John Galen Howard and Mark H. White
864 Francisco St.

1979, Don Knorr
888 Francisco St. (Knorr house)

1914, Ward & Blohme
898 Francisco St. (Patigian house)

This block has a remarkably varied group of houses ranging from one of the city's oldest at 825, through almost every period and style to Don Knorr's late seventies contemporary.

52 Houses
c 1926, Winfield Scott Wellington
2423, 2455 Leavenworth St.
Were these houses stuccoed, their cubistic geometry would reveal their modernity. Shingled and weathered, they blend in perfectly with their context.

57. National Maritime Museum

53 Studio
1961, Clark & Beuttler
Charles W. Moore, designer
2508 Leavenworth St.
This studio addition to an older house is ingeniously angled to catch the view and define the entry.

54 Cottage row
c 1900, Lucius Solomon, builder
2540-50 Hyde St.
An engaging gable-roofed row.

55 Terraced houses
1850s
Rem. 1937, William W. Wurster
757-63, 765 Bay St.
House
1937, William W. Wurster
737 Bay St.
The first group is beautifully sited to step down the hill. All are deceptively simple early Wurster.

56 Church house
c 1860
Rem. 1954, Thomas Church
2626 Hyde St.
Freely remodeled with a miniature formal court and branching staircase by famed landscape architect Thomas Church, this charming Gothic Revival house has a whimsical scale that goes well with the Gothic ornament.

57 National Maritime Museum
1939, William Mooser Sr. & Jr.
680 Beach St. at Polk St.
Looking appropriately like an oceanliner's superstructure, this streamlined Moderne landmark houses historical material on West Coast shipping, including a fine collection of models and photographs. The murals are by Hilaire Hyler and Sargent Johnson.

58 Ghirardelli Square
1860-1916
Tower Building
1915, William Mooser
Rem. 1962-67, Wurster, Bernardi & Emmons
Polk St. to Larkin St., Beach St. to North Point St.
Deservedly one of the great tourist landmarks, this collection of old (and one new) brick buildings originally housed the Ghirardelli Chocolate Company. It was taken over and remodeled into restaurants and shops by developer William Matson Roth as an almost nonprofit venture. The fountain is by Ruth Asawa, the landscaping by Lawrence Halprin.

59 Hyde Street Pier
(San Francisco Maritime Historical Monument)
End of Hyde St. at Jefferson St.
Administered by the state, the pier has a fascinating collection of old vessels open for visit.

60 Haslett Warehouse Building (Fromm & Sichel Headquarters)
c 1880
Rem. 1973, Wong & Brocchini
NE and SE cors. Hyde and Beach sts.
Old and new brickwork at one of the city's busiest corners, terminus of the Hyde Street cable car.

The Cannery
c 1909
Rem. 1968, Joseph Esherick & Assoc.
2801 Leavenworth St.
An old warehouse was gutted and given a whole new interior structure to house shops and restaurants on three levels with an interior court.

61 Cost Plus Imports
Taylor St., Bay to North Point sts.
An amazing institution—which has spawned many others— that sprawls through a number of old warehouse buildings. Not much architecture, but inventive merchandising.

Longshoremen's Hiring Hall
1959, Henry Hill
400 North Point St. at Mason St.
A polygonal mansard-roofed concrete structure.

62 North Point Public Housing
1950, Ernest Born and Henry Gutterson
Bay St. and Columbus Ave.
These now somewhat battered balcony-access apartments reflect International-style housing design of the post-World War II era. A block south and east on Water Street is a row of simple but charming shanties that were built to rehouse people after the 1906 fire.

56. Church house

5
Pacific Heights
Inner Marina

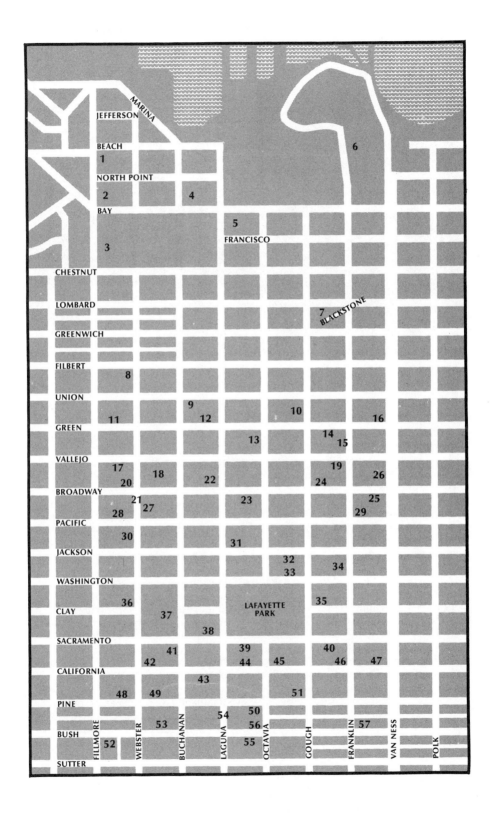

5 Pacific Heights/Inner Marina

Panama-Pacific International Exposition, 1915 (Photo courtesy San Francisco Public Library)

Though the city annexed Pacific Heights as part of the Western Addition in the early 1850s, it became a neighborhood in its own right by the turn of the century. Before that, the hollow north of the ridge was called Golden Gate Valley, an appropriately pastoral name for the vegetable and dairy farms that dotted the landscape. The so-called Laguna Pequena by the Bay shore drew the first settlers because of its fresh water supply from springs. Here laundries and dairy farms flourished, the latter so much so that by the 1870s the area was called, as it is today, Cow Hollow. By this time too, the heights above began to be built up with more pretentious homes whose owners, unable to find space in other fashionable areas of the city, were attracted by the splendid views. They were not pleased, however, by the barnyard aromas from Cow Hollow. In 1891, the city shut down the dairy industry and gave prisoners the task of filling the lagoon with sand from the nearby dunes. Still, Cow Hollow remained a zone of modest residences compared to the Heights.

During the fire that raged for days after the 1906 earthquake, Van Ness Avenue, which runs north-south in a valley, was the first natural break along which the Army Engineers could dynamite to stop the blaze. The resulting destruction of the mansions that lined the boulevard prepared the way for the street's transformation from a prime residential area to the commercial strip it has been ever since. For it was here that the retailers found space to relocate their businesses.

San Francisco's drive to rise phoenixlike from the ashes coincided happily with the completion of the Panama Canal. The dual triumph was celebrated in 1915 with the splendiferous Panama-Pacific International Exposition. The site, located between Black Point and the Presidio, was created by a massive tidal-land fill project carried out by the Army Corps of Engineers. The Exposition was the last of the great fairs to be planned and designed in the Beaux-Arts Classical style initiated by the 1893 Columbian Exposition in Chicago.

According to Louis Christian Mullgardt, who wrote the introduction to *The Architecture and Landscape Gardening of the Exposition*, "the arrangement of this Exposition is

5 Pacific Heights/Inner Marina

distinctive because of its Court Composition. Eight Palaces seemingly constitute a single structure, containing five distinct courts or places for large public gatherings, which are open to the sky." The Expo's Architectural Commission was composed of Willis Polk, chairman; Clarence Ward; W.B. Faville; George W. Kelham; Louis C. Mullgardt of San Francisco; McKim, Mead & White; Carrere & Hastings; and Henry Bacon of New York. John McLaren was in charge of landscaping, Karl Bitter and A. Stirling Calder of sculpture, Jules Guerin of color and decoration. There was also a Department of Travartine Texture to supervise the composition of colored surface materials in order to unify the buildings and sculpture. The most spectacular structure was Carrere & Hasting's glittering, central Tower of Jewels, but the entire complex celebrated the consumption of energy through spectacular night illumination and fireworks displays. The only structure to survive on the site was the beloved Palace of Fine Arts, 6:1.

The Marina, as the greensward bordered by walks and roadways that skirted the Bay was called, remains; its name was given to the district as a whole following the demolition of the fairgrounds. What replaced the great stucco palaces of the Expo was a small-scale stuccoed Mediterranean village with scenographic charm but no great architectural distinction. The neighborhood was first populated—and still is in part—by Italian families.

Today Pacific Heights is one of the city's most richly varied residential areas, with houses of every size and pretension, and a remarkable collection of churches and temples. Its chief commercial strip, along Union Street, has a variety of shops and restaurants catering largely to the upper-class neighborhood around it, as does the other shopping area along Chestnut in the Marina. Fillmore is the main north-south shopping artery spanning Pacific Heights and the Western Addition. Because of the steepness of the slope down to the north from the ridge, most of the great mansions have spectacular views of the Golden Gate and Marin County. It is wise to plan walking tours in an east-west direction (although there are some steep surprises even here) and to travel north and south in a car with good brakes.

1 **Apartment houses**
   1936, 1931, Richard R. Irvine
   1600, 1695 Beach St.
   Double houses
   1935, S.A. Colton
   1627-9 Beach St.

   1939, Oliver Rousseau
   1633-7 Beach St.

2 **Apartment house**
   1933, Richard R. Irvine
   3650 Fillmore St.
The characteristic building types in the Marina are apartment houses, double houses and flats, and single houses; the dominant styles are the range of Mediterranean Revival modes from Spanish to French, and the Modernistic or Moderne styles, which use the vocabulary of stylized ornament associated with Art Deco.

In general, simplified planar forms with ornament restricted to openings and edges, a pastel palette, and a uniform height and scale contribute to the homogeneity of the district. Although the first impression may be one of sameness, there is considerable variation from the Bay to Chestnut Street, abetted by curving streets in part of the area. It is all very walkable.

3 **Marina Middle School**
   1936, George W. Kelham/William P. Day
   3500 Fillmore St. at Bay St.
One of the few large-scale public schools built in the Depression; the stylized decorative detail reflects the influence of Le Style Moderne.

Marina Branch Library
1955, Appleton & Wolfard
Chestnut and Webster sts.
A pleasant, informally scaled branch library with a Mark Adams tapestry in the reading room.

**4   Former San Francisco
Gas Light Company**
1893
3640 Buchanan St.
This brick Richardsonian block is the lone survivor of a former gasworks. It has a walled garden and a handsome interior space.

5   Heritage Retirement Community
1924-25, Julia Morgan
3400 Laguna St.
Julia Morgan designed a number of buildings for benevolent organizations; they are remarkable for their well-worked-out plans and quiet dignity. The Heritage organization, originally a refuge for homeless Gold Rush children, has an L plan with a pleasant and protected south-facing garden court.

6   Fort Mason
The Spanish armed Black Point, or Punta Medanos, as they called it, with a few guns in 1797. By 1822 only one was left. Although the point was declared a U.S.

6. Fort Mason

military reservation in 1850, the Army did not occupy it until the Civil War. In the meantime, several houses were built by squatters, the most famous of whom was John C. Fremont, whose house was demolished in 1864 for a Civil War gun battery. Although they have since been altered, three other houses remain from the pre-Army days. They form an irregular row north from the gate on Bay Street, as follows:

Quarters 2, Brooks house
1855
Quarters 3, Moody house
1855
Quarters 4, Haskell house
1855
In 1877 the larger residence just south and east of these was built as the commanding general's house; it was later converted to an officers' mess.
The fort was used for coast defense batteries until the turn of the century, but its most important function was as port of embarcation for overseas forces from 1912 through the Korean War. Today the piers at the lower (northwest) level that served this function have a new life as the Fort Mason Center, home to a variety of civic cultural activities as well as some shops and restaurants. This portion of the site is accessible from Marina Boulevard. The remaining buildings on the upper level are mostly WPA Mission Revival structures. One of them houses a youth hostel. The entire site is now part of the Golden Gate National Seashore under the direction of the National Park Service.

7   Blackstone house
1851-52
11 Blackstone Ct.
A simple cottage with a two-story porch, one of the city's oldest houses.

**8   Old Headquarters
of the Vedanta Society**
1905, Joseph A. Leonard
2963 Webster St. at Fillmore St.
A meeting of the mysterious East and the uninhibited West.

8. Old Headquarters of the Vedanta Society

Orson Fowler's best selling book, *A Home for All, or The Gravel Wall and Octagonal Mode of Building,* first published in 1849, was the inspiration for about seven octagonal houses in San Francisco. Only two remain, and of the two only this one preserves most of its original appearance despite being moved across the street and remodeled. Now a museum, it is open to the public.

9 Bank of America Branch
1974, Sandy & Babcock
1995 Union St.
Victorian shop front
1981 Union St.

10 The Octagon/National Society of Colonial Dames
1857
Rem. 1953, Warren Perry
2645 Gough St.

10. The Octagon/Society of Colonial Dames

11 Leander Sherman house
1879
2156 Green St.
Built by the founder of the city's leading music store, this large Mansard house has a three-story music room in its west wing where Paderewski, Schumann-Heink, and Lotta Crabtree (a next-door neighbor) performed.

12 Flats
1875
1950-80 Green St.
This early row of apartments was moved here in 1891, reversing what was originally the back elevation for the front.

**13 Golden Gate Valley
Branch Library**
c 1910, Coxhead & Coxhead
Green and Octavia sts.
This terra-cotta-clad branch library shows Ernest Coxhead in a less inventive format than his other, more free-wheeling works that draw on Classical sources.

14 House
1940, William W. Wurster
1641 Green St.
A vintage Wurster house, which demonstrates that unpretentious design can still be assertive.

15 Apartments
c 1915, James F. Dunn
2415 Franklin St.
One of the most elegant of Dunn's essays in this imported Belle Epoque style. For others see 4:4 and 4:20.

14. House, 1641 Green

16. Holy Trinity Russian Orthodox Cathedral

17. Apts, 2255-63 Vallejo

16 Holy Trinity Russian Orthodox Cathedral
1909
1520 Green St.
The city is rich in wood vernacular buildings for almost every religious sect and nationality. This one replaces an earlier church lost in 1906.

17 Apartment group
1909, Stone & Smith
2255-63 Vallejo St.
California's version of the Craftsman style lent itself to picturesque massing and interesting off-street court spaces.

18 Sara Dix Hamlin School
1965, Wurster, Bernardi & Emmons
2129 Vallejo St.
(Second) James L. Flood Mansion
1900-01
2120 Broadway
The imposing Mannerist mansion on Broadway is backed up by WBE's simple and straightforward classroom building below.

19 Apartment group
1920s
1737-57 Vallejo St.
The city's only version of the then-popular Norman farmhouse compound. The court spaces are similar to contemporary Craftsman apartment groups.

Burr house
1875, Edmund M. Wharff
Rem. 1941, W.W. Wurster
1772 Vallejo St.

20 Convent of the Sacred Heart
Andrew Hammond Mansion
1905
2252 Broadway
(Third) James A. Flood Mansion
1912, Bliss & Faville
2222 Broadway
Joseph D. Grant Mansion
1910, Hiss & Weekes (N.Y.)
2200 Broadway
Over the years this school has acquired three of the city's most imposing houses, of which the Italian Renaissance palazzo by Bliss & Faville is the prize.

21 Mansion
1914, G. Albert Lansburgh
2201 Broadway
Italian Consulate
2151 Broadway

Two more handsome brick mansions. The Lansburgh design is notable for its restraint and strong geometry.

22 Apartment buildings
1973, Backen, Arrigoni & Ross
2000 Broadway

Luxury apartments in Brutalist concrete.

23 Two apartment buildings
c 1925, H.C. Baumann
1945, 1955 Broadway

Baumann designed so many white stuccoed Churrigueresque apartment houses all over the city that they have become a distinctive part of its image. Two more are up the hill at 2070 and 2090 Pacific. (Note also the Classical details of the house at 1905 Broadway.)

24 House row
1895, George Hinkel
2414-24 Gough St.
House
1904, Howard White
2340 Gough St.

A characteristic Queen Anne row by a member of a prolific family of late 19th-century builders, and an elegant Spanish Colonial-style house show how tastes changed in the period around the turn of the century.

25 St. Brigid's Church
1900, H.A. Minton
Broadway and Van Ness Ave.

A Romanesque Revival that looks as though it was taken from a steel engraving.

26 Houses
1901
2209 Van Ness Ave.

1908, Moses Lyon
2256 Van Ness Ave.

Two big, flamboyant houses, in different styles, survivors of the once-proud stand on Van Ness Avenue. Another by Moses Lyon is at 2134, and an older Italianate of 1875 is at 2826, moved there from Larkin and Broadway.

27 Bourn Mansion
1896, Polk & Polk
2550 Webster St.

A compact clinker-brick block with Polk's bold and distinctive Classical detailing, this was designed for the president of the Spring Valley Water Company for whom Polk also designed two great estates: Filoli, near Woodside, and the so-called Empire Cottage at his Empire mine near Grass Valley.

27. Bourn Mansion

20. Convent of the Sacred Heart

Leale house
c 1853
2475 Pacific Ave.
One of Pacific Heights's early dairy farm-
houses, which had its facade modernized
c 1875.

28 Apartment building
2340 Pacific Ave.
Representative Art Deco styling.

29 Talbot-Dutton house
1875
Add. 1905
1782 Pacific Ave.
This elegant Italianate was a wedding
present from a lumber tycoon to his
daughter. In 1905, it acquired a matching
wing that created the unusual double-bay
facade.

30 Apartment house
c 1915, James F. Dunn
2411 Webster St.
Dunn's Francophilia varied from the
tasteful, as in entry I5, to the extravagant, as here.

31 California Historical Society
(Whittier house)
1894-96, E.R. Swain & Newton J.
Tharp
2090 Jackson St.
Imported brownstone and a composition
that recalls the early work of McKim,
Mead, & White contribute to the eastern
look of this rather somber mansion. Now
a museum, the interior is well worth a
visit to understand why this house cost
$150,000 in 1894. The former John
Spreckels, Jr., house at 2099, now serves
as the society's library.

32 Greenlee Terrace Apartments
1913, Arthur J. Laib
1925-55 Jackson St.
A densely packed complex in the picturesque Mission Revival style.

Houses
c 1900 brown-shingled double house
2576 Washington St.

33. Spreckels Mansion

1887 Stick style
2527, 2531 Washington St.

1879 Italianate
2560 Washington St.

This block has a good range of older
houses, from the exuberantly painted
towered Queen Anne house to the handsome dark-shingled double house.

33 Spreckels Mansion
1913, MacDonald & Applegarth
2080 Washington St.
A French palace for French Alma de Bret-
teville Spreckels, for whom Applegarth
also designed the Palace of the Legion of
Honor.

34 Haas-Lilienthal house
1886, Peter R. Schmidt
2007 Franklin St.
One of the great monuments of the city's
Victoriana, this queen of Queen Anne
villas is owned by the Foundation for San
Francisco's Architectural Heritage and is
open for tours. (Call 441-3000 for information.) The Haas and Lilienthal families
were among the founders of the city's influential Jewish community and were related to the owners of the cluster of
houses at California and Franklin streets,
entry 46.

35 House
1889, T.C. Matthews & Son
2004 Gough St.
A Queen Anne house with a variety of
plaster reliefs affixed to the facade like
patterns appliqued on a Victorian
sampler.

36 Italianate row houses

1878-79, Henry Hinkel
2209-35, 2239-53 Webster St.

1878-79, The Real Estate Assoc.
2244-50, 2315-21 Webster St.

This fine row by the oldest of this famous family of five brothers is part of a historic district that extends along Webster from Jackson to Clay. Of the 25 houses included in the district, 12 are by Henry Hinkel and 5 by the Real Estate Associates, his competitors. Other builders are also represented. Since all the houses were built between 1878 and 1880, the street has a rare period homogeneity.

37 Presbyterian Medical Center

Webster St. to Buchanan St. bet. Sacramento St. and Washington St.
An outgrowth of the old Stanford University Medical School, founded here in the 1880s, whose original buildings have been demolished. This is an example of the scale and circulation problems brought on by large institutions with heavy parking requirements in a residential area. Skidmore, Owings & Merrill did a master plan for the expansion of the hospital after Stanford moved to Palo Alto in the 1960s, and designed two buildings, the Dental School of the University of the Pacific at 2155 Webster Street (1965) and the Research Building at 22 Webster Street (1963). Stone, Marraccini & Patterson then took over and did the massive new hospital in 1972. One of the most interesting buildings is the old Health Sciences Library at 2395 Sacramento, designed c 1905, which has murals by Arthur Matthews.

38 House

1903
2245 Sacramento St.
Georgian Revival.

House

1895, A. Page Brown
2212 Sacramento St.
A huge Colonial Revival-style box with the requisite Palladian window.

Mansion Hotel

1887
2220 Sacramento St.
A house in transition from Queen Anne to Colonial Revival that has suppressed its towers.

39 House

1881
Rem. c 1910
2151 Sacramento St.
The remodeling of this house, briefly the home of Arthur Conan Doyle, has been attributed to Willis Polk.

40 Five houses

c 1870-1895
1911-21 Sacramento St.
A varied group, ranging from Italianate to early Classic Revival, in an area otherwise largely built up with apartments.

35. House, 2004 Gough

41 Barreda house
1880
Rem. 1904, Willis Polk
2139-41 Buchanan St.
Owned by Fernando Barreda, minister from Spain and Peru to the Court of St. James and the United States, this was remodeled by Polk when he married Barreda's daughter.

42 Temple Sherith Israel
1905
California and Webster sts.

43 Houses
1882, S. & J.C. Newsom
2129 California St.

1882, S. & J.C. Newsom
2145-49 California St.

1880s
2151, 2159 California St.

1882, McDougall & Sons
2165 California St.

1879
2175-87 California St.
The first two houses by the Newsoms have distinctive decorative detail. Note the leatherlike strap work in the spandrel of 2129 and the flat-sawn, cut-out stencil forms on 2145. Nos. 2151 and 2159 have the kind of elegance associated with the Hinkels, while 2165 has urns and garlands. Altogether an unusually cohesive row on a stretch of California Street rich in late 19th-century houses.

44 Houses
1880-90
2018-26 California St.
No. 2026 was updated after the 1906 fire with curved glass windows in the front bay and the addition of carved panels below the cornice. The other two houses have both extravagant forms and paint jobs.

45. Atherton house

45 Atherton house
1881-82, Moore Bros., Charles Tilden, builders
1990 California St.
House
1883, Schmidt & Havens
1976 California St.
Two of California Street's most exuberant Victorians, showing the transitions from Italianate to Stick-Eastlake and Queen Anne. The Atherton house was enlarged and restyled a decade after it was built (the date 1881 appears over a pair of upper-story windows). The California Street addition completely changed the orginal house and gave it the scale of a rural Queen Anne villa that appears to be almost bursting out of its site. In 1923, Charles J. Rousseau, member of an important family of architects, bought the house, which was home to his heirs for more than 50 years.

Tobin house
1913, Willis Polk
1969 California St.
Half of a Gothic double house Polk designed for the de Young sisters, one of whom moved away and never built her half.

46 Wormser-Coleman house
1876
Rem. 1895, Percy & Hamilton
1834 California St.
Lilienthal-Pratt house
1876
1818-20 California St.
Coleman house
1895, W.H. Lillie
1701 Franklin St.
Bransten house
1904, Herman Barth
1735 Franklin St.
This corner announces Pacific Heights as an area of stately mansions as you come from downtown. The families were interrelated, which permitted the last house to be oriented toward a communal south garden. The styles range from full-blown Queen Anne on the corner to Georgian Revival at 1735.

47 First Church of Christ Scientist
1915, Edward Matthews
1700 Franklin St.
Polychromed terra-cotta and varicolored brickwork enrich this otherwise staid Lombard- Gothic Revival church. For a similar design see 8:41 in the Haight, also by Matthews. The interior is worth seeing.
Pine Street is the northern boundary of the Western Addition. The Bush-Pine corridor was developed in the 1870s and 1880s when the cable and streetcar lines were extended westward. The small tracts on typically long narrow lots, 25 by 100 feet, were financed by the popular building societies of the building and loan associations. Apparently some lots were even offered by lottery. When the automobile replaced rail transit and the more western neighborhoods became accessible, the streetcar suburb declined. As the A-2 Redevelopment Area's block-by-block demolition proceeded, community protest increased; the destruction finally stopped near Bush, giving a reprieve to the outstanding blocks listed below. Alas, much of what was destroyed was often equally fine and finer.

48 Houses
1877
2208 Pine St.

1875
2210 Pine St.

1877
2212-14 Pine St.

1872
2231 Pine St.

1880, S. & J.C. Newsom
2255 Pine St.

1880
2256-58 Pine St.
No. 2231 has a New England farmhouse look that suggests an earlier date than 1872, but the owners may just have wanted a simple house. No. 2255 by the Newsoms resembles their house at 2129 California Street.

49 Berge house
1884, B.E. Henrickson
1900 Webster St.
An unusual blind-window treatment, doubtless designed to enliven the side elevation while maintaining privacy, distinguishes the side of this elegant town house.

50 Taylor house
1880, Wolfe & Son
1911 Pine St.

51 Houses
1890
1837 Pine St.

1873
1843 Pine St.

1876
1855 Pine St.

1875
1703 Gough St.

1875
1705 Gough St.

1885
1707 Gough St.

1875
1709 Gough St.
Public Housing for the Elderly
1972, Marquis & Stoller
1880 Pine St.
An exposed-concrete high rise with staggered massing to give optimum orientation to the units.

52 Houses
1874, The Real Estate Assoc., builder
2115-25 Bush St.

1874
2103-7 Bush St.

1883, S. & J.C. Newsom
2100-2 Bush St.

1884, Wolf & Son
2104 Bush St.

1882 John Nash, builder
1-6 Cottage Row
The south side has one of the best flat-front Italianate rows in the city. The whole block gives a good idea of the scale and character of tract development in this streetcar suburb, by some of the most active real estate developers and builders of the last quarter of the 19th century.

52. Houses, 2115-25 Bush

53 Stanyan house
1852
2006 Bush St.
Though it is well known that many pre-fabricated houses were shipped to San Francisco from New England during the Gold Rush era, this house is one of the very few that have been so identified. The interior has typical mid-century detail but is scaled down, as are the room sizes, to New England proportions. The Stanyans, who owned the house from 1854 to 1974, replaced their large garden with the flats next door in 1892. Then as now, open space was vulnerable to real estate pressures. The exterior and interior detail was prefabricated in New England and sent around the Horn. The flats next door were built on speculation by the Stanyan family in the 1880s.

54 Houses
1889, William Hinkel
Odd side, Laguna St.

1877, The Real Estate Assoc.
Even side, Laguna St.

5 Pacific Heights/Inner Marina

Two of the most entrepreneurial of the 19th- century builder-developers created this harmonious street. TREA's simple Italianate houses give way to fancier variations on the theme a decade or so later, as taste demanded more complicated frills.

55 Pacific Hall
(Congregation Ohabai Shalome)
1895, Moses J. Lyon
1881 Bush St.
Hebraic-Victorian-Byzantine. 1828-28 Pine Street is a fine row of 1870s houses opposite

Green's Eye Hospital
1915, Frederick Meyer
1801 Bush St.
The gigantic eucalyptus trees in front of this reticent Classical building are said to have been planted by Mary Ellen "Mammy" Pleasant, San Francisco's most mysterious and sinister 19th-century madam, and housekeeper to Thomas Bell, whose mansion stood on this site.

56 Morning Star Church
1715 Octavia St.
A tasteful design in the Japanese manner with fine terra-cotta tiles and decorative detail.

57 Trinity Church
1893, A. Page Brown
1666 Bush St. at Gough St.
A massive fortresslike Gothic Revival church. The large square tower is open to the interior.

57. Trinity Church

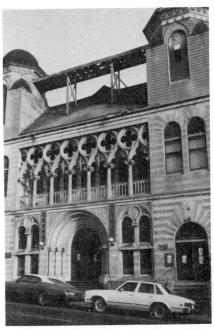

55. Pacific Hall

6
Pacific
Heights
Outer
Marina

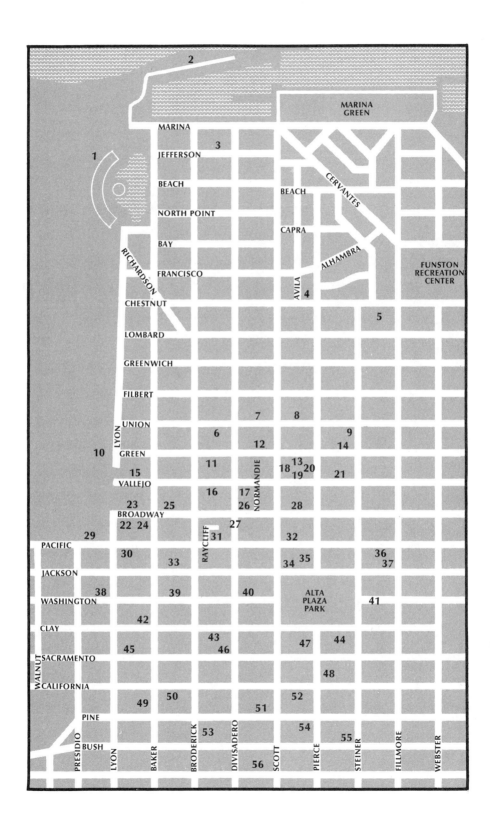

MARINA GREEN

MARINA

3

JEFFERSON

1

BEACH

BEACH

NORTH POINT

CERVANTES

CAPRA

BAY

FRANCISCO

CHESTNUT

ALHAMBRA

AVILA

4

5

FUNSTON
RECREATION
CENTER

RICHARDSON

LOMBARD

GREENWICH

FILBERT

UNION

7   8

6

9

LYON

12   14

10   GREEN

11

NORMANDIE

13
18 19 20   21

15

VALLEJO

16   17
        26   28

23   25

BROADWAY

22 24

27

29

PACIFIC

30

RAYCLIFF

31

32

33

34 35

36
37

JACKSON

38

39

40

ALTA
PLAZA
PARK

41

WASHINGTON

42

CLAY

43

45

46

47   44

WALNUT

SACRAMENTO

48

CALIFORNIA

49 50

52

51

PINE

PRESIDIO

BUSH

LYON

BAKER

BRODERICK

53

DIVISADERO

56

SCOTT

54

PIERCE

55

STEINER

FILLMORE

WEBSTER

6 Pacific Heights/Outer Marina

1. Palace of Fine Arts

1   Palace of Fine Arts
1915, Bernard Maybeck
Baker St. at Beach St.
In 1915, Louis A. Mullgardt described the Palace's design as a free interpretation of Roman forms and a "purely romantic conception, entirely free from…obedience to scholastic precedent. Its greatest charm has been established through successful composition; the architectural elements have been arranged into a colossal theme…into which the interwoven planting and the mirror lake have been incorporated in a masterful way."
Until 1962 the crumbling stucco original of this beloved relic of the 1915 Exposition survived in the melancholy state Maybeck said was the right mood for the fine arts. Then, thanks largely to the generosity and persistence of Walter Johnson, who matched the funds raised by the city, it was restored in concrete and given a new life as a home for the Exploratorium, an auditorium, and other cultural activities.

2   St. Francis Yacht Club
1828, Willis Polk
Rem. 1978, Marquis Assoc.
The Marina
This venerable San Francisco institution suffered severe fire damage in 1976; the interior was redone by the Marquis office.

3   Double house
(Dr. William Schiff)
1937, Richard Neutra & Otto Winkler
2056-58 Jefferson St.
A steel and glass facade of standard industrial sash members. Like the Kahn house on Telegraph Hill, 3:30, it had almost no influence in the Bay Area.

4   Moderne commercial group
1933, Frederick Quandt
2240-68 Chestnut St. at Avila St.
A rare row of almost intact Moderne shop fronts.

5   Crocker Bank, Marina branch
1973, Wong & Brocchini
2055 Chestnut St.
A redwood pavilion with a metal tent roof at the east end of the Marina's bustling shopping strip along Chestnut Street.

6 Rosstown Townhouses
1967, John L. Field
2600 block Union St. near Divisadero St.
A somewhat mannered row, designed to relate to its older neighbors.

7 House
1890, A.C. Schweinfurth
Rem. 1955, John Funk
2516 Union St.
A simplified Colonial Revival house of quiet distinction, by an architect who belonged to the group of architects—Coxhead, Polk, Maybeck, etc.— who forged the Bay Area's first regional approach to design. Funk remodeled the interior for Walter Landor, one of the city's leading graphic and industrial designers.

8 House
c 1872
2460 Union St.
An unusual mansard-roofed house with paired dormers and a central gable.

9 St. Mary the Virgin Episcopal Church
1891
Rem. 1953, Warren Perry
2301 Union St.
The courtyard fountain is fed by one of the springs that nourished Cow Hollow's early dairies. The informal shingled church also reflects the area's pastoral past. Warren Perry's sympathetic remodeling shifted the entrance from Steiner to Union Street.

10 Spanish group
c 1920
2517-25 Lyon St.

1912, S.G. Holden
2535-37 Lyon St.

1915, William F. Knowles
2545-47 Lyon St.

c 1920
2601 Lyon St.

A Mediterranean enclave perched on the Presidio wall. No. 2601 forms a handsome terminus for Green Street.

11 House
1939, William W. Wurster
2633 Green St.
One of Wurster's few overt nods toward the International style.

12 House
1901, Edgar Matthews
2508 Green St.
A half-timbered Craftsman house, whose mate to the left is almost certainly also by Matthews, a prolific designer of shingled houses and apartments in Pacific Heights.

13 Two Houses
1893, 1895, Ernest Coxhead
2421, 2423 Green St.
The quiet exterior of Coxhead's own house at No. 2421 conceals an ingenious interior, with a long glazed entrance gallery on the west side running from a high-ceilinged living room on the street to the dining room on the rear garden. Upstairs the master bedroom has a select view through the corner bay window.

14 St. Vincent de Paul
1916, Shea & Lofquist
Green and Steiner sts.
The exaggerated scale of the pseudo half-timbering, the gabled gambrel roofs, and the tower of this huge church make it unusual among the many Roman Catholic churches designed by this firm in the city. It is stylistically related to the smaller-scale San Anselm's in San Anselmo.

15 House
1950, Joseph Esherick
2960 Vallejo St.
This Shingle house carries on the Cow Hollow tradition of *rus in urbe*. The south court below street level creates an inviting entrance.

16 Two houses
c 1905
2727, 2737 Vallejo St.
House
1938, Wurster, Bernardi & Emmons
2795 Vallejo St.
A pair of dark-shingled houses of the First Bay Tradition, and an originally dark Wurster, Bernardi & Emmons box with the stairway expressed by a diagonal through the hall window.

17 House
1938, John E. Dinwiddie
2660 Divisadero St.
A lone example in San Francisco of the residential work of this prominent local Modernist. The canted, boxed view window was so much imitated by tract builders that it became a cliche.

18 House
1938, Gardner Dailey
2750 Scott St.
A Bay Region adaptation of the European International style, with less rigorous geometry and a pleasant courtyard plan. Dailey was fond of framing windows with half-round moldings.

17. House, 2660 Divisadero

12. House, 2508 Green

19 Warren Perry house
1925, Warren Perry
2530 Vallejo St.
A quiet shingled house, more academically "eastern" than most local work.

20 Casebolt house
1865-66
2727 Pierce St.
Set back in the center of the block, this great Italianate was once the manor house of Cow Hollow. Henry Casebolt, a Virginia blacksmith who arrived and made his fortune during the Gold Rush era, used salvaged ship timbers for much of his mansion's structure. The white exterior was once speckled with dark tones to mimic stone, which, for eastern pioneers, was a higher-class material than wood.

21 House
1968, John L. Field
2440 Vallejo St.
A contemporary version of the l9th-century slanted-bay town house. Field has designed several town houses that draw on familiar prototypes to strengthen their architectural context.

22 House
c 1920
2330 Lyon St.
A rambling Mediterranean-style house with an arcaded entrance court on the uphill side. In plan, if not in style, this is kin to the post- World War II ranch house.

23 Napthaly house
1913, Willis Polk
2960 Broadway
A pink Mediterranean villa.

24 House
1926, Henry Smith
2901 Broadway
An example of determined neo-Classicism prevailing over almost all odds. This Renaissance palace is perched on a cliff and is approached by a complicated ramp from below.

6 Pacific Heights/Outer Marina

20. Casebolt house

22. House, 2330 Lyon

26. Heil house

25 House
1900, Willis Polk
2880 Broadway
A neo-Classical manor house that recalls
the London work of John Nash.

House
1913, Walter Bliss
2898 Broadway
An elaborate Dutch Colonial manor
house that contrasts wonderfully with
Polk's pastel palace next door.

26 Heil house
1941, Gardner Dailey
2674 Broadway
Designed when Joseph Esherick worked
in Dailey's office, this house shows
Esherick's hand in its clear geometry and
simplicity of detail. When built it was a
milestone of Modernism.

House
1968, Bull, Field, Volkmann &
Stockwell
2635 Broadway
Grover house
1939, William W. Wurster
2666 Broadway
A classic early Wurster town house, with
a studied lack of pretension in its form
and materials and a hint of rural simplicity. The practical plan put the garage
and service rooms on the street and left a
sheltered court before the main part of

the house. Also practical was the placement of the living rooms on the upper
floors to gain the maximum view. The
Heil house employed the same plan with
a more cubistic, Modern form.

House
1968, Bull, Field, Volkmann &
Stockwell
2635 Broadway
Similar to entry 21 in its respect for local
prototypes.

House
1953, Wurster, Bernardi & Emmons
10 Normandie Terr.
House
1939, Gardner Dailey
Adds. 1960s, Joseph Esherick
44 Normandie Terr.
A vertical box with a lid, a hallmark of
early Bay Region Modernism. However,
the pronounced picture frame moldings
around the large windows look back to
more traditional detail. The cylindrical
stair tower is a nice foil for the main, rectangular mass. The entrance composition
was added by Esherick, who originally
worked on the house in Dailey's office. A
comparison with the later WBE house at
10 Normandie Terrace shows both the
strong influence of the work of Europeans
like Walter Gropius on early Bay Region
Modernism, and the overtones of rural
suburbia that characterized the main-
stream post-World War II stage of
Modernism.

27 House
1939, William W. Wurster
2560 Divisadero St.
A simplified Regency Revival house with
well- proportioned massing on the site of
an older mansion. Wurster appears to
have favored brick for his more traditional designs and wood for his more informal and more personal work (see
entry 26, the Grover house).

House
1966, John L. Field
2512 Broadway
House
c 1930, Paul Williams
2555 Divisadero St.
A rare northern California work by one of
the country's first prominent black architects, who practiced in Los Angeles and
exported this narrow bit of Hollywood
Regency style to San Francisco.

28 House
1981, J. Ream
2776 Broadway
A futuristic solar house, which looks star-
tling among its staid neighbors.

29 House
1912, Ernest Coxhead
3151 Pacific Ave.
The exigencies of hillside sites encouraged a remarkable freedom in plan and
massing that, when combined with fine
traditional detail as in Coxhead's work,
produced houses that were truly original
without making a great point of it.

House
c 1900
3198 Pacific Ave.
An outstanding example of the plasticity
often achieved by wrapping with shingles
the curved and angled forms of houses
that mixed Queen Anne and Colonial Revival elements.

30 House
1959, Wurster, Bernardi & Emmons
3095 Pacific Ave.
A late Wurster, Bernardi & Emmons box,
when the simplicity of this style was beginning to be mannered.

House
1953, Joseph Esherick
3074 Pacific Ave.
In his third San Francisco town house,
Esherick spaced four-by-fours across the
facade to express the structural module of
the frame. It is interesting to compare this
very restrained structural decoration with
the 19th-century designers' elaboration of
structural members as surface ornament
in the so-called Stick style.

29. House, 3198 Pacific

33. Howard house

31 Houses
1951, Gardner Dailey
1 Raycliff Terr.

1959, Wurster, Bernardi & Emmons
25 Raycliff Terr.

1957, rem. Germono Milono
55 Raycliff Terr.

1951, Joseph Esherick
75 Raycliff Terr.

1890, Arthur Brown, Jr.
2889 Pacific Ave.

1937, Wurster, Bernardi & Emmons
2870 Pacific Ave.

1910, Albert Farr
2830 Pacific Ave.

1912, Willis Polk & Co.
2820 Pacific Ave.

1910, Albert Farr
2810 Pacific Ave.

1899, Ernest Coxhead
2800 Pacific Ave.

A catalog of two generations of local domestic architecture, Raycliff Terrace is a rare collection of Bay Region Modernism that reveals its evolution over two important decades. The other houses provide the more or less traditional context against which Modernism took its stand.

32 House
1904, Newsom & Newsom (Sidney B. and Noble)
2698 Pacific Ave.
The sons and successors to the original Newsoms, following the turn-of-the-century trend to Classicism with a near caricature of entry 34.

House
1937, Wurster, Bernardi & Emmons
2600 Pacific Ave.

33 Howard house
1939, Henry T. Howard
2944 Jackson St.
One of the best of the city's few examples of streamlined Moderne.

34 Music & Arts Institute
(former residence)
1894, Willis Polk
2622 Jackson St.
Probably Polk's first major independent commission, this sandstone house has his characteristic rather heavy, spare Classical detailing.

House
1897, Ernest Coxhead
2600 Jackson St.

35 Houses
c 1910, Edgar Matthews
2415-21 Pierce St.

38. Swedenborgian Church

36 Leale house
c 1853
2475 Pacific Ave.
One of Pacific Heights's early dairy farm-houses, which had its facade modernized c 1875.

37 Calvary Presbyterian Church
c 1900
Christian Education Building
1979, Robinson, Mills & Williams
Fillmore and Jackson sts.
The original church stood at Powell and Geary on Union Square. When it was demolished c 1898, the materials and some of the interior woodwork were reused in the new building at this location. The old school building was replaced in 1979 with a design that strengthens the composition of the block in a contemporary way.

38 Swedenborgian Church
1894, A. Page Brown
2107 Lyon St.
A beloved landmark of the early Crafts-man era, this church brought together the talents of A. Page Brown; Bruce Porter, who sketched the original design and did

the stained glass; Bernard Maybeck; and A.C. Schweinfurth, who did the drawings in Brown's office. The prime mover behind it all was the Rev. Joseph Worcester, pastor of the church and friend and patron of the artists and architects who fostered the Bay Area branch of the California Arts and Crafts Movement. The lovely garden provides the appropriate introduction to the church interior, a living room with a roof supported by untrimmed madrone tree trunks and a great brick fireplace opposite the sanctuary. The stained-glass windows by Porter are complemented by landscape paintings by William Keith. The pegged wooden chairs with seats and backs of woven rushes were credited by Gustav Stickley as the inspiration for Mission furniture. Rarely have nature and architecture been so well married.

Flats
c 1905, E. Matthews
2106-10 Lyon St.
An appropriately Craftsman group of flats across from the church.

39. Engine Company 23 Firehouse

39 Engine Company 23 Firehouse
(now residence)
1893
3022 Washington St.
This churchlike Victorian firehouse with its hose-tower steeple has become a studio-residence like most of the city's old firehouses.

40 Shingle apartments
c 1905, E. Matthews
2874-76 Washington St.
The multidormered roofscape of this shingled apartment group is magnificent.

41 Houses
Brown-shingled double house
2576 Washington St.

1887 Stick style
2527, 2531 Washington St.

1879 Italianate
2560 Washington

This block has a good range of older houses, from the exuberantly painted towered Queen Anne house at No. 2527, to the handsome dark-shingled double house at No. 2576.

42 Houses
1897, McDougall & Son
3100 Clay St.
An elaborate towered Queen Anne house in transition to the Colonial Revival style. Across the street at 3101 Clay is an apartment house with an amazing cornice.

43 Apartment house
c 1900
2971-73 Clay St.
This Queen Anne apartment house has impressive Classical ornament.

44 Victorian row houses
1875, The Real Estate Assoc., builders
2637-73 Clay St.
A vintage row of Italianate houses from this famous firm of builders.

45 Pacific Heights Townhouses
1979, Daniel Solomon & Assoc.
1900 block Lyon St.
These stylish taut-skinned new condominiums fit very well into the old neighborhood.

46 Five cottages
c 1890
1805-17 Baker St.
The smaller cottage-scale streetscape was handled with real grace by Victorian builders.

47 House
1883
2131 Divisadero St.
A corner turret, possibly added later, on a Stick- style cottage.

48 Houses
1882
2002 Pierce St.

c 1875
2006-12 Pierce St.

1894
2028-32 Pierce St.

1894
2695 Sacramento St.

1894
2029-32 Pierce St.

1892, Henry A. Schultze
2031-41 Pierce St.

The three earlier flat-front Italianates on the even side contrast with the more exuberant later Queen Annes around them.

49 Houses

1885, Henry Geilfuss
1705-7 Baker St.

c 1885, John Hinkel, builder
1709 Baker St.

1889, John Coop, developer
1716 Baker St.

1888
1718-24, 1730-32 Baker St.

An unusually fine group of Stick-style cottages.

50 Double house

1892
2915 California St.
Note the gable with a balcony on this double house.

51 Ortman-Schumate house

1870
1901 Scott St.
One of San Francisco's Victorian landmarks, this freestanding house with elaborate gardens gives a hint of what this part of the city looked like in the 1870s.

52 Selfridge house

c 1878
Rem. 1930s, Julia Morgan
2615 California St.
Selfridge was the builder of 2603-13 California as well as this fine Stick-style mansion.

53 Houses

1883, Charles Hinkel, builder
1703-19 Broderick St.
These seven houses were built at the same time by the ubiquitous Hinkels although they show a transition from Italianate to Stick style.

40. Apts, 2874-76 Washington

51. Ortman-Schumate house

55. St. Dominic's Church

54 Mary Ann Crocker
Old Ladies' Home
1890, A. Page Brown
Pine and Pierce sts.
A very unusual Queen Anne/Shingle-style
building for the west, this looks like Richardson or early McKim, Meade, & White
in its long wrapping shinglework. Originally there were two stories.

55 St. Dominic's Church
1927, Beezer Bros.
Bush and Steiner sts.
Crisp, dry, but scholarly Gothic, lavishly
executed throughout with an unusually
generous budget for the West.

56 Unity Hospital
(orig. Maimonides Health Center)
1950, Eric Mendelsohn & Michael
Gallis
Rem. 1953, Hertzka & Knowles
2356 Sutter St.
Designed for the chronically ill, this
once- elegant building had to be remodeled because of code changes. The
balconies were glazed in, and the rhythm
of their curving lines was lost. One of
Mendelsohn's relatively few works in this
country, the building figured prominently
in the New York Museum of Modern Art's
exhibition on post-war Modern architecture.

7
Civic Center
Western Addition I

1 Houses, 1700 block Webster; apts, Sutter
2 Houses, 1700, 1800 blocks Sutter
3 Red Cross bldg & apts, 1550, 1590 Sutter
4 Thomas Payne house, 1409 Sutter
5 Commercial bldgs, 1335, 1337 Sutter
6 Regency Theatre, 1320 Van Ness
7 Japantown Redevelopment
8 Century Club, 1335 Franklin
9 Japanese Cultural Trade Center
10 The Sequoias, San Francisco, 1400 Geary
11 First Unitarian Church, 1187 Franklin
12 Mansard loft bldg, 1117 Geary
13 Harcourt Brace Jovanovich, 1001 Polk
14 Apts, 825, 850 Geary
15 Rossmoor Apts, 765 Geary
16 St. Francis Square
17 Laguna Heights, Laguna-O'Farrell apts
18 St. Mary's Cathedral
19 St. Mark's Church, apts; 1100 block Gough
20 Moderne apts, 1050 Franklin
21 Car showrooms, 999, 1000 Van Ness
22 British Motors showroom, 901 Van Ness
23 Western Addition, A-2 Area
24 Western Addition, A-2 South
25 SF Redevelopment Agency, 939 Ellis
26 Family Service Agency, 1010 Gough
27 St. Pauls Lutheran Church & apts, Eddy
28 F.C. Stadmuller house, 819 Eddy
29 House, 807 Franklin
30 German Assn, 601 Polk
31 Opera Plaza, Golden Gate & Van Ness
32 McDonald's, Van Ness & Golden Gate
33 Federal Office bldg, 450 Golden Gate
34 Motion picture studio, 125 Hyde
35 Hastings Law Center, 200 McAllister
36 Church & hotel, 100 McAllister
37 Cathedral, 858 Fulton; Friendship Village
38 State Bar Association, SF Ballet Center
39 Civic Center
   a City Hall
   b Veterans bldg & Opera House
   c State Office bldg
   d SF Museum of Modern Art
   e SF Public Library
   f Civic Auditorium
   g Public Health bldg
40 Federal bldg, Civic Center
41 UN Plaza & Civic Center BART
42 City offices, 101 Larkin
43 Orpheum Theatre
44 Davies Symphony Hall
45 Fox Plaza
46 State Insurance bldgs & Merchandise Mart
47 Bank of America Computer Ctr & Muni
   station
48 California College of Law, 42 Fell
49 Masonic Temple, 25 Van Ness
50 SF Board of Education, 135 Van Ness
51 Blatte Ctr, 45 Franklin
52 Church of the Advent, 261 Fell
53 Shop & flats, Fell & Laguna
54 Houses, 700 block Grove
55 House row, 700 block Webster
56 Bannecker homes

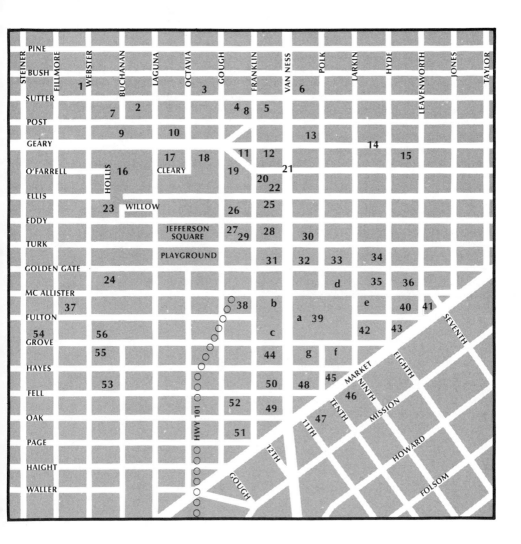

This is an area of great architectural, social, and historical interest. It is full of contrasts. Some are wonderful, others are painful to those who care about cities. The area contains one of the noblest monuments of the City Beautiful Movement—the San Francisco Civic Center—and some of the sorriest examples of failed urban renewal, all interspersed with a a fascinating array of 19th-century single- and multi-family residential architecture. Parts of the area are as a safe for walking as any in the city; parts of it are definitely not, especially for the solitary walker.

San Francisco pushed more or less evenly westward, where the terrain did not interfere. The Van Ness Ordinance, ratified in 1858, extended the grid pattern of streets and designated the public squares of Jefferson, Alamo, Hamilton, and the so-called Hospital Lot, now part of Duboce Park. Hayes Valley, a 160-acre tract owned by Mayor Tom Hayes, lay between Alamo and Duboce parks on the western edge. Hayes built his estate to include a pleasure garden with an art gallery and a concert hall, a kind of forerunner to the Civic Center; it burned in 1872.

The great surge of residential development that accompanied the laying of streetcar lines created a homogenous middle-class suburb that endured until the period following the 1906 earthquake and fire, when dislocated downtown populations moved to the

93

area in droves. These included the Jews, who moved from south of Market to the Fillmore area, and a smaller number of Japanese who established "Little Osaka" nearby between Post and Sutter streets. The area east of Van Ness was rapidly rebuilt after the fire with hotels and apartment blocks to rehouse those who had been burned out, and to accommodate the anticipated flood of visitors to the 1915 Panama-Pacific Exposition. For a while after the Exposition, this was a typical close-to-downtown, medium-to-high-density residential area—and like all such places, it was increasingly vulnerable to decline as the housing stock aged and automobile use increased the attractiveness of the outer suburbs. For many years known as the Tenderloin, the area today is home to derelicts and the elderly poor, who make good use of the Civic Center's open spaces.

To the north and east the area grades upward toward Nob Hill. The Polk Street "gulch" is the major shopping street. Although nothing this side of Van Ness antedates 1906, the variety of ornament on the stock, typically four-story wood-frame apartment houses, is remarkable.

Until urban renewal struck in the 1950s, the western part of the Western Addition had the city's most exuberant stand of late 19th-century houses. Most of it was in sorry shape, having gone from middle-class respectability through shabby gentility to outright slum. This progress is, of course, what led to "renewal." Although the 280-block area was designated "blighted" in 1948—a decision that activated the Redevelopment Agency to undertake a project there—it was not until 1956 that the Board of Supervisors accepted a formal plan for redevelopment of the 28 blocks called Area A-1. Meanwhile, under sentence by the agency, the housing declined precipitously, making later preservation efforts nearly impossible. The neighborhood today is a textbook example of the triumphs and tragedies of the country's post-World War II efforts to revitalize its cities. The A-1 project area, a swath on either side of Geary Boulevard from Franklin to Fillmore, contains a mix of upper-, middle-, and lower-income housing. To atone for their wartime relocation, the Japanese were given an enclave north of Geary. The Longshoremen's Union built a model cooperative project called St. Francis Square, and the rest was a mix of high- and low-rise market-rate housing. All of it was, of course, too expensive for the former residents, the black population that came to the Bay Area to work in the defense plants. In the course of their removal from the area, this group got a political education that helped to blunt the thrust of the next renewal offensive in the A-2 area. By the time the area was built out in the 1960s, there was disenchantment with the sweep-clean approach, and the Redevelopment Agency bowed to pressures from both upper-class preservationists and lower-class residents to save a portion of the houses in the A-2 area.

For a while the redevelopment looked like a model procedure in which almost all of the salvageable 19th-century houses were either restored in place or moved to form groups. New projects for the residents were built to the scale of the old neighborhood. Yet today there are still wastelands of cleared but unbuilt sites, and the crime rate is so high that outsiders are warned to stay away. Strong community organizations such as the Western Addition Project Area Committee struggle to stabilize the area socially. Planning goes on. But, setting social concerns aside, nearly everyone mourns the loss of the congenial scale and the streetscape of the old Western Addition.

1 Houses
1875
1717 Webster St.

1885, Samuel & J. C. Newsom
1737 Webster St.

One of the Newsoms' minor masterpieces of the 1880s rectilinear style called Stick. The interlocking of ornament with form is particularly masterful. This is one of the houses restored under the auspices of the San Francisco Redevelopment Agency and the Foundation for San Francisco's Architectural Heritage. It was moved here from 773 Turk Street in 1975.

Houses
1881
1771 Webster St.

1885
1781-87 Webster St.

1880
1809-11 Webster St.
Sakura Apartments
1973, Van Bourg Nakamura
1840 Sutter St.
Redevelopment market-rate housing with a contemporary Japanese flavor.

3. Red Cross Building

7. Nihonmachi Mall

2   **Houses**
1880s
1745, 1771-75, 1781-87 Sutter St.
Satow Building
c 1970
1765 Sutter St.
Houses
1880s
1809, 1811-15, 1825 Sutter St.
A group of restored buildings that preserve the character of old Japantown.

3   **Red Cross Building**
1950, Gardner Dailey
1550 Sutter St.
Americanized International style enlivened by board- form concrete texture and some Bay Region touches such as small-paned windows. There is a pleasant court and an elegant stairway in the lobby.

Queen Anne Apartments
c 1900
1590 Sutter St.
A fine, freshly restored example of its namesake period.

4   **Thomas Payne house**
c 1880, William Curlett
1409 Sutter St.
A candle-snuffer corner tower distinguishes this Stick-style house.

5   **Commercial buildings**
c 1900
1335, 1337 Sutter St.
A couple of quirky Classic Revival facades.

6   **Regency Theatre**
1911, O'Brien & Werner
1320 Van Ness Ave.
This former Scottish Rite Temple is one of several designed by this firm. The Masons seem to have favored Florentine palaces around the turn of the century (see also entry 49). The opulent auditorium is now the movie theater.

7   **Nihonmachi Mall**
1976, Okamoto & Murata/Van Bourg Nakamura
Buchanan St. bet. Post and Sutter sts.

Kokusai Theatre
1971, Okamoto & Murata/Van Bourg Nakamura
Post and Buchanan sts.

Soko Hardware Co.
1980, Van Bourg Nakamura
1698 Post St.

Before renewal, Japantown was commercially vital but structurally decrepit. Now it is less interesting but more sound, and is still well worth visiting for food and shops. The mall is well scaled and has fountain sculpture and street furniture designed by Ruth Asawa. The Soko Hardware Company still has an amazing variety of wares, and the architecture of the area succeeds in expressing ethnicity while blending in with the restored 19th-century neighborhood around it. What has vanished are the nontourist shops that catered to the former residents.

8   Century Club of California
1905
Rem. 1914, Julia Morgan
1335 Franklin St.

A chaste Classic Revival facade, originally a private home that for two years after 1906 housed the State Supreme Court.

**9   Japanese Cultural
& Trade Center**
1968, Minoru Yamasaki/Van Bourg Nakamura

None of the excitement of architecture in Japan of the same period.

10 The Sequoias, San Francisco
1969, Stone, Marraccini & Patterson
1400 Geary Blvd.

A concrete high-rise retirement community.

11 First Unitarian Church
1887-89, George W. Percy
Add. 1967-79, Callister, Payne & Rosse
1187 Franklin St.

Thomas Starr King, famous preacher and civic leader of the 1860s, was associated with this congregation; his tomb is in the churchyard. The church mixes Romanesque and Gothic Revival elements. The contemporary concrete and redwood

14. *Castle Apts*

11. *First Unitarian Church*

buildings used for offices and the church school form a remarkably harmonious complex that holds its own amidst the asphalt roadways around it.

12 Mansard loft building
c 1906
1117 Geary Blvd.

An unusual survivor of an old commercial type, probably built right after the fire to rehouse displaced businesses.

13 Harcourt Brace Jovanovich
1915, John Galen Howard
1001 Polk St.

This Classic Revival automobile showroom, originally for Pierce Arrow, has been restored as a publisher's offices.

15. Rossmoor Apts

16. St. Francis Square Photo: Karl Riek

14 Castle Apartments
c 1920
825 Geary St.
Alhambra Apartments
1914, James F. Dunn
850 Geary St.
Two of the more exotic examples of local apartment house architecture. The ever-inventive Mr. Dunn here turns his hand to Moorish.

15 Rossmoor Apartments
c 1915
765 Geary Blvd.
A small elegant Renaissance Revival block in rough brick with white trim.

16 St. Francis Square
1961, Marquis & Stoller
Geary Blvd. bet. Webster and Laguna sts.
The outstanding social success of Western Addition renewal, this project was sponsored and subsidized by the Longshoremen's Union and had an income ceiling for residents. Its internal garden courts are particularly attractive and its simple architecture has worn well.

17 Laguna Heights
1963, Claude Oakland
85 Clay St.
Laguna-O'Farrell Apartments
1960, Jones & Emmons
66 Clay St.
Two of the first center city projects by Joseph Eichler, a suburban developer famous for the architectural quality of his tracts.

18 St. Mary's Cathedral
1971, Pietro Bellushi/Pier Luigi Nervi/McSweeney, Ryan & Lee
Geary Blvd. at Gough St.
In 1960, after this site had been "renewed" with a supermarket, a fire completely destroyed the old cathedral on Van Ness Avenue. A quickly arranged trade demolished the year-old market, giving the Archdiocese a suitably prominent site in exchange for its Van Ness property. Four 190- foot hyperbolic paraboloids roof the 2,500-seat space over a base that contains meeting rooms, a rectory, a convent, and, to the south, a paro-

chial high school. The stained glass is by Gyorgy Kepes, the baldachino by Richard Lippold, and the organ was designed by Father Robert F. Hayburn.

19 St. Mark's Lutheran Church
1894, Henry Geilfuss
1111 O'Farrell St. bet. Franklin and Gough sts.

A High Victorian Romanesque-Gothic church in red brick by an architect mostly known for his houses.

The Carillon Retirement Apartments
1970, Donald Powers Smith
1100 Gough St.

20 Moderne apartments
c 1925
1050 Franklin St., corner O'Farrell St.

The medium-sized freestanding apartment house, richly ornamented and painted white, is a hardy building type that enriches many of the city's older neighborhoods.

21 Cadillac Showroom
1923, Weeks & Day
1000 Van Ness Ave.
European Motors (Ernest Ingold) Showroom
c 1950, J.E. Dinwiddie
999 Van Ness Ave.

A pair of automobile palaces, one elegantly backward-looking and the other appropriately forward-looking. Note also the extravagant cornice of the Grosvenor Inn next to European Motors.

22 British Motors Showroom
(orig. Earle C. Anthony Packard)
1927, Bernard Maybeck/Powers & Ahnden
901 Van Ness Ave.

The queen of all the Van Ness Avenue automobile palaces, built for one of Maybeck's great clients, the showroom once more features cars that measure up to the space.

18. St. Mary's Cathedral

22. British Motors Showroom

23 Western Addition A-2 Area (to North)

The following are typically block-sized low-rise apartment projects typical of l960-70 housing design, not bad and not good and hampered by low-budget standardization.

Marcus Garvey Square
1971, Whisler-Patri Assoc.
Pierce St. to Steiner St., Eddy St. to Ellis St.
Martin Luther King Square
1970, Kaplan & McLaughlin
Pierce St. to Steiner St., Turk St. to Eddy St.

26. Family Service Agency/ 27. St. Paul's

Malcolm X Square
1973, Whisler-Patri Assoc.
Webster St. to Buchanan St., Turk St. to Eddy St.
Thomas Paine Square
1971, McGuire & Catough
Webster St. to Laguna St., Turk St. to Golden Gate St.

24 Western Addition A-2 South
Margaret & Hayward
Playground Building
1972, Willis & Assoc.
Laguna St. and Golden Gate Ave.
Prince Hall Apartments
1971, Kennard & Silvers
Fillmore St. to Webster St., Golden Gate Ave. to McAllister St.
Frederick Douglas Haynes Gardens
1973, Marquis & Stoller
Golden Gate Ave., Laguna and McAllister sts.
Freedom West
c 1970, Krisel, Shapiro & Assoc.
460 Fulton St.

25 San Francisco
Redevelopment Agency
c 1915
939 Ellis St.
This looks as if it has been fortified to defend the inmates from the slings and darts of outraged citizens.

26 Family Service Agency
1928, Bernard Maybeck
1010 Gough St.
Maybeck's personal stamp on this Mediterranean-style building is evident in the handling of such elements as the spiral fire escape in its slot, the fenestration on the west facade, and the fence motif.

27 St. Paul's Lutheran Church
& Rectory
1894, J.A. Krafft
Gough and Eddy sts.
Apartment building
951 Eddy St.
A version of Chartres Cathedral in wood flanked by an unusual columned-balcony apartment house with a sandstone base.

28 F.C. Stadmuller house
1880, P.R. Schmidt
819 Eddy St.
A fine Italianate survivor of a time when this was a palm-lined street of single-family houses.

29 House
c 1875
807 Franklin St.
Another lonely Italianate.

30 German Association
1913, Frederick H. Meyer
601 Polk St.
More or less straight from old Munich, with a rathskeller in the basement.

31 Opera Plaza
1982, Jorge de Quesada/Warnecke Assoc.
Golden Gate Ave. bet. Franklin St. and Van Ness Ave.
This luxury condominium development marks a major change in the character of the area around the Civic Center.

32 McDonald's
1980, Whisler/Patri Assoc.
Van Ness and Golden Gate aves.
The first venture into golden-archless contemporary design for this famous chain.

33 Federal Office Building
1959, Albert F. Roller/Stone, Marraccini & Patterson/John Carl Warnecke
450 Golden Gate Ave.
A blockbuster expressing all too well the contemporary scale of government.

34 Motion picture studio
1930, Wilbur Peugh
125 Hyde St.
A fine Art Deco facade. See also two former film depots of 1930 by the O'Brien Brothers at 245-51 and 255-59 Hyde—this area was once the center of the city's film industry.

35 Hastings College of Law
1950, Master & Hurd
Add. 1967, Gwathwey, Sellier & Crosby
198 McAllister St.

1980, Skidmore, Owings & Merrill
200 McAllister St.

Of this campus of modern buildings, the Law Center by Skidmore, Owings & Merrill is the most recent and the most distinguished.

**36 William Taylor Hotel
& Methodist Church**
1929, Miller & Pflueger/Lewis Hobart
100-20 McAllister St.
A building serving an unusual combination of functions, both of which failed because of the Depression. It then became a federal office building for many years and is now back in residential use for Hastings College of Law.

37 Friendship Village
1971, Buckley & Sazevich
Fillmore St. to Webster St., McAllister St. to Fulton St.
Old Holy Virgin Russian Orthodox Cathedral
1880
858-64 Fulton St.
Friendship Village is perhaps the most successful of all the Western Addition A-2 efforts to get in scale with the neighborhood. Several 19th-century facades are integrated into an interesting and varied site plan, with sympathetic shingled units surrounding interior courts. On the same block is a several-times-recycled Gothic Revival church taken over by the Russians in 1930.

34. Motion picture studio

35. Hastings College of Law

38 State Bar Association
(two buildings)
1962, Hertzka & Knowles
601 McAllister St.
1979, Hertzka & Knowles
555 Franklin St.
San Francisco Ballet Center
1984, Beverly Willis
Cor. Franklin and Fulton sts.

**39 Civic Center:
Franklin St. to McAllister St., Market St. to Hayes St.
a. City Hall**
1915 (competition 1912), Bakewell & Brown
b. Opera House & Veterans Building
1932, Brown & Lansburgh
Opera House Addition
1977, Skidmore, Owings & Merrill
c. State Office Building
1926, Bliss & Faville
**d. San Francisco Museum
of Modern Art & Bookstore**
(in Veterans Building)
Rem. 1971-2, Robinson & Mills
Herbst Hall
Rem. 1977, Vincent J. Raney

39. Civic Center

e. San Francisco Public Library
1916 (competition 1915), George Kelham
f. Civic Center Auditorium
1915, John Galen Howard, Fred Meyers & John Reid,Jr.
Rem. 1964, Wurster, Bernardi & Emmons and Skidmore, Owings & Merrill
g. Public Health Building
101 Grove St.

40 Federal Building
1936, Bakewell & Brown
Civic Center

41 United Nations Plaza Building
1980, Whisler/Patri & Assoc.
10 United Nations Plaza
United Nations Plaza
and Fountain
1980, Lawrence Halprin
Civic Center Muni/BART Station
1973, Reid & Tarics
The Civic Center is not only a crowning achievement of City Beautiful Movement design in this country (along with the Washington Mall and the great turn-of-the-century fairs), but also the only really

first-rate example of French High Baroque Revival carried out in detail and with loving care. The City Hall itself is the jewel, inside and out— don't miss the rotunda. Although the other buildings are Depression products they do not show it. The Opera House is modeled on Garnier's Paris Opera and has a circulation system nearly as impressive. The Veterans Building, erected without a clear program, was later occupied on the upper floors by the San Francisco Museum of Modern Art; it recently had its small auditorium restored as a recital hall. The other Civic Center buildings follow the general plan set forth by the advisory commission headed at first by John Galen Howard and later by Bernard Maybeck, and listing among its members Willis Polk, Ernest Coxhead, G. Albert Lansburgh, John Reid, Jr., Frederick H. Meyer, and Arthur Brown, Jr. The contemporary part of the complex, the plaza and axis east to Market Street, has been the subject of many designs and imperfect realizations. There is indeed a gulf between us and Arthur Brown, Jr.

42 City offices
1941
101 Larkin St.
The visitor information center for the 1939 Golden Gate International Exposition on Treasure Island, reworked into city offices.

43 Orpheum Theatre
1925, B. Marius Priteca
1192 Market St.
Churrigueresque ornament prodigally applied over a very glassy curtain wall. The city and the owners each thought the other would pay to have the blank back wall finished to match the character of the Civic Center—neither did.

44 Davies Symphony Hall
1981, Skidmore, Owings & Merrill
SW cor. Van Ness Ave. and Grove St.
A thoughtfully done bridge between the French Classicism of the rest of the Civic Center and the architecture of today, this building is not quite comfortable with either, but has the strength of its convictions. The interior is most successful spatially and acoustically.

45 Fox Plaza
1967, Victor Gruen & Assoc.
Market, Grove, and Larkin sts.
The city's first mixed-use retail office and apartment complex. It occupies the site of one of the West Coast's great movie palaces, which had a whole make-believe Spanish village built along its auditorium walls.

46 State Compensation Insurance Fund Office Building
1976, J.C. Warnecke & Assoc.
1275 Market St.
Giant steps sheathed in red granite, an example of the new style of broken massing for large buildings.

Merchandise Mart
1937, The Capitol Co.
1355 Market St.

47. Bank of America Computer Center

47 Bank of America Computer Center buildings
1960, Wurster, Bernardi & Emmons
1979, Skidmore, Owings & Merrill
1455-1525 Van Ness Ave.
The first building was designed to expand vertically, but never did, partly because of changes in computor technology. The huge gleaming white building is designed to expand by the addition of another octagonal tower.

Van Ness Muni Station
1972, Reid & Tarics
Van Ness Ave. and Market St.

48 California College of Law
1932, Willis Polk
42-58 Fell St.
A residentially scaled complex in the Spanish- Mediterranean idiom, with a forecourt that seems a luxurious use of space today.

49. Masonic Temple

49 Masonic Temple
1910, Bliss & Faville
25 Van Ness Ave.
A prominent Florentine Renaissance palazzo, which is to be refurbished by Tanner & Van Dine.

50 San Francisco Board of Education
(High School of Commerce)
1927, John Reid, Jr.
135 Van Ness Ave.
For another exercise in this richly ornamented mode by John Reid, Jr., once official architect for the district, see 9:29.

51 Blatte Center
1981
45 Franklin St.
This handsomely painted apartment building has a battery of solar collectors on the roof that go very well with the faceted bays.

52 Church of the Advent of Christ the King
1910
261 Fell St.
The "highest" of San Francisco's Episcopal Churches, liturgically speaking, this Spanish Colonial Revival church was built for the Cowley Fathers from Boston. It has a quietly elegant interior.

53 Commercial building
c 1900
Cor. Fell and Laguna sts.
A favorite turn-of-the-century building type that may come back with the gentrification movement.

54 House row
c 1880
700 block Grove St.

55 Houses
c 1880
701, 709, 717, 721, 725, 735, 737, 741 Webster St.

56 Bannecker homes
1970, Esherick, Homsey, Dodge & Davis
Lawrence Halprin & Assoc., landscape architect
Webster St. to Buchanan St., Fulton St. to Grove St.
One of the more successful Western Addition renewal projects.

8
Haight
Ashbury

Western
Addition II

The following map labels appear on the image:

PINE, BUSH, SUTTER, POST, GEARY, O'FARRELL, ELLIS, EDDY, TURK, GOLDEN GATE, MC ALLISTER, FULTON, GROVE, HAYES, FELL, OAK, PAGE, HAIGHT, WALLER, HERMANN, DUBOCE, FREDERICK, CARL, PARNASSUS, BEULAH

MASONIC, PRESIDIO, LYON, BAKER, BRODERICK, DIVISADERO, SCOTT, PIERCE, STEINER, FILLMORE, WEBSTER

BAKER, ST JOSEPH'S, BEIDEMAN

STANYAN, SHRADER, FULTON, GROVE, HAYES, FELL, OAK, PAGE, HAIGHT, WALLER

ASHBURY, MASONIC, CENTRAL, COLE, BELVEDERE, CLAYTON, DOWNEY, DELMAR, BUENA VISTA WEST, JAVA

BUENA VISTA PARK, CASTRO, ROOSEVELT, MARKET, FILLMORE

1, 2, 3, 4, 5, 6, 7, 8, 9, 10, 11, 12, 13, 14, 15, 16, 17, 18, 19, 20, 21, 22, 23, 24, 25, 26, 27, 28, 29, 30, 31, 32, 33, 34, 35, 36, 37, 38, 39, 40, 41, 42, 43, 44, 45, 46, 47, 48, 49, 50, 51, 52

T he outer Western Addition focuses on Alamo Square, the counterpart of Alta Plaza in Pacific Heights. It is a high and empty plaza, a true breathing space, surrounded by a prime collection of the kind of late 19th-century houses that fill the blocks in a steady progression westward to Golden Gate Park. South of the Panhandle is the notorious Haight Ashbury district, now recovered from the late- sixties invasion of the flower children and becoming gentrified, as evidenced by extensive painting and refurbishing.

Before the march of the streetcar suburbs began, these sparsely populated western lands were dairy farms and ranches. The Big Four of the Southern Pacific Railroad, particularly William Crocker, owned large tracts of land along with other wealthy citizens.

8 Haight Ashbury/Western Addition II

After the Southern Pacific ran the first cable car line out Haight from Market to Stanyan in 1883, the area developed rapidly, partly because of the tourist traffic to Golden Gate Park and the Chutes, a typical 19th-century amusement park. As more streetcar lines were laid both on the flat streets and running up hill to fashionable Ashbury Heights, more blocks were built up with houses. The disproportionate number of 1890s Queen Anne-style structures in the district testifies to the peak of the boom. As the area filled, apartment houses and flats were built in the transitional styles from Queen Anne to Colonial and Classic Revival after the turn of the century. The enormous housing shortage after the 1906 disaster caused the conversion of many of the huge single-and two-family houses to multiple- rental units. The more transient population brought about a decline in status for the area. As the single-family population got into their automobiles in increasing numbers and moved to the western suburbs, the area completely changed character. At the end of the post-World War II suburban expansion period it housed a mixture of members of the Beat Generation, blacks displaced by urban renewal in the Western Addition,and others who had either been long-time residents or who had moved in to take advantage of the low rents. It seems unlikely that the district will return to its original state, but like the other former streetcar suburbs it is closer to it today than it has been for years.

Because of limits of space it is not possible to present a comprehensive tour of the area here. It is most walkable and will reward the reader with serendipity.

1 Fillmore Auditorium
c 1900
Geary Blvd. near Fillmore St.
This former synagogue, designed in a medley of mostly medieval styles, had a few years of international fame in the mid-sixties when rock impresario Bill Graham operated it as the first great rock dancehall. It is now a deserted, vandalized hulk awaiting another rebirth.

2 Beideman Place
c 1875-95
Eddy St. to O'Farrell St., Scott St. to Divisadero St.
A mixed group of 11 late 19th-century houses, three of which were moved here in 1976 and offered for sale by the Foundation for San Francisco's Architectural Heritage. A mixed-use project with low- and moderate-income housing, it is the city's only restoration effort of this kind.

3 Holy Cross Parish Hall
1854
1822 Eddy St.
The city's oldest church—on the exterior—is this simple frame building, formerly St. Patrick's. It once stood on Market Street where the Palace Hotel is

1. Fillmore Auditorium

today, and was part of St. Ignatius College, founded by the Jesuits as the city's first institution of higher education. It was moved here in 1873 and remodeled in 1891 as a parish hall.

4 Town houses
1981
1965-97 Eddy St.
A rhythmically composed, contemporary shingled complex with solar greenhouses at the back.

5 House
1895, Henry W. Cleaveland
1825 Turk St.
A Queen Anne house of noble proportions on a large lot.

6 House
c 1880
1671 Golden Gate Ave.
While Moorish was stylish for firehouses
(10:46) and apartment houses (7:14), this
seems to be the only Moorish house
around.

7 House row
1875, The Real Estate Assoc.
1513-31 Golden Gate Ave.
A row of typical tract houses of the day
by this most entrepreneurial firm; three
have been stuccoed.

8 Andreozzi house
1886, John W. Dooley, contractor
1016 Pierce St.
A 1880s house with a typical rectangular
bay and particularly fine decorative detail. Happily, it survived the urban renewal bulldozer that claimed other
equally fine houses in this area.

9. Apts, 1400 block Golden Gate

**9 Missionary Temple,
house row, and apartments**
c 1900
1400 block Golden Gate Ave.
The Classic Revival building at 1455
looks very like a branch library. Next to it
are some amazing c 1890 castellated
Queen Anne apartment houses, and
across the street is a newly refurbished
row of speculative flats, designed by John
P. Gaynor and built in 1884 for a total
cost of $30,000.

10 Commerical-residential building
c 1905
1801 McAllister St.
A tastefully refurbished example of a
standard building type that affords what
Jane Jacobs calls "eyes on the street."
Down McAllister at No. 1833 and around
the corner at Nos. 623-29 Baker Street
are some Queen Anne cottages to add to
your checklist.

11 Public Housing for the Elderly
1974, Marquis & Stoller
1715-17 McAllister St.
A successful design, thoughtfully sited,
with pleasant public areas.

12. Apts, 1347 McAllister

12 Apartments
c 1900
1300 block McAllister St.
A splendid row of late Chateauesque
Queen Anne flats. Across the street at
No. 1347 is one of James F. Dunn's elegant Parisian Belle Epoque designs. One
wishes Mr. Dunn had had a block to himself somewhere. In any case, this is a
block worth seeing for its complexity and
contradiction.

13 Houses
1895, Cranston & Keenan, contractors
700-18, 701-11 Broderick St.
There is nothing like the Queen Anne style for bringing plasticity and rhythm to a streetscape. Plaster decorative motifs like those on 707 and 714 could be ordered by the piece from catalogs. It must have been fun putting them on.

14 House
c 1895
1255 Fulton St.
Yet another brightly painted towered Queen Anne.

15. House, 120l Fulton

15 House
c 1895, A. Page Brown
1201 Fulton St.
A cottage inspired by the English Arts and Crafts Movement, which looked back to medieval vernacular building types like the Cottswold cottage. When the house was refurbished it unfortunately lost its copper roof finials, but otherwise it is intact. The other local architect who seemed particularly fond of this style was Edgar Matthews, who adapted it for a house in Pacific Heights, 6:12.

Westerfield house
1889, Henry Geilfuss
1198 Fulton St.
Geilfuss's style is particularly marked by a linear or modular organization of the elevations emphasized by vertical decorative wood strips. This so-called San Francisco Stick or Strip style is a variation on the eastern style Vincent Scully termed Stick, a more generally direct though complicated expression in which the hidden structural frame of the house was restated on the exterior as decoration.

16 House
1894, A.J. Barnett
809-11 Pierce St.
Another towered Queen Anne.

17 Houses
c 1895, Martens & Coffey
910, 915, 921 Steiner St.

1888
908 Steiner St.

This was one of the first blocks to be refurbished. In 1967, No. 908 became the first and most famous of a wave of super-colorful paint jobs. Since then taste has quieted down.

18 Houses
1890s
Steiner St. bet. Hayes and Fulton sts., and 900 block Grove St.
A rich and varied stand of houses, some built on speculation and others custom designed for the affluent.
Nos. 710-20 Steiner (1894-95), developed by Matthew Kavanaugh, are among the city's most published "painted ladies." No. 940 Grove, on the corner of Steiner (1895, Pissis & Moore), is now the French- American Bilingual School and was added to in 1971 by Beebe & Hersey. No. 814 Steiner dates from 1895, and No. 850, by T. Patterson Ross, dates from l899. The Koster manse at No. 926 Grove (1897) is an imposing early Classic Revival design. No. 975 Grove sports a California golden bear on the chimney, while No. 957 (1886) is a characteristic composition by Samuel and Joseph Cather Newsom, which cost all of $5,000.

19 Houses
1895, Martens & Coffey
820, 833-35 Fillmore St.
More examples of late Queen Anne exuberance.

20 Native Daughters of the Golden West
1920, Julia Morgan
500 Baker St.
A reserved Mediterranean villa tied to California by little golden bears perched on the balcony, this is another of Morgan's many small institutional designs.

21 Gadatsu Church
c 1891
401 Baker St.
This former house is an unusually large Queen Anne with two towers and a notable profusion of plaster ornament.

22 House
c 1895
1588 Fell St.
House
c 1895, William Curlett
301 Lyon St.
These two Queen Anne-style houses are typical of the scale of residences in this prime location on the panhandle to Golden Gate Park. The Panhandle, as it was officially called, was landscaped in the 1870s under the park administration of William Hammond Hall. The eucalyptus trees are the park's oldest; they shade a curving drive that was crowded with the carriages of the wealthy on Sundays. The park was private at first and fenced. The pretentious houses that lined the one- by-eight-block park are the measure of the streets' former status.

Harkness Hospital
c 1905
Baker and Fell sts.
This long-deserted Classic Revival building will be converted to 185 units of Section 8 housing for the elderly by Lanier/Sherrill/Morrison.

23 Ohloff house
1891, Charles I. Havens
601 Steiner St.
Another fine towered Queen Anne house, now owned by the Episcopal Diocese of San Francisco.

24 Houses
c 1890
411-15, 426 Shrader St.
The first house dates from 1890 and was built by Cornelius Murphy; the second is a particularly fine work by Samuel and Joseph C. Newsom. It shows the influence of C.F.A. Voysey and other architects of the the so-called English Domestic Revival Movement, which drew on medieval vernacular buildings and used such quaint detail as the roughcast plasterwork in the gable ends that incorporates pouchlike swallows' nests.

25 Apartments
c 1895
1899, 1907 Oak St.
A matching pair.

26 House
1895, Coxhead & Coxhead
400 Clayton St.
Ernest Coxhead's manipulation of Classical ornament was so personal as to defy classification. He delighted in overscaling and intertwining traditional motifs and imposing them on plain, boxlike forms.

27 Phelps house
1850s
Rest. 1976, The Preservation Group
1111 Oak St.
Mish house
1885, McDougall & Son
1153 Oak St.
The Abner Phelps house was long thought to have been prefabricated and shipped from New Orleans, but in the course of its restoration it was found to be of local construction. Originally a farmhouse and probably built from a carpenter's plan book, it was moved more than once, ending up in the middle of this block, where for years it was invisible from the street. Now turned to face Oak Street and given a front yard, the house can be appreciated for its early Gothic Revival style, unique in the city.
The Mish house next door is a grand Stick-style town house, also restored in 1976 as part of this small office park called Phelps Place.

Firehouse
1893, Henrickson & Mahoney
1152 Oak St.

28 House
1896
729 Oak St.
Another elaborate town house, with its
interior intact.

29 House
1896, Edward J. Vogel
1901 Page St.
A transitional style, called Queen Anne
for its finely scaled plaster decorative detail, and Colonial Revival for its neo-
Georgian form. Novelist Kathleen Norris
once lived here.

30 House
c 1890, Cranston & Keenan
1777 Page St.
These designers spiced up their otherwise
typical Queen Anne houses with unusual
plaster ornament such as the owls used
here. For other motifs, see entry 13 and
the row listed below.

31 Houses
c 1890
1542-48, 1550 Page St.
The first houses (1891) are by Cranston &
Keenan; the house at No. 1550 is either
by them or by the Newsoms, and is very
handsome in either case.

32 Houses
1899, Newsom & Myer
1478-80 Page St.
The taming of the Queen Anne style as it
merged with Colonial Revival at the century's turning.

33 Haight Ashbury
Children's Center
1906
1101 Masonic Ave.
A substantial Classic Revival house, typical of the period and type.

34 Apartments
c 1900
1390-2 Page St.
Craftsman-style apartment houses that
look like the work of Edgar Matthews, but
are not identified as such.

35 Former telephone exchange
1890
865 Page St.
The city's earliest known example of the
Mission Revival style.

36 Houses
c 1890, Cranston & Keenan
500-6, 508-16 Cole St.
The first house is an interesting switch in
scale of the usual components of the
Queen Anne house: a small tower is
squeezed between two large gables. The
developers were clearly getting their
money's worth out of this large corner
lot.

37 Flats
c 1910, James A. Dunn
1677-81 Haight St.
Parisian-style flats. For others in this
mode see entry 12.

Commercial building
1907
1660 Haight St.
A rare Art Nouveau storefront; there is
one other at 225 Frederick Street, designed by August Nordin (1912), which is
not so dramatic.

38 House row
1896-97, Cranston & Keenan
1214-56 Masonic Ave.
Another wonderful row of towered
Queen Anne houses— note especially
No. 1226—by these contractors, who
were particularly active in the area at this
time.

39 House row
1899, Daniel Einstein
142-60 Central Ave.
The towers have been merged with the
bays so that the houses look as though
they have helmets.

36. Houses, 500-6, 508-16 Cole

44. House, 833 Ashbury

40. Apts, 91 Central

40 Apartments
1904
91 Central Ave.
An extraordinary Classic Revival facade embellished with plaster heads.

41 Houses
1896, Fred P. Rabin
1894, John J. Clark
1080, 1081 Haight St.
The Haight is introduced appropriately at this edge of the park by towered Queen Anne houses, perhaps the most typical— and certainly the most spectacular— building type in the area. In the next block is the Third Church of Christ Scientist, 1918, by Edgar Matthews, very like the one at California and Franklin streets.

42 Apartments
c 1907, Charles J. Rousseau
135-39 Pierce St.
Combination Mission Revival and Art Nouveau.

43 Houses
c 1910
762, 777 Ashbury St.

44 Houses
1908-12
806, 821-25, 857-61
880 Ashbury St.
A wonderful potpourri of early 20th-century styles: No. 806 is a squeezed Classic Revival villa; Nos. 821-25 show French influence; No. 833 (1908), by Beasley & Beasley, is planned around a pleasant inner court; No. 857-61 is Elizabethan Revival enriched with plaster male faces; No. 880 (1908), by A.A. Cantin, is vintage Mission Revival. Mixed in are Colonial Revivals and other styles that defy description.

45 House
c 1910, T. Patterson Ross
1370-2 Masonic Ave.
A rather staid house; across the street at Nos. 1322-42 is a row of identical c 1885 houses.

46 Richard Spreckels Mansion
1897-98, E.J. Vogel
737 Buena Vista Ave. West
A more imposing Queen Anne-Colonial Revival house than Vogel's other work in the neighborhood, entry 29, but also with literary associations: both Ambrose Bierce and Jack London stayed here. It is now a bed and breakfast inn. Up the hill at No. 595-97 Buena Vista West is a pair of flats (c 1950) by Henry Hill, one of the post-World War II generation of Modern architects. For another of his works see 3:33.

47 Casa Madrona Apartments
c 1920
110-16 Frederick St.

An unexpected oasis of Spanish Colonial Revival- styled apartments, with a tropically landscaped courtyard. Just down the block at 130 Frederick is an apartment block of 1919 by A.H. Larsen, who did the much larger Clay-Jones Apartments on Nob Hill. And at No. 191 Frederick is the Crossways, a vaguely Mediterranean apartment block. This cluster is evidence of the increasing population density in the Haight and the shift from single- family homes to apartment houses.

47. Casa Madrona Apts.

48 Houses
c 1900
1430, 1450, 1482 Masonic Ave.

Three remarkable houses. No. 1450 (1891) is by A.J. Barnett; No. 1482 is an unusual shingled Queen Anne with a corner dome.

49 House
1910, Bernard Maybeck
1526 Masonic Ave.

A subtle composition in staggered roof planes and voids where the balcony and entrance stair occur. Maybeck's deft touch in a modest shingled house.

49. House, 1526 Masonic

50 Apartments
c 1925, H.C. Baumann
555 Buena Vista Ave. West

One of Baumann's many neo-Churrigueresque apartment blocks.

51 Apartments
c 1910
1077-81 Ashbury St.

A successful handling of a narrow lot. This group of Mission Pueblo Revival apartments nearly comes to a point at the corner.

52. Cottage, 439 Roosevelt Way

52 Cottage
c 1910
439 Roosevelt Way

Anchored to the shelf of the hill by a Corinthian- columned portico, this house is actually larger than it appears because it steps down the hill behind.

9
West
Mission

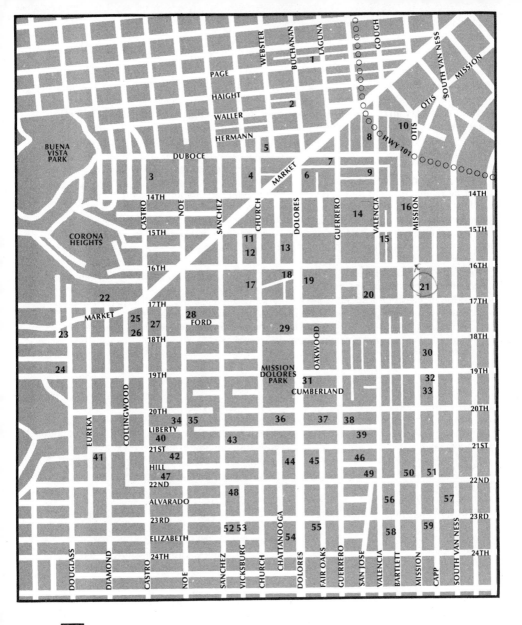

The Mission district, one of the city's largest, has two fairly distinct parts. While the eastern part, covered in Section 10, has always mixed industrial and residential uses—and originally large farms—the inner or western Mission grew in a more urban and residential way as a streetcar suburb. The mission itself, founded in 1776, was well sited on the banks of the Laguna de Manantial, which roughly covered the city blocks now bounded by 15th, Guerrero, 23rd, and Harrison streets. The lake was fed by the Arroyo de Nuestra Senora de los Dolores. In time the mission acquired the name of the stream. The wisdom of the Franciscan padres, who founded the mission in the most benign part of what they regarded as a generally bleak and unfriendly peninsula, was ignored by the early Yankee settlers, whose ties were to trade, not agriculture. Although the mission's long decline following the Secularization Act of 1834 freed a great deal of land, the area was so remote from the new city center that it preserved its pastoral quality until the streetcar era began in the 1860s. Mission Street, originally the plank road that linked the mission with downtown, served as the main development channel. Once the streetcars began to run, the pleasure seekers discovered the balmy climate. Roadhouses and an elaborate entertainment park called Woodward Gardens at Mission and Duboce responded to their needs. From about 1870 to the early 1900s, the area filled up with a rich variety of single- and multi-family dwellings, many of which survive and are being refurbished. Several small hills add variety to the relatively flat terrain. Dolores Park is a welcome green open space stretched along Dolores Street by John McLaren's march of palms, planted in the median strip after the fire. Mission Street itself is one of the most colorful and lively of the city's major neighborhood shopping streets. Although it is slowly showing signs of gentrification, it is distinctly multinational Latin and wonderfully untidy—so far.

Noe Valley, named for a tract laid out in the 1850s by Jose Noe, extends roughly west of Sanchez Street to Douglass and from Market to about 30th Street. The neighborhood has two thriving shopping streets, 18th and 24th, on either side of the hill that rises up in the center. Of all the South of Market districts, this one gentrified most rapidly during the 1970s. Not only is it the heart of the city's internationally known gay community, but it is also home to a mixed professional and working-class population that has contributed to the strong neighborhood identity.

1 **Zen Center**
1922, Julia Morgan
300 Page St.
Dietle house
1888, Henry Geilfuss
294 Page St.
Houses
c 1875, c 1885
273, 287 Page St.

c 1880
251 Laguna St.
Houses
1880s
319-23 Haight St.

c 1885
395 Haight St.
This cluster is well worth a detour: one of Morgan's most gracious small institutional buildings, originally designed as the Emanuel Sisterhood; a noble Stick-style mansion by Geilfuss; and a varied group of other Victorians.

2 **Nightingale house**
1882
201 Buchanan St.
A sprightly corner-bayed Stick-style cottage— perfect for a witch with a small family.

3 **St. Francis Hospital**
1970, Stone, Marraccini & Patterson
Castro St. and Duboce Ave.

4 **St. Francis Lutheran Church**
(St. Angsar)
1905-07
152 Church St.
Stern Nordic Gothic, originally built for a Danish congregation.

5 **San Francisco Funeral Service**
1954, Jones & Emmons
1 Church St.
Owner Nicholas Daphni, determined to bring contemporary architecture into a notably conservative business, first tried Frank Lloyd Wright, then settled on Jones & Emmons. This may be the first Modern funeral parlor.

**6 California Volunteers'
Memorial**
1903, Douglas Tilden, sculptor
Base, Willis Polk
Dolores St. at Market St.
A superior equestrian statue by the city's
greatest outdoor sculptor, this is perfectly
placed at the head of Dolores's stately
row of palms, although the surrounding
buildings don't give it much help. Gilbert
Stanley Underwood's mighty fortress for
the U.S. Mint (1937) destroyed the scale
of this important intersection.

7 House
1873, Henry Geilfuss
Rest. 1980, Roy Killeen
102 Guerrero St.
One of Geilfuss's most refined facades.
The slender colonnettes that divide the
windows of the polygonal bays are an
unusual feature.

House row
c 1876, TREA
120-6 Guerrero St.

8 Baha'i Center
1932, Harold Stoner
170 Valencia St.
This remarkable facade is tucked under
the curve of the freeway. It was designed
for the Woodmen of the World.

**9 Levi Strauss Factory
& Playground**
1906
Rest. 1970, Howard Friedman
250 Valencia St.
So freshly painted and lovingly maintained that it seems like a bit of Disney-
land, this is where all those jeans started.

**10 Juvenile Courts
& Detention Home**
1914, Lewis Christian Mullgardt
**San Francisco Social
Services Building**
1980, Garo Dorian
150 Otis St.
A high-rise version of the bungalows that
Mullgardt designed in the East Bay; the
wall articulation was well ahead of its

12. Church Street Terrace

time. The monolithic mass of the new
welfare building is, alas, a fitting expression for the bureaucracy. It is ironic
that, architecturally at least, the new
structure has made the older one seem
more humane.

**11 St. Nicholas Russian
Orthodox Cathedral**
(orig. St. Luke's German Evangelical
Church)
c 1903
2005 15th St.
A Carpenter Gothic church unexpectedly
converted to orthodoxy by the addition of
a cocktail-onion dome on its spire.

12 Church Street Terrace
1981, Stephen Allen Roake
350-60 Church St.

13 Tanforan cottages
c 1853
214, 220 Dolores St.
Two very early small cottages, one with a
carriage house behind, preserve the look
of the early Mission district.

14 Valencia Gardens
1943, W.W. Wurster & Harry
Thomsen
Sculptor, Beniamino Bufano
15th, Valencia, and Guerrero sts.
One of the real landmarks of public
housing from the days when that was far
from a derogatory term; this simple group
has had its ups and downs with vandal-
ism but is presently well painted and
maintained.

18. Mission Dolores

7. House, 102 Guerrero

22. Shop and flats, 4200 17th St.

15 St. John the Evangelist Episcopal Church
1909
1661 15th St.
English country Gothic done in shingles.

16 Armory
1909, Woollett & Woollett
14th and Mission sts.
A clinker-brick bastion.

17 Everett Middle School
1925, John Reid, Jr.
Church St. bet. 16th and 17th sts.
Although the design has some elements of the Mission Revival style, it also speaks strongly of Moorish- Byzantine. The lavishness of the decorative detail shows to what degree urban public schools once counted as cultural institutions.

18 Mission San Francisco de Asis
(Mission Dolores)
1782
Rest. 1918, Willis Polk
Mission Dolores Basilica
1913
16th and Dolores sts.
These two make an eloquent pair. The humble mission with its powerfully crude, stumpy columns marching up and down the gable, and the overwhelming Mission-style basilica next door bespeak altogether different institutions. The interior of the mission should be seen, that of the basilica should not. The peaceful, time-worn cemetery with its lush vegetation blurs the harsh existence of the original mission population: 5,000 Indians were buried here.

19 Center of Arts & Education
(Old Notre Dame School)
1907
347 Dolores St.
This graceful building, which housed the city's first girls' school, has a composite style that may simply represent the rebuilding of an already modified older structure. Its scale is complementary to the old mission.

St. Mark's Lutheran Church
1901
3281 16th St.
This late Carpenter Gothic church still has services in German.

20 Duggans Funeral Service
c 1900, Ernest Coxhead
3434 17th St.
Coxhead again, pre-posting the post-Modernists at their own (and his) game of distorting Classical elements.

21 Mission Plaza
1981, Jorge de Quesada
Capp and Mission sts.
A cleanly done mixed-use residential and commercial development, one of the first significant responses to the 16th Street BART station (designed by Hertzka & Knowles, as is the 24th and Mission Station).

22 Shop and flats
c 1890
4200 17th St.
The Victorian shop and flats combination is one of the city's great vernacular building types. This is one of the best, with its residential box soaring off the hillside above an almost transparent base.

23 Apartment house
c 1900
4600 18th St.
An elegant late Queen Anne, nicely painted.

Mural house
c 1885
4550 18th St.
How to liven up nondescript architecture.

24 Nobby Clarke's Folly
1892
250 Douglass St.
This imposing pile was built with the earnings of thirty years' service as clerk to the chief of police in the Vigilantes era. It originally had a 17- acre estate to go with it.

25 Castro Condominiums
1982, Dan Solomon
2425 Market St.
A skeletal fence-gate on Market Street marks this gleaming white cluster of stepped boxes, nicely arranged on an awkward site.

26 Sushi-Gen
c 1900
4248 18th St.
An outstanding Victorian shop front.

24. Nobby Clarke's Folly

27 Castro Theatre
   1923, T. Pflueger
   429 Castro St.

According to Steven Levin, movie theater historian, the Castro was the flagship of the extensive operations of the Nasser family, a pioneer motion picture family who built their first theaters in Noe Valley. For their young architect, Timothy Pflueger, this was the first of the seven movie palaces his firm was to design. (For another see 4:38.) Though it seats 1,800, it was never the largest neighborhood theater; however, it was one of the most ornate. The Spanish Baroque style of the facade is carried out on the interior, but the auditorium is an extravaganza all by itself, with its ceiling cast in plaster to resemble a tent with swags, ropes, and tassels. Appropriately, the Castro is one of the homes of the San Francisco Film Festival.

28 Corner houses
   c 1890
   437, 451 Noe St.

Two Stick-style towered corner houses show how to do streetscape on a domestic scale. Across the street, Nos. 460-76 were built by Fernando Nelson, local resident and prolific city builder, who finished his career with Presidio Terrace, 12:34.

29 Mission High School
   1926, John Reid, Jr.
   Rehab. 1972-78, J. Martin Rosse
   18th and Dolores sts.

A Mission district landmark that competes in prominence with the basilica. The polychromed tile domes and expert Spanish Baroque detailing make this the most sumptuous of the city's public schools.

30 Mission Neighborhood Center
   c 1900, Ward & Bloom
   362 Capp St.

A residentially scaled shingled Craftsman community center.

29. Mission High School

30. Mission Neighborhood Center

31. Flats, 96, 98 Cumberland

31 Flats
c 1900
96, 98 Cumberland St.
An unusual pair of gambrel-roofed flats.

Ascension Lutheran Church
(Mission Park Congregational Church)
c 1900
19th and Dolores sts.

32 Russian Orthodox Convent of Our Lady of Vladimir
1914
19th and Capp sts.
The blue and white color scheme, appropriate to the Russian Church, heightens the festive quality of this decorated box, originally built for the Emanuel Evangelical Church.

33. El Capitan Theatre

32. Russian Orthodox Convent

33 El Capitan Theatre
c 1930
2361 Mission St.
The scale of this combination theater and hotel with its abundant ornament testifies to the importance the Mission district had attained by the 1930s as a self-sufficient suburb with all the conveniences of downtown.

34 Houses
1898-99 Fernando Nelson
4100 block 20th St.
Nos. 4100-38 and 4119-41 were built by Nelson in two styles that, according to Judith Lynch, an authority on Nelson's work, he called simply A and B. The idea, of course, was to give variety to the block and some choice to the client.

35 Moderne apartments
c 1940
741 Noe St.
White stucco boxes stepping down the hillside.

Houses
1961, 1963, George Homsey
4067-69 20th St.
These two houses are sophisticated commentaries on the traditional San Francisco bay-windowed row house. Homsey is one of the originators of the shed-roofed cut-out box style that began in the 1960s and is particularly apt for steep and difficult sites.

36 House
c 1910
3851 20th St.
This chaste Classic Revival box with a Corinthian columned side porch looks like a transplant from Pacific Heights.

37 House
c 1880
3755 20th St.

38. House, 827 Guerrero

41. House, 4015 21st St

38 House
1881
Rem. 1890, Samuel Newsom
827 Guerrero St.
The original house was enlarged and transformed by Newsom into a rather ponderous but inventive version of a Queen Anne, with a gambrel roof and exotic touches like the "moon gate" entrance, a hallmark of Newsom design.

39 Houses
1877
23-25 Liberty St.

1898, R.H. White
27 Liberty St.

1892, J.E. Kraft
31 Liberty St.

c 1875
37 Liberty St.

1870
49 Liberty St.

1876
58 Liberty St.

1870
70 Liberty St.

1870
109 Liberty St.

1878
159 Liberty St.
One of the Mission's best groups of Italianates and one imposing Queen Anne line a street that was obviously a choice place to live from early on. The houses on the south side are set high on the hill to catch the view.

40 Houses
1897, Fernando Nelson (his own house)
701 Castro St.

c 1890
712 Castro

1894, Charles Hinkel (he lived in 740)
740- 6 Castro
Two of the city's leading late 19th-century builders lived on this block. No. 701 was originally on the back lot and was moved forward over the later garages. By that time Nelson had moved to his fashionable development, Presidio Heights, in the Richmond.

41 House
1952, Wurster, Bernardi & Emmons
4015 21st St.
A fine example of the kind of informal yet clearly defined house done in many variations by this firm from the 1930s through the 1950s.

42 House
1892, Charles Rousseau
3833 21st St.
An ornate Queen Anne-Italianate, to be compared with 835 South Van Ness, also by Rousseau.

43 Casa Ciele
1930
3698 21st St.
Built by famed Mayor "Sunny Jim" Rolfe, this secluded English cottage in the pines has a superb view of downtown.

Houses
1966, 1974, Lanier & Sherrill
3616, 3637 21st St.
Two well-sited houses that fit nicely into the neighborhood; the entrance landscaping is about all that can be seen of No. 3637—but it is very nice to look at.

44 Edison School
1927
Reconst. 1974, Eden & Eden
3531 22nd St. at Dolores St.

45 House
1888, A.R. Denke
68 Fair Oaks St.
A Stick-style house with an unusual porch with flat-sawn balusters, looking more like an eastern farmhouse than a city house. Fair Oaks has many interesting Victorians along its five-block length; note No. 92, for example.

51. St. John's Lutheran Church

46 Hill St. houses
1878, The Real Estate Assoc.
14-28, 30 Hill St.

1883, Charles Geddes
25 Hill St.

1885
49 Hill St.

1883
77 Hill St.

1884, T.J. Welsh
83-91 Hill St.
Another fine group—Italianate on the even side and Stick on the odd.

47 Firehouse No. 44
c 1910
Rem. 1962, Lanier & Sherrill
3816 22nd St.
A Mission Revival firehouse elegantly remodeled into an artist's studio.

48 Houses
1875
2-6 Vicksburg St.

c 1910
22-24 Vicksburg St.
No. 2-6 is a lofty Italianate with a five-sided corner bay. No. 22-24 is a Craftsman double house.

49 Hibernia Bank
c 1910
22nd and Valencia sts.
One of several exemplary Classic Revival banks in the Mission district.

50 Mission Market Mall
c 1900
22nd and Mission sts.
This very sprightly restoration of a turn-of-the- century commercial building into a food market- mall is next door to the site of the Old Mission Market, the last of the city's great concession food markets to disappear.

51 St. John's Lutheran Church
c 1895
3126 22nd St.
A naive Carpenter Gothic facade, like a child's drawing of a Gothic cathedral.

53. House, 160 Vicksburg

52 Noe Valley Ministry
c 1890
1021 Sanchez St.
A commendable conversion of an old church into a community center.

53 House
1907
160 Vicksburg St.
A rich man's Classic Revival palace as seen through a reducing glass.

54 Row of houses
1889, Percy & Hamilton
1000 Dolores St.

1883
1010 Dolores St.

1887, S. & J.C. Newsom
1037 Dolores St.

1904
1041 Dolores St.

1885, Schmidt & Havens
1074 Dolores St.

c 1880
1080 Dolores St.

1890
1083 Dolores St.
A vintage block from the Mission's heyday as a suburban "zone of better residence," as the real estate brochures used to say.

55 House
1886
200 Fair Oaks St.
A Stick-style house, handsomely painted.

56 Collegio de La Mission
(old S. Gompers High School)
1939, Masten & Hurd
22nd and Bartlett sts.
This former high school has a streamlined Moderne rear elevation facing Valencia Street, with rounded glass-block stair towers.

57 Houses
1889, T.J. Welsh
703-9, 731-65 Capp St.
Fifteen Stick-style houses, all by the same hand, ten of which are intact.

58 Horace Mann Middle School
1924, John Reid, Jr.
Reconst. 1976, Hardison & Komatsu
3351 23rd St.
Another school by John Reid to compare with entries 17 and 29.

56. Collegio de La Mission

Mission Branch Library
c 1910
24th and Bartlett sts.
A branch library in the form of a small
Italian Renaissance palazzo.

Houses
1877
3350 23rd St.

1882
3336 23rd St.

1886
3330 23rd St.

1877, John Hinkel
3326 23rd St.
A fine group of late 19th-century houses
that span a decade but keep the same
style. The Hinkels may have done them
all.

59 Bank of America
c 1925
23rd and Mission sts.
A late version of the Italian Renaissance
palace that was for so long the favorite
image for the palaces of finance.

Corner commercial-flats
c 1898
23rd and Mission sts.
A typical building type of the times, now
called "mixed use," but then just known
as "living over the store."

10
South of
Market

East
Mission

Potrero
Hill

1 Hills Bros Coffee Factory, 2 Harrison
2 Union Oil & Sailor's Union
3 PT&T, 611 Folsom
4 Brick bldg, 657 Howard
5 Condos, 3rd St & Folsom
6 Senior Activities Ctr, 360 4th St
7 Dettner Printing Co, 835 Howard
8 Crocker Bank Computer Ctr, 155 5th St
9 Calif Casket Co, 965 Mission
10 Media bldg, 943 Howard
11 Hotel Orlando, 995 Howard
12 Eng-Skell Co, 1035 Howard
13 Koret of California, 1130 Howard
14 PG&E Substation; Magrun & Otter Co
15 Phillips Hotel, 201 9th St
16 People's Laundry, 165 10th St
17 St. Joseph's Church, 1415 Howard
18 More Paper Co, 1489 Folsom
19 Foremost Dairy bldg & Le Du bldg
20 Ukrainian Orthodox Church, 345 7th St
21 South Park
22 Fire Dept Pumping Station, 698 2nd St
23 Warehouses, 600 block 3rd St
24 Warehouses, 100 block Townsend
25 Industrial bldgs, 224, 264 Townsend
26 Warehouses, 310, 350 Townsend
27 China Basin bldg, 185 Berry
28 Warehouses, 650, 700-68 7th
29 Galleria, Kansas; Showplace Sq, Brannan
30 Greyhound Garage, 8th St & Hooper
31 Far West Labs, 1855 Folsom
32 House, 573 South Van Ness
33 St. Charles School, 18th St. & Shotwell
34 Project Artaud, 599 Alabama
35 House, 19th St & Florida
36 Houses, 900 block South Van Ness
37 Apts, 1080 South Van Ness
38 Double house, 772 Shotwell
39 Apts, 1201 South Van Ness
40 Houses, 2733, 2735 Folsom
41 Houses, 1348, 1381 South Van Ness
42 House row, 1100 block Shotwell
43 Apt complex, 26th St & South Van Ness
44 House row, 1200 block Treat
45 Housing, 23rd & Potrero
46 Former fire station, 2501 20th St
47 SF General Hospital, 1001 Potrero
48 Neighborhood house, 953 De Haro
49 Victoria Mews, 20th St & Wisconsin
50 Potrero Hill Middle School, 18th St
51 Pioneer Square & Anchor Brewing Co
52 Cottages, 559-609 Arkansas
53 Houses, 512-26 Connecticut
54 Daniel Webster School, 465 Missouri
55 Houses, 300, 301 Pennsylvania
56 House, 400 Pennsylvania
57 Esprit de Corps Park, 900 Minnesota
58 Cottages, 1100 block Tennessee
   Old Irving Scott School, 1060 Tennessee
59 Muni Maintenance Depot, 1100 block 23rd
60 Potrero Hill Police Sta, 3rd Ave & 20th St
61 American Can Co, 3rd bet 20th & 22nd sts
62 Bethlehem Steel Yards, 20th & Illinois

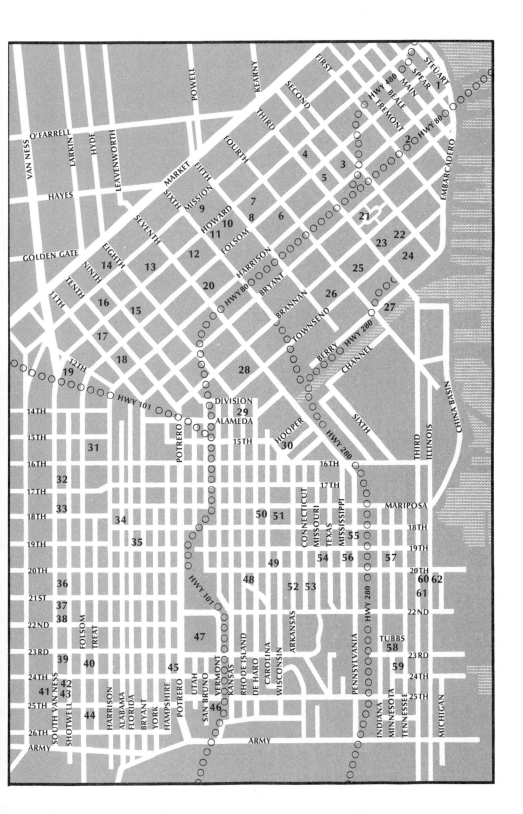

When Jasper O'Farrell gave the city its first formal survey in 1847, he decided that the existing street grid north of Market was too confining, and so made the blocks south of Market roughly four times as large—too large, in fact, for residential development. This decision consigned the area's flatlands to light industry beginning in 1851, when several foundries and shipyards were established along the shore beyond First Street. The city's first working-class neighborhood occupied the vale between the sandy hills on Market and Howard, euphemistically called Happy Valley. Looming over Happy Valley was Rincon Hill, where the rich lived until the late 1860s when Second Street was cut through, fracturing the hill and abetting the industrialization of the area. A forelorn reminder of its fashionable history is the remnant of South Park, entry 21. When the cable car made Nob Hill accessible, the social climbers left Rincon for good. The hill itself departed when it was cut down to serve as the springing point for the Bay Bridge, completed in 1936.

Potrero Hill, former pastureland as the name implies, rises out of the flats south of Market Street. Though surrounded by freeways and industrial areas, the hill quickly becomes residential as it rises. A few early settlers such as Captian Adams, whose house stands at 300 Pennsylvania, saw the advantages of this secluded hill and its fine weather. They settled on the Bay side in the 1860s and 1870s. In the 1880s when the Union Iron Works, now Bethlehem Steel, moved to the base of the hill, it was known as Scotch Hill because of the many Scots who lived and worked there. After 1905, Russians were the largest immigrant group and remained so until the 1930s. Potrero Hill is still something of a backwater. While most of the houses, both old and recent, are relatively small and unpretentious, the views of downtown and the Bay are spectacular. The industrial belt adjacent to the waterfront and stretching south and east of the freeway is a treasure trove for fanciers of industrial architecture, see entries 23-31.

1   Hills Bros. Coffee Factory
   1933, George Kelham
   2 Harrison St.
A visual and olfactory landmark for those crossing the Bay Bridge.

2   Union Oil Co.
   1940, Lewis P. Hobart
   425 First St.
   Sailor's Union of the Pacific
   1950, William G. Merchant
   450 Harrison St.
The Union Oil Company digital clock tower is another landmark for the Bay Bridge traffic. The building was designed as a billboard to advertise the company's products to the crowds attending the Golden Gate International Expo of 1939-40 on Treasure Island. The Sailor's Union is post- Moderne.

3   Pacific Telephone Building
   1972, McCue, Boone & Tomsick
   611 Folsom St.
A well-detailed brushed-aluminum box for delicate and complex telephone switchgear. The program resulted in the windowless paneled skin interrupted only by glazed indentations where personnel circulation and lunchrooms occur. This is one of a group of telephone buildings strung along Folsom. No. 633 is by John Carl Warnecke & Associates.

4   Building
   1925
   657 Howard St.
An old industrial building handsomely converted to offices and shops.

5   Condominiums
   1980s, Kaplan, McLaughlin & Diaz
   Third and Folsom sts.
This project will occupy the last of the large land parcels in the Yerba Buena Redevelopment Area and, when completed, will establish a sizable 24- hour resident population for the first time since the heyday of Happy Valley and Rincon Hill.

13. Koret of California

6   Senior Activities Center
1925
360 Fourth St.
A residentially scaled Spanish Colonial Revival building that is a real surprise in this area, fortunately put to a good use.

7   Dettner Printing Co.
1909, Coxhead & Coxhead
835 Howard St.
The architect's fondness for exaggerated detail appears here in the giant keystone over the entrance, perhaps the only opportunity afforded by the budget to add a little drama to a typically utilitarian building type. The metal-framed ground floor is handsome and well- proportioned.

8   Crocker Bank Computer Center
1974, Skidmore, Owings & Merrill
155 Fifth St.
The building as container says little and so says much about the anomie of the computer age.

**9   California Casket Co.
Office Building**
1909, Albert Pissis
965 Mission St.
An appropriately dignified Classical facade. For a neo-Classical work of considerably more opulence by this prominent early 20th-century architect, see the Hibernia Bank, 1:59.

10   Media Building
1973
943 Howard St.
A contemporary shed-roofed brick building that fits well on the street.

11   Hotel Orlando
c 1910
995 Howard St.
The corner hotel with a dome to advertise its importance was a popular building type before the advent of giant signs designed to be visible at auto speed.

12   Eng-Skell Co.
1930, A.C. Griewank, engineer
1035 Howard St.
One of the several fine Art Deco industrial facades in the South of Market area. Griewank, an engineer-designer of industrial buildings, also did the Harband Building at 1126 Howard in 1930.

13   Koret of California
c 1935
Rem. 1972, Beverly Willis & Assoc.
1130 Howard St.
With its almost playfully fortified parapet, sunburst entrance, and other detail redone in contrasting paint, this decorated box has the swank associated with the geometric ornament of the 1920s and 1930s.

14   PG&E Substation
1947, William G. Merchant
66 Eighth St.
Mighty and ponderous, this massive block with its muscular sculpture is a far cry from the graceful Classical designs of Willis Polk; see the Jessie Street Substation, 1:48.

Magrun & Otter Co.
1928, Bliss & Faville
1235 Mission St.
A great display of the decorative possibilities of terra-cotta.

15   Phillips Hotel
1907, Fabre Mohr
201-6 Ninth St.
A newly refurbished corner-domed hotel; see entry 11.

16   People's Laundry
1906, J. Dolliver
165 Tenth St.
Originally the Lick Baths, this picturesque complex was built to serve those rendered bathless by the earthquake.

20. Ukrainian Orthodox Church

17 St. Joseph's Church
1912, John J. Foley
1415 Howard St.
St. Joseph's imposing twin-towered neo-Baroque facade looms over the loft buildings of this now largely industrial area, testifying to the staunch Italian neighborhood that was once here. The Templo Calvario next door is an older Carpenter Gothic church, which has lost half its spire.

18 More Paper Co.
c 1910
1489 Folsom St.

19 Le Du Building
c 1930
123 South Van Ness Ave.
Foremost Dairy Building
c 1930
1675 Howard St.
Two more Moderne-style buildings that testify to the industrial growth of this area when on the verge of the Great Depression.

20 Ukrainian Orthodox Church
of St. Michael
1906, S. Ardrio
345 Seventh St.
With its lively twin-towered facade approached by a double-branching stair and flanked by palm trees, this oasis in the industrial neighborhood proves that the cultural institutions of strong ethnic groups can endure even when their residential context disappears.

21 South Park
1856, George Gordon
Second St. to Third St., Bryant St. to Brannan St.
One of San Francisco's first upper-class residential developments, South Park was a speculative tract laid out by an Englishman with similar London developments in mind. Though a few of the town houses that were meant to encircle the elliptical drive were built, the project as a whole never really got off the ground because of the declining status of Rincon Hill in the 1870s. The short row of London-style town houses has disappeared, but the mid-block park still sparks memories and plans for recapturing its former ambience.

**22 S.F. Fire Department
Pumping Station**
c 1920, Frederick H. Meyer
698 Second St.
Given the right paint job, this building could make the cover of *Progressive Architecture* as the latest in post-Modernism.

23 Warehouses
1880s, 1890s, 1900s
615, 625, 660 Third St.
A good collection of brick warehouse buildings; the oldest in the vicinity and the most structurally interesting is the Oriental Warehouse, 1867, at 650 First Street.

24 Warehouses
1890s-1900s
100 block Townsend St.
Another good block—notice the buildings with scalloped parapets.

25 Industrial buildings
c 1930, c 1890
224, 264 Townsend St.
This and the following row are being converted from industrial to office use. In general, the rash of office conversion is a response to the skyrocketing rents for downtown space.

26 Warehouses
c 1900
310, 350 Townsend St.
Tasteful conversions of brick warehouse buildings using a design approach that might now be called "conversion vernacular."

27 China Basin Building
1922, Bliss & Faville
Rem. 1973, Robinson & Mills
185 Berry St.
The office conversion of this enormous warehouse building, originally built for the Pacific Steamship Company, started the now well- established trend.

22. SF Fire Department Pumping Station

28 Warehouses
c 1890
650 Seventh St., Sixth and Bluxome sts.
Baker & Hamilton Warehouse
1905, Albert Pissis
700-68 Seventh St.
More noble brick storage palaces.

29 The Galleria
c 1900
Rem. 1973, Wurster, Bernardi & Emmons
101 Kansas St.
A spectacular joining of two brick warehouses by a steel and glass atrium.
Showplace Square
1970s
Brannan St. bet. Seventh and Eighth sts.
Two of the major buildings housing the showrooms of interior design firms.

30 Greyhound Maintenance Garage
c 1947, Skidmore, Owings & Merrill
Eighth and Hooper sts.
SOM's first job in San Francisco was a staightforward piece of long-span steel industrial design.

31 Far West Labs
c 1900
Rehab. 1972, Esherick, Homsey, Dodge & Davis
1855 Folsom St.
Another brick warehouse conversion, this time to offices and laboratories for educational research. The 300 block of Shotwell has an almost intact row of 1880s houses on the even-numbered side.

32 House
c 1890
573 South Van Ness Ave.
A grand and lonely Queen Anne house.

33 St. Charles School
c 1880
18th and Shotwell sts.
A rare survivor of wooden Italianate
school design.

34 Project Artaud
c 1900
599 Alabama St.
One of several conversions of industrial
buildings to artists' studios and housing.

35 House
1981, Jeremy Kotas
Near cor. 19th and Florida sts.
In spite of a very tight budget the architect managed to give this house painterly
panache in the post-Modern manner.

36 Houses
c 1890
919, 920, 943, 959, 989 South Van
Ness Ave.
A varied group of late 19th-century
houses, some of them very imposing,
such as No. 943. Note the very ornate
plasterwork on No. 959.

37 Apartments
c 1900
1080-6 South Van Ness Ave.
Unusual rounded-corner, flat-faced bays
distinguish this combination commercial-
residential building. It and the house next
door are nicely painted.

38 Double house
c 1875
772-74 Shotwell St.
The twin-bay Italianate at its best—a classic San Francisco row house type. The
block as a whole is representative of this
era of tract housing; many similar to it
may be found in the Western Addition.

33. St. Charles School

38. Double house, 772-74 Shotwell

39 Apartments
c 1885
1201 South Van Ness Ave.
Another unusual corner apartment house,
this one with heavy gable hoods. The
second floor was restored by San Francisco Victoriana, the city's leading Victorian restoration firm, after a 1976 fire.

40 Houses
1880s
2733, 2735 Folsom St.

41 House
1886, Seth Babson
1348 South Van Ness Ave.
One of the state's first professionally
trained architects designed this great
Stick-style pile for Frank M. Stone, a
prominent lawyer. The richly detailed interior is apparently intact.
House
1884, Charles I. Havens
1381 South Van Ness Ave.

43. Apts, 26th St and South Van Ness

44. House row, 1200-2, 1232 Treat

41. House, 1348 South Van Ness

42 House row
c 1885
1110-28, 1136-38, 1140-2 Shotwell St.
A fine row, nicely painted. The roundels with knobs in their centers used in the frieze were called *pies* although it is not clear why.

43 Apartment complex
c 1910
26th St. and South Van Ness Ave.
One of the city's best pieces of Craftsman, clinker-brick, and Shingle apartment designs, this has a lively facade and a carefully scaled interior court.

44 House row
1890, John McCarthy
1200-2, 1232 Treat St.

c 1885
1256 Treat St.

The first two buildings were built by an owner- developer who apparently wanted something fireproof for himself and so put up this unusual brick Italianate. No. 1256 has fine ornament.

45 Housing
1980, Burger & Coplans
23rd St. and Potrero Ave.
Compatible contemporary Shingle-style housing.

46 Former fire station
1917
2501 20th St.
Moorish Romanesque Revival—there is a fire station in San Francisco in almost every style.
The open space in this bend of Potrero Avenue is the Knudsen-Bloom Park, designed by Esherick, Homsey, Dodge & Davis, whose offices are nearby at 2789 25th Street. There is an entry plaza off Utah Street.

47 San Francisco General Hospital
1909-15, Newton Tharp, city architect/John G. Howard/Frederick H. Meyer/John Reid, Jr.
1976, Stone, Marraccini & Patterson
1001 Potrero Ave.
A huge campus occupied by hospital buildings designed over a period of about

47. SF General Hospital

53. Houses, 512-26 Connecticut

49. Victoria Mews

60. Potrero Hill Police Station

50 years. The progression from a rich selection of materials and a relatively small scale to the inhuman scale of modern medical technology in concrete is clear.

48 Potrero Hill
Neighborhood House
1922, 1925, Julia Morgan
953 De Haro St.
This neighborhood house was established in 1919 by the Presbyterian Church to serve the Russian immigrants who had been settling on the hill since 1905. Morgan's reputation for designing successful small institutional buildings won her this job, which she executed with her usual concern for context in the informal design of this rustic shingled building with a welcoming entry and lobby areas.

49 Victoria Mews
1979
20th and Wisconsin sts.
Movie-set Victorian well done but best viewed from a distance, where the general mass merges with the older row housing in the hillside.

50 Potrero Hill Middle School
1968, Faulk & Booth
18th and De Haro sts.

51 Pioneer Square &
the Anchor Brewing Co.
c 1915
Mariposa, Carolina, 18th sts.
Industrial buildings, one converted to mixed use and one housing the city's most famous local brewery.

52 Cottages
1885
559-609 Arkansas St.

53 Houses
1885
512-26 Connecticut St.
Two fine streetscapes From the 1880s.

54 Daniel Webster
Elementary School
1974-75, Wong & Brocchini
465 Missouri St.
Exposed steel frame with panel infill designed to be readily expanded or contracted.

55. Adams house

55 Adams house
1868
300 Pennsylvania St.
Richards house
1866
301 Pennsylvania St.
Captain Adams bought this 13-acre tract in the 1860s and built his home there, probably from a carpenter's plan book from the east. The older Richards house seems very simple and chaste, having lost its entrance porch and its octagonal cupola, from which there must have been a fine view of the Bay.

56 Crowell house
c 1870
400 Pennsylvania St.
Similar to the Adams house. Across the street is a contemporary Shingle-style villa designed by its owner.

57 Esprit de Corps Park
1982
Minnesota St. to Indiana St., 19th St. to 20th St.
A wonderful community contribution by a clothing and accessory design firm adjacent to the park at 900 Minnesota.

58 Cottages
c 1885
1100 block Tennessee St.
Old Irving Scott School
1895
1060 Tennessee St.
The old wooden school building is a particularly choice piece of old Potrero Hill.

59 S.F. Muni Maintenance Depot
1980, Rockrise Odermatt Mountjoy Assoc.
1100 block 23rd St. at Tennessee St.
A fine work of contemporary industrial architecture.

60 Potrero Hill Police Station
c 1910
Third Ave. and 20th St.
A box wrapped in the Mission Revival style.

61 American Can Co.
c 1905
Third Ave. bet. 20th and 22nd sts.
A two-block-long concrete-frame industrial plant built from stock company plans used across the country, now converted to mixed use.

62 Bethlehem Steel Yards
c 1880-1910
20th and Illinois sts.
Of all the industrial compounds at the base of the hill, this may be the prize. The buildings date from the arrival of the Union Iron Works at this site and are thus among the first industrial structures in the area. There is also a San Francisco Ship-building office and an old powerhouse. Alas, the complex may not be around much longer.

11 Presidio

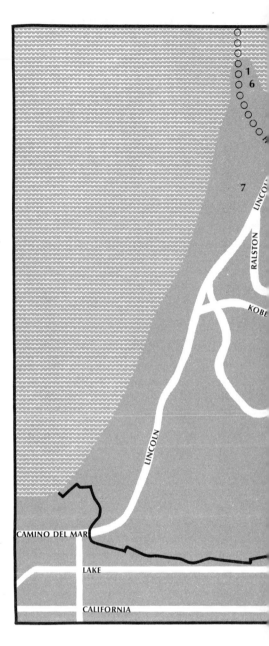

1 Golden Gate Bridge
2 Officers' Club, Moraga at Arguello
3 Army Museum, Funston at Lincoln
   Officers' housing, Funston
4 Barracks row, Montgomery S of Funston
5 Religious Activities Ctr, Lincoln
6 Fort Point, end of Marine
7 Coastal artillery batteries, Lincoln
8 Fort Winfield Scott, Ralston
9 Officers' housing, Kobbe
10 Family housing, Hoffman & New Road C

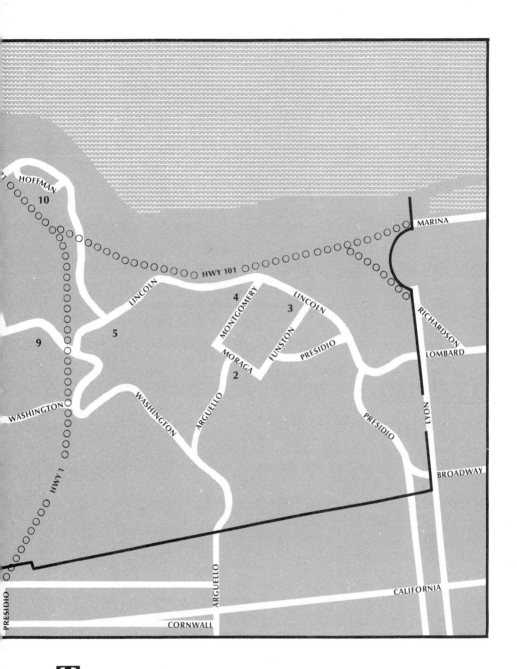

The first Spanish settlement in San Francisco was the military stockade built in 1776 around the site of the present officers' club at Moraga Avenue and Arguello Boulevard, which incorporates some of the adobe walls of the first commander's house. By the time the United States Army arrived in 1846, the Presidio was largely in ruins. The Army substantially rebuilt the fort, only to abandon it again in 1849, when most of the troops deserted for the gold mines. The present officers' club is interesting as a 1934 WPA interpretation of the Spanish Mission style.

11 Presidio

The oldest intact building on the fort is the present Army Museum, originally Wright General Hospital, built in 1863 at Funston Avenue and Lincoln. With its elegant attenuated three- story galleries, it is also one of the handsomest of the Presidio's buildings. Behind it along Funston Avenue is a row of officers' housing of the same period, which lined the original parade ground. Northwest along Montgomery Street, facing the present parade ground, is a fine group of brick barracks from 1895, now used as administrative offices. Driving along Lincoln Boulevard toward the Golden Gate Bridge, you pass the Religious Activities Center on a knoll next to the Highway 1 viaduct. It is a white frame structure from about 1900, with a veranda on three sides. A turnoff to the north slightly farther on leads to Fort Point, a polygonal brick coast- defense fort of 1853-61, now a museum. One of the finest surviving examples of a group that includes Fort Sumter in Charleston Harbor, it is well worth a visit and affords a wonderful view from below the Golden Gate Bridge.

Continuing westward along Lincoln Boulevard past the bridge, you come to a string of abandoned coastal artillery gun emplacements facing the Pacific; and inland of the road is Fort Winfield Scott, most of whose buildings date from 1908 to 1912. They mark one of the earliest appearances of Spanish Mission style in U.S. military architecture. Turning east, along Kobbe Avenue is a handsome row of Classic Revival officers' housing of 1912. Recent housing groups by George Matsumoto are at Hoffman and New Road C and on Lincoln Boulevard.

Apart from its interest as a historic military post, the Presidio has some of the finest scenery in the Bay Area, with matchless views of the Golden Gate and great windswept stands of Monterey cypress. It is also evidence that military reservations are one of the great ways of conserving natural sites, for it would long since have been built over had the Army not clung to it.

1 Golden Gate Bridge
1937, Irving Morrow, consulting
architect
Joseph Strauss, chief engineer
The 4,200-foot clear span was, until
1959, the longest in the world. The great
achievement of placing tower foundations in the swirling currents of the
Golden Gate, the superb setting, and the
red color of the bridge make it one of the
landmarks of bridge building. Moderne
detailing remarkably adapted to heavy
steel construction makes it an equally
clear expression of its time.

2 Officers' Club
1934, Quartermaster Capt., Barney
Meeden
Moraga Ave. at Arguello Blvd.

3 Presidio Army Museum
1863
Funston Ave. at Lincoln Blvd.
Officers' housing
1862
Funston Ave.

1. Golden Gate Bridge

4. Barracks row

5. Presidio Religious Activities Center

3. Presidio Army Museum

4 Barracks row
1895
Montgomery St. south of Funston Ave.

5 Presidio Religious Activities Center
c 1900
Lincoln Blvd.

6 Fort Point
1853-61
End of Marine Dr.

7 Coastal artillery batteries
1893-1908
Lincoln Blvd.

8 Fort Winfield Scott
1912
Ralston Ave.

9 Officers' housing
1912
Kobbe Ave.

10 Family housing
1968, George Matsumoto & Assoc.
Hoffman St. and New Road C

12
Inner Richmond
Presidio Heights

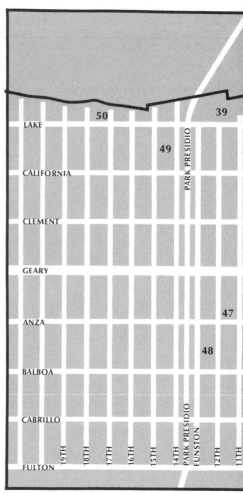

1 Lincoln University, 281 Masonic
2 University of SF, 501 Parnassus
3 Columbarium, end of Loraine
4 Double house, 21 Presidio
5 Houses, 3200 block Pacific
6 Houses, 3300 block Pacific
   House, 2 Laurel
7 King house, 50 Laurel
8 House, Locust at Presidio Wall
9 Roos house, 3500 Jackson
10 House, 3550 Jackson
11 Rosenberg house, 3630 Jackson
12 Wm. Hammond Hall house, 3855 Jackson
13 Batten house, 116 Cherry
14 House, 145 Cherry
15 House, 3820 Washington
   Koshland Mansion, 3800 Washington
16 Russell house, 3778 Washington

12 Inner Richmond/Presidio Heights

The original part of the Richmond extends from Arguello Boulevard to 15th Avenue between California and Geary. Despite the barrier posed by Lone Mountain and its cemeteries (now occupied by USF, entry 2), the availability of cheap land with some transportation encouraged a few of the builders who were working in the Mission and other expanding neighborhoods in the 1890s to buy up small parcels in these outside lands and build modest cottages. J. R. Chapton (entry 40) may have been the first, but he was soon followed by Fernando Nelson, who created Jordan Park, 28, and later his most ambitious project, Presidio Terrace, 34. In the general exodus from the inner city caused by the 1906 disaster, the Richmond developed more rapidly. Joseph Leonard, another major home builder, contributed blocks of substantial houses in a free-wheeling mix of styles (entry 46). Still, there was more lot-by-lot construction of single houses and flats in the inner than in the outer Richmond. The dead-end blocks adjacent to the Presidio, enjoying the same parklike scenery as Presidio Heights, have more custom-designed homes. Today, the rustic flavor is largely gone. Mountain Lake Park, which runs from Eighth Avenue to Funston Avenue, is an unexpected natural preserve hidden behind a wall of buildings; it may have been more obvious to Juan Bautista De Anza when he camped there in 1776.

One great boon to development came in 1912 with the opening of the Municipal Railway line on Geary Boulevard, which provided good transit to downtown. In 1917 the area was officially named Park Presidio, partly to avoid confusion with the city of Richmond across the Bay and partly because the new connection prompted a desire to discard the past, when the area was known as the Great Sand Waste. In any case, the new name did not stick. Until the Great Depression and World War II, development proceeded with deliberate speed. But the real boom followed the war and succeeded in filling all the blocks to the ocean as well as the leftover pockets. Recent years have witnessed major battles to stop increasing density by down-zoning the area. So far this tactic has worked, but one has the feeling that large-scale development still lurks in the wings.

Even the most casual visitor is struck by the ethnic variety of the Richmond. In the late teens and twenties, immigrant Russians and East European Jews settled here. Businesses, restaurants, bookstores and the Russian Cathedral on Geary still testify to their presence. The post-World War II influx was composed of Jews from the declining Fillmore area and Japanese who returned from relocation camps to find their Western Addition neighborhood occupied by blacks who had migrated to the Bay Area to work in the defense plants. The largest ethnic minority is the Chinese, who, overflowing from Chinatown, found it easier to acquire property here than in the inner- city neighborhoods. The commercial strips along Geary, Clement, and California from Presidio Boulevard to Arguello are the new Chinatown. Though this rich ethnicity has not stamped the area in any architecturally significant way, its gastronomic impact is considerable. Hunger pangs produced by sightseeing can be happily assuaged.

1 Lincoln University
c 1900
281 Masonic Ave.
The city's earliest black educational institution.

2 University of San Francisco
1927-30, master plan
1948, 1967, 1975, Milton T. Pflueger/
Pflueger Architects
501 Parnassus Ave.

In 1855 the Jesuits founded the city's first college, St. Ignatius, located on Market Street. Its church, St. Patrick's, now stands at 1822 Eddy Street. The next campus at Hayes and Van Ness Avenue, established in 1880, was destroyed by the 1906 fire. In 1927, the college moved to its present site; it became the University of San Francisco in 1930. The imposing St. Ignatius Church, designed by Patrick J. Devlin, was the largest on the West Coast

12 Inner Richmond/Presidio Heights

when it was built in 1914. The neo-Baroque structure, with its 210-foot towers, is a landmark visible from practically everywhere in the western part of the city. The modern campus, designed by the Pflueger family firm, occupies most of the hilltop. Lone Mountain College has been part of USF since 1937; it once hosted four of the city's early cemetaries: Laurel Hill (1854), Calvary, the Masonic, and the Odd Fellows.

**3 San Francisco
Memorial Columbarium**
1898, B.J.S. Cahill
End of Loraine Ct.
Originally designed as three buildings connected by a colonnade, the only one that was completed is this imposing neo-Classical structure. It once stood in the the middle of the Odd Fellows Cemetery.

4 Double House
c 1900
Rem. 1915, Bruce and Robert Porter
21-23 Presidio Ave.
A quietly elegant facade by a talented amateur, Bruce Porter, who contributed to the First Bay Tradition in architecture, stained glass, and landscape design. Two houses designed for him by his friends, Willis Polk and Ernest Coxhead, are around the corner in the 3200 block of Pacific Avenue.

5 Houses
1918
3200 Pacific Ave.

c 1890
Rem. c 1904, Willis Polk
3203 Pacific Ave.

1902, Ernest Coxhead
Rem. 1959, John Funk
3232 Pacific Ave.

1909, Bernard Maybeck
3233 Pacific Ave.

1902, Ernest Coxhead (Bruce Porter house)
3234 Pacific Ave.

c 1910, William F. Knowles
3235 Pacific Ave.

5. House, 3233 Pacific

5. Houses, 3236-40 Pacific

c 1910, William F. Knowles
3236-40 Pacific Ave.

c 1910, Ernest Coxhead
Rem. Willis Polk
3255 Pacific Ave.

This steep block is an architectural treasure trove. Nowhere else in the city is there such a harmonious stand of houses from what has been termed the First Bay Tradition, a West Coast "Shingle style" that mixes elegance of detail with informality in materials and form—don't miss the back side for real vernacular informality. The designers' names are a roster of the turn-of-the- century group of eastern migrants who brought forth a first flowering of regional design.

6 Houses
c 1945
Rem. Clark & Beuttler
2 Laurel St.

1908, Julia Morgan
3377 Pacific Ave.

1925, Louis M. Upton
3355 Pacific Ave.

1903, Albert Farr
3343 Pacific Ave.

1903, Albert Farr
3333 Pacific Ave.

1963, Joseph Esherick
3323 Pacific Ave.

Though not a showcase for idiosyncratic design like the previous block, the houses in this block quietly affirm the strength of the tradition; 2 Laurel and 3323 Pacific are respectful modern additions.

7 Frank King house
1917, Bliss & Faville
50 Laurel St.
A huge Georgian Revival mansion shoe-horned into its site.

8 House
1918, Julia Morgan
Locust St. at the Presidio Wall
The reliable English Cottage style much favored by Morgan and her clients (see also entry 11), but barely visible behind its shroud of foliage.

9 Roos house
1909, 1925, Bernard Maybeck
3500 Jackson St.
Maybeck's most lavish city residence, for which he designed all the interior appointments including furniture. The half-timbered English Tudor mode, called Stockbrokers' Tudor in eastern circles, is enlivened by Maybeck's personalized Gothic details in the roof brackets and balcony railing.

10 House
1940, Michael Goodman
3550 Jackson St.
A self-conscious expression of the International style, which later softened into a more regional interpretation. For another similar example of this early, European-influenced design, see 4:45, Montclair Terrace on Russian Hill.

9. Roos house

11 Rosenberg house
1916, Julia Morgan
3630 Jackson St.
A large but very subdued residence in the so-called English Cottage style, which shows the enduring fashionableness of English prototypes for the substantial American middle-class dwelling.

12 William Hammond Hall house
1912, William Hammond Hall
3855 Jackson St.
Hall, superintendent of Golden Gate Park and its principal engineer, designed this multilevel house and equipped it with such innovative features as air conditioning, an intercom system, and an earthquake shelter.

13 Batten house
1892, Willis Polk
116 Cherry St.
A study in the subtle manipulation of facade elements to create balanced asymmetry.

16. Russell house

17. Goldman house

14 House
1916, Hermann Barth
145 Cherry St.
A Colonial Revival house with the requisite three-part Palladian window with fan tracery in the center of the facade. A comparison with Barth's most important residential commission, the Bransten house (5:46), shows the ease with which architects of this generation shifted from one style to another.

15 House
1959, Campbell & Wong
3820 Washington St.
Koshland Mansion
1902, Frank Van Trees
3800 Washington St.
The Petit Trianon transplanted. A comparison with Mendelsohn's Russell house across the street reveals how the mansion image changed in 50 years.

16 Russell house
1952, Eric Mendelsohn
3778 Washington St.
Except for the trace of early Mendelsohn streamlining in the rounded corner bay and porthole windows, this house, well sited in its parklike setting, is a perfect example of the second wave of Bay Area regionalism.

17 Goldman house
1951, Joseph Esherick
3700 Washington St.
Compared to Mendelsohn's design above, Esherick's is a more straightforward rendition of a wooden box that balances the barnlike informality of vertical siding and double-hung windows with delicate railings and concrete sonotube columns. The L plan creates an elegant side garden court and processional entranceway sheltered from the street.

18 House
1928, Arthur Brown Jr.
3690 Washington St.

19 House
c 1900, Bliss & Faville
3638 Washington St.
Two houses that draw on the Classical vocabulary of forms in different ways. The latter has particularly delicate ornamental detail, comparable to the decorative motifs on Wedgwood porcelain. Note the stair windows on the side elevation—the variety of windows creates a catalog effect.

20 House
1929, Willis Polk
3450 Washington St.

21 House
1912, Oliver Everett
3340 Washington St.
A lavishly detailed town house in a version of the French Second Empire style that seems *retarditaire* for the date.

22 House
1895, Coxhead & Coxhead
3362 Clay St.

21. House, 3340 Washington

25. House, 301 Locust

23 Jewish Community Center of San Francisco
1932, Arthur Brown Jr./Hyman & Appleton
3200 California St.
Menorah Park Housing for the Elderly
1979, Stoller & Friedman/Segar/McCarthy & Miller
Sacramento and Walnut sts.
The housing for this well-known cultural institution is linked to the older building through a series of sheltered courtyards that have turned the interior of the block into a well- orchestrated set of protected and inviting spaces.

24 House
1909, Bliss & Faville
3581 Clay St.

25 Houses
1945, Wurster, Bernardi & Emmons
250 Locust St.

1954, Wurster, Bernardi & Emmons
301 Locust St.

26 House
1942, Wurster, Bernardi & Emmons
3655 Clay St.
Three houses that show a range of expressionism from Modernistic formality at 250 Locust to Bay Region Modern informality at 301 Locust and 3655 Clay Street.

27 House
1907, Stone & Smith
3779 Clay St.
A quirky corner-lot house that combines elements of the Craftsman and the Mission Revival styles.

28 Jordan Park
1900-1920s, Joseph Leonard, Urban Realty Co.
California St. to Commonwealth Ave., Arguello Blvd. to Geary Blvd.
A small tract built on cemetary property and named for the family who bought it after the 1906 earthquake and fire. The developer, Joseph Leonard, was also responsible for Ingleside Terrace (15:34). The uniformly set-back detached houses compose a suburban streetscape with landscape amenities such as the palm trees on Palm Avenue. The individual houses listed here were chosen both for architectural interest and to present the range of styles in Jordan Park. The selection is not comprehensive.

a. 12 Jordan Ave.
b. 55 Jordan Ave.
c. 57 Jordan Ave.
d. 71 Jordan Ave.
e. 85 Jordan Ave.
f. 20 Palm Ave.
g. 104 Palm Ave.
h. 129 Palm Ave.
i. 30 Euclid Ave.
j. 620 Euclid Ave.

29 Roosevelt Middle School
1934, Miller & Pflueger
460 Arguello Blvd.
Fine constructivist brickwork reminiscent of Dutch Expressionist buildings of the late teens and twenties. One of the city's most distinguished works of public school architecture.

30 Camp Fire Girls
Golden Gateway Council
1929, Henry Gutterson
325 Arguello Blvd.
A residentially scaled complex with an inviting forecourt and a rich combination of the kind of Arts and Crafts materials that are so precious today.

32. Temple Emanu-El

28. House, 12 Jordan

31 St. John's Presbyterian Church
1905
SW corner Arguello Blvd. and Lake St.
A fine brown-shingled church with a country parish look that reflects the Richmond's state of development in 1905. The building incorporates pews, pulpit furnishings, and the rose window from the original church of c 1870, which stood at Post and Mason. Other fine stained-glass windows come from a second church of 1888, which was at California and Octavia streets.

32 Temple Emanu-El
1924-26, Arthur Brown, Jr., John Bakewell, Jr., Sylvan Schaittacher Bruce Porter, interior decorator Bernard Maybeck, G. Albert Lansburgh, Edgar Walter, consultants
NW cor. Arguello Blvd. and Lake St.
A monumental neo-Byzantine Roman temple with a handsome forecourt. The interior is richly appointed and well worth visiting. The stained- glass windows, *Fire* and *Water*, installed in 1972-73, are by Mark Adams. A history of the Congregation Emanu-El is available at the temple office.

33 House
c 1903, Newsom & Newsom
166 Arguello Blvd.
Not Samuel and Joseph Cather, but the younger Newsoms, Sidney B. and Noble, designed this high, narrow, vaguely Elizabethan house.

34 Presidio Terrace
1905, Fernando Nelson, developer
This exclusive development was the crowning achievement of Nelson's prolific building career. No. 30, his own home, occupies the most important site on the left just past the entrance; it was designed by W.R. Yelland in 1930. Many prominent architects designed houses here. A selection follows:

c 1910, Albert Farr
9 Presidio Terr.

c 1910, Charles Whittlesey
10 Presidio Terr.

1905, Bakewell & Brown
16 Presidio Terr.

c 1910, Charles Whittlesey
19 Presidio Terr.

1910, Lewis Hobart
20 Presidio Terr.

c 1910, J.E. Krafft & Sons
23 Presidio Terr.

1908-9, A.F. Whittlesey
28 Presidio Terr.

1909, W.R. Yelland (Fernando Nelson house)
30 Presidio Terr.

c 1910, Charles Whittlesey
32 Presidio Terr.

c 1910, George Applegarth
34 Presidio Terr.

1911, Julia Morgan
36 Presidio Terr.

35 Apartments
c 1910, Earl B. Scott
121-25 Lake St.
Bold detail and form in a Secessionist-Prairie School styling.

36 St. Anne's Home
1903, Pissis & Moore
1981, Anshen & Allen
300 block Lake St.
The site of a recent lengthy preservation battle to save a set of handsome Neo-Georgian institutional buildings that were finally judged too outmoded to serve. History and aesthetics lost; functionalism survives.

37 Houses
1898-1905
5, 7, 15, 19, 23, 27, 37, 53-55 Seventh Ave.
An outstanding block of shingled Craftsman houses, which convey the rustic simplicity that the early Richmond afforded its residents.

38 Apartment house
1912, Albert Farr
SE cor. Eighth Ave. and Lake St.
A reserved Classical design that reveals the change from rustic simplicity to suburban sophistication in the expansion following the earthquake and fire.

39 Apartment house
c 1915, Houghton Sawyer
1-3 12th Ave.
Another example of the neighborhood change mentioned above. For a more luxurious work by this architect see Nob Hill, 4:10.

40 House row
1893, J.R. Chapton
211-17 Third Ave.
The area's earliest surviving cottage row.

41 House rows
c 1900, Fernando Nelson
500-700 Second Ave.
Those who have seen Nelson's houses in the Mission district will recognize these; one signature detail is the row of "doughnuts" across the entry porches. At 99 Cabrillo there is a shingled Queen Anne-Colonial house that may have been Nelson's; it is certainly an unusual type in this area.

42 Clement Hall
(Richmond Hall)
1897
301-05 Clement St.
An early neighborhood center.

43 French Hospital
1969, John Carl Warnecke & Assoc./ Rex Allen, Drever, Lechowski
1970-01, Paffard Keatinge Clay
4100 block Geary Blvd.
Institutional monumentality expressed by the boldly scaled exposed-concrete frame with glass infill walls.

44 Houses
c 1900
606-14 Eighth Ave.
A pair of outrageous Queen Anne houses that reveal this most popular 19th-century style in its final convulsions.

46. Houses, 500 block 12th Ave.

47. Christ the Saviour Greek Orthodox Church

45 Park Presidio Baptist Church
1908, Frederick Boese
850 Cabrillo St.
Wooden Gothic Revival churches were built in San Francisco long after the style had declined elsewhere. This one seems to look back to early Richmond and may well have stood alone like a rural parish church when it was built for the Zion Lutheran congregation and stood two blocks away. The 700 block of Tenth Avenue leading to the park was probably developed by Fernando Nelson around 1910; No.745 is known to be by his firm.

46 Houses
1911, Joseph Leonard
900 block Balboa St., 500 blocks
Tenth and 12th aves.
Most of the houses in these blocks were built by Leonard, a major home builder who originally came from Alameda. A few, such as 579 12th Avenue by Charles Rousseau, are by other builders. As is the case with most mass-produced products, the styling is homogenous, stressing theme and variation rather than distinctive individual design. Here there is an amazing fusion of Mission, Craftsman, Prairie, and Tudor executed with an attention to a picturesque variety of compositional elements that disguise the standard plans. The one stylistic exception is 900 Balboa, also by Leonard, which relies on the enduring authority of the Classical style to advertise the prestige of this corner lot.

47 Christ the Saviour
Greek Orthodox Church
1966, Esherick, Homsey, Dodge & Davis
490 12th Ave.
A serenely simple design that effectively communicates its purpose through the small blue onion dome.

48 Houses
c 1915, Pockman & Co., developers
500 block Funston Ave.
Another symphony of styles in the same key as entry 46 by Leonard. The only custom-designed house is No. 556, by Meussdorffer; it is noticeably simpler than the rest.

49 Houses
c 1914
100 blocks 14th and 15th aves.,
Lake St. to California St.
More vintage styling by an unknown developer. We have tried to select the most representative blocks, but urge you to explore others if your enthusiasm for typology is strong.

50 Apartments
1600, 1601 Lake St.
An elegant pair of Regency-inspired apartment houses.

13
Outer
Richmond

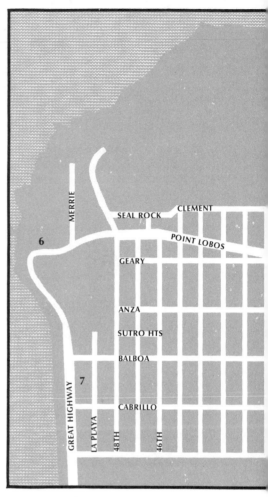

1 Sea Cliff, El Camino Del Mar
2 Houses, 9, 25, 45 Scenic
3 House, 850 El Camino Del Mar
4 House, 895 El Camino Del Mar
5 Lincoln Park; Palace, Legion of Honor
6 Sutro Heights, Cliff House, Sutro Baths
7 Ocean Beach condos, Great Hwy
8 House, 726 34th Ave
9 George Washington High School, 32nd Ave
10 Washington Hghts Condos, 31st & Geary
11 Presidio Middle School, 400 block 30th Ave
12 Apts & Cathedral, 6200 block Geary
13 Firehouse No. 14, 26th bet Anza & Geary
14 Cottage, 451 25th Ave
15 Santa Monica's Church, 470 24th Ave
16 Cabrillo School, 700 block 25th Ave

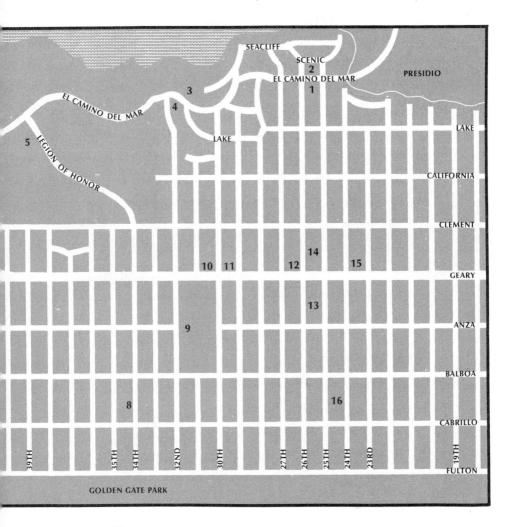

1 Sea Cliff

1912, Mark Daniels, planner
Gates on El Camino Del Mar at 25th,
26th, and 27th aves.

A garden suburb planned by Mark
Daniels, who also laid out Forest Hill.
Streets follow the contours and afford op-
portunities for panoramic views of the
Bay, the Marin Headlands, and the
Golden Gate. The architecture is blandly
Mediterranean for the most part, the ambience redolent of privacy. Though large
trees would have diminished the view,
the kind of integrated landscaping that
distinguishes St. Francis Wood would
have enhanced Sea Cliff as well. The
houses listed below are a sampling of
those by the better- known architects:

2 Houses

1914, Willis Polk & Co.
9, 25, 45 Scenic Way

Polk's late Classical style exhibits none of
the idiosyncracies of his early work.

3 House

1958, Wurster, Bernardi & Emmons
850 El Camino Del Mar

4 House

1963, Esherick, Homsey, Dodge &
Davis
895 El Camino Del Mar

There are few contemporary houses in
the area, for the simple reason that it was
rapidly built up in the teens and twenties,
leaving only a few lots. These two houses
reveal the evolution of Modern architecture over half a decade.

13 Outer Richmond

5. Lincoln Park, Legion of Honor Palace

5 Lincoln Park
Palace of the Legion of Honor
1916, George A. Applegarth
Across from 34th Ave. and Clement
St. or El Camino Del Mar

Lincoln Park occupies the top of the Point
Lobos Headland. Like Lone Mountain, it
once had a cemetary—aptly called the
Golden Gate—where the golf course is
now. Near the first tee an arch from a
Chinese tomb commemorates this piece
of the past. Matchless views of the
Golden Gate Bridge, the Marin Headlands, and the city to the east delight
those who walk along the north edge of
the park.

The California Palace of the Legion of
Honor, a city art museum devoted largely
to European painting of the 16th to 18th
centuries and a sculpture collection star-
ring Rodin, was given to the city by Adolph and Alma de Brettville Spreckels as a
memorial to the World War I dead. The
building is a modified copy of the Paris
palace of the same name, here given a
country rather than a city setting.

6 Sutro Heights
The Cliff House
Sutro Baths Ruins

Adolph Sutro began developing his
1,000-acre oceanfront estate in the
1880s. He purchased the burned-out hulk
of the 1863 Cliff House and rebuilt it into
one of the most fanciful seaside confec-
tions on the West Coast. Adjacent at the
waterline were the glazed domes of the
six indoor saltwater pools of the Sutro
Baths, a veritable pleasure palace on the
Pacific. Sutro planted thousands of eucalyptus trees with labor provided by
convicts and schoolchildren and laid out
exclusive gardens with specimen trees,
statuary, fountains, and so on. Being a
practical man, he initiated a steam railroad line that visitors could ride for a
nickel out to the Cliff House and a Sun-
day tour of his gardens. When the line
was sold to the Southern Pacific and the
fare raised, he laid down another line on
California Street, which also cost passengers a nickel. By the end of the century, transit from most of the city to the
ocean was no problem. Excursion cars
were common, and the scenic Lands End
line ran until a landslide closed it down
in 1925. Sutro's mansion overlooking the
Cliff House and the ocean, remodeled
and enlarged several times, was more
like a rustic lodge than a Mediterranean
chateau. In 1907 both the Sutro house
and the Cliff House burned; the latter was
partially rebuilt in 1908. Today there are
few physical remains to aid the imagination in reconstructing the grandeur that
was. But try anyway—the setting still hath
charm of the scenic variety and the ocean
hasn't changed.

7 Ocean Beach Condominiums
1982, Donald Sandys
The Great Highway bet. Balboa and
Cabrillo sts.
The first high-density housing to be built
on the oceanfront, formerly the site of
Playland Amusement Park.

8 House
1905, Willis Polk
726 34th Ave.
A modest but interesting shingled cottage
that suggests a much different lifestyle
than that of its neighbors, built in the
1930s.

9 George Washington High School
1936, Miller & Pflueger
500 block 32nd Ave.
One of the San Francisco School District's most impressive school complexes,
on a commanding site.

10 Washington Heights Condominiums
1982, Daniel Solomon and Assoc./
John Baumann
31st Ave. and Geary Blvd.
Straightforward but elegant design by an
architect whose several small-scale multiunit housing projects have maintained
the city's tradition of good design in this
field. For others see 4:43 and 3:39.

11 Presidio Middle School
1930, W.H. Grim, Jr./E.J. Rising
400 block 30th Ave.
Another example of distinguished public
school design that exhibits the high level
of craftsmanship available in the period
when most of San Francisco's schools
were built.

12 Apartment house
c 1925, Hermann Baumann
Geary Blvd. and 27th Ave.
Holy Virgin Russian Cathedral
1962, Oleg Ivanitsky
6210 Geary Blvd.
Perhaps because of the availability of
large parcels of land in the flatlands and/
or the lack of development on the major
commercial strips, there is a procession
of monumental institutional buildings on
Geary Boulevard. The Russian Cathedral
is one of the most culturally important, as
any visitor on feast days can attest.

2. House, 25 Scenic

8. House, 726 34th Ave.

13 Firehouse No.14
c 1975, Jacques de Brer
26th Ave. bet. Anza St. and Geary
Blvd.

14 Cottage
1890s
451 25th Ave.
A good example of the kind of small cottage that was built, probably on speculation, to entice the inner-city dwellers to
the Outside Lands.

15 Santa Monica's Church & School
1907, Shea & Lofquist
470 24th Ave. at Geary Blvd.
A monumental ecclesiastical complex,
designed by the leading Irish Catholic architects but with stylistic references to
Italy, homeland of many of the original
parishioners.

16 Cabrillo Elementary School
1973, Bowles & Marshall
700 block 25th Ave.
A well-sited, compact school built as a
result of the Field Act. This act set seismic
safety standards for the aging stock of city
schools, which, in many cases, could
only be met by new construction.

14 Golden Gate Park

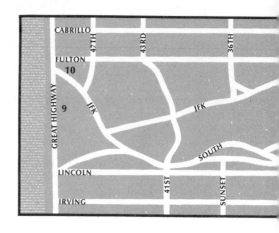

1 McLaren Lodge (Park Hdqtrs)
2 Alford Lake Bridge
3 Children's Playground
   Sharon Children's House
4 Conservatory
5 California Academy of Sciences
   Planetarium, Aquarium & Hall of Science
   Cowell Hall
6 Music Concourse
7 M.H. de Young Memorial Museum
8 Japanese Tea Garden
9 Beach Chalet
10 Dutch and Murphy windmills

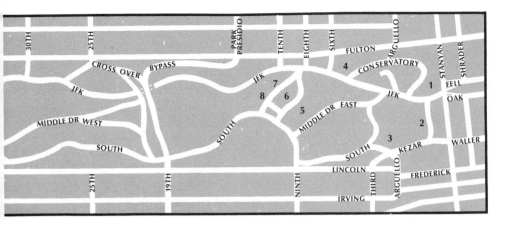

T o create one of the world's more verdant parks out of miles of shifting sand dunes is no mean achievement. To do so in the face of parsimonious budgets and endless political intrigue is even more impressive. This was the task of the man responsible for Golden Gate Park, now such a beloved and well-used part of the city that most residents take it for granted.

The idea of the park began in the 1860s. Frederick Law Olmsted, creator of New York's Central Park, was invited by the Outside Lands Commission to give his advice. He pronounced the prospective site hopeless, but, happily, his advice was ignored. In 1871, the remarkable William Hammond Hall, an ex-Army engineer, was appointed the park's first superintendent. In five years, in spite of inadequate support, he had designed the park, figured out how to anchor the sand dunes by planting imported sand grass and how to make the trees grow, and had begun at the east end to landscape the barren waste. But he was no politician and, after struggling vainly against budget cuts, resigned in disgust. Five years later he was wooed back, but accepted only long enough to hire his successor, the famous "Uncle John" McLaren, who is now widely and erroneously assumed to have designed the park.

The facts are remarkable enough. McLaren was superintendent from 1886 to 1943, when he died in office at the age of 96. Sage, tyrant, superb gardener, and adroit politician, he completed the park, landscaped the Panama-Pacific International Exposition, planted Dolores Street's parks, and generally dominated the city's landscape for 60-odd years.

The park that Hall designed and McLaren built is one of the great monuments of romantic landscape design. Long and narrow, it provides maximum green frontage to the city on either side and, thanks to careful grading and planting, a great variety of sheltered and secluded areas. Because of the fog the lawns survive intensive use far better than do the lawns of eastern parks. Since much of the vegetation is not deciduous, the park is perennially green. Major museums occupy the park along with monuments and notable works of architecture. But above all it is, as all great urban parks are, a piece of the country in the city.

7. Court of the Ages, Panama-Pacific Exposition

1   McLaren Lodge
(Park Headquarters)
1895, E. R. Swain
North of John F. Kennedy Dr. at east
entrance

Rusticated sandstone with a tile roof; the
Romanesque Revival style is reminiscent
of H. H. Richardson's work and of Stanford University. Percy & Hamilton set the
style with their Children's House, entry
3, in 1886.

2   Alford Lake Bridge
1889, Ernest Ransome
Pedestrian underpass, Kezar Dr. opposite Haight St.

The first reinforced concrete bridge in the
United States, although the design does
its best to conceal the fact. Instead, the
material mimics stones dripping with
mossy stalactites.

3   Children's Playground
Sharon Children's House
1886, Percy & Hamilton
Kezar Dr. near First Ave.

The playground occupies the site of a
lake filled by the leveling of a nearby hill.

The precedent for a children's playground came from New York's Central
Park; the concept was typical of the social planning of the time and gathered
great popular support. The Children's
House, which holds all manner of child-oriented delights, is the city's purest surviving example of Richardsonian Romanesque. Heavily damaged in the
earthquake, as were other masonry structures in the park, it was rebuilt within the
year. The carousel dates from c 1892. In
1978, Michael Painter & Associates redesigned the playground.

4   Conservatory
1878, Hammersmith Works, Dublin,
Ireland
John F. Kennedy Dr. opposite Fourth
Ave.

James Lick died before the magical
greenhouse he had ordered for his San
Jose estate could be erected. Leland Stanford and others bought it for the park.
The building, its setting, and its contents
marvelously preserve the ambience of the
19th century.

5 California Academy of Sciences
1915-31, Lewis P. Hobart
**Planetarium, Aquarium,
and Hall of Science**
1951, Weihe, Frick & Kruse
Cowell Hall
1968, Milton Pflueger
Whales Fountain
1939, Robert Howard
South side of the Music Concourse
A successful integration of old and new
buildings.

6 Music Concourse
The sculptural rhythm of the pollarded
plane trees makes this great formal space
a perfect contrast to the surrounding lush,
romantic landscape. The focus is the Music Pavilion, given by Claus Spreckels
and designed by the Reid Brothers in
1899.

7 M.H. de Young Memorial Museum
1916, Louis Christian Mullgardt
Rem. Arthur Brown, Jr.
Brundage Wing
1965, Gardner Dailey & Assoc.
De Young, founder of the *San Francisco
Chronicle*, insisted that the museum he
gave to the city be modeled on
Mullgardt's Court of the Ages at the
1915 Panama-Pacific International Exposition. The elaborate Spanish-style ornament that originally encrusted the
museum walls had to be removed for
seismic safety, leaving its form in the
nude. Arthur Brown then remodeled it in

his late stripped Spanish mode, a la Stanford's Hoover Tower. While neither the
original museum nor the more recent
Brundage wing are distinguished architecture, the collections are well worth a
visit.

8 Japanese Tea Garden
1874, George Turner Marsh
This Victorian idea of a Japanese garden,
designed by an Australian who was the
country's first Oriental-art dealer, attracts
a major share of the park's visitors—it is
definitely a must. Originally built for the
1894 Mid-Winter Fair, the park's first major
public event, the garden proved so popular that it was preserved. From 1907 to
1942, one family, the Hagiwaras, ran the
concession, inventing fortune cookies
along the way. In 1942 they were de-
ported. In 1978 Ruth Asawa, who was a
victim of the World War II Japanese-re-
location program, designed a bronze
plaque honoring the Hagiwaras, which is
located near the entrance. The garden
has many features, properly marked for
visitors.

9 Beach Chalet
1921, Willis Polk
A hipped-roof pavilion, which houses a
remarkable set of WPA murals by Lucien
Labaudt, executed in 1936-37, illustrating
recreational activities in San Francisco.
Polk was also the architect for the Portals
of the Past on Lloyd Lake, an Ionic colonnade that originally graced a Nob Hill
mansion designed by him that burned in
1906.

**10 Dutch Windmill
      & Murphy Windmill**
1903, 1905
These two great windmills at the western
edge of the park were built to pump its ir-
rigation water. The Murphy has recently
been restored; there is hope that the
other one soon will be.

4. Conservatory

15
Outer
Sunset

1 Shriners Hospital, 1701 19th Ave
2 SF Conservatory of Music, 1201 Ortega
3 Apts, 1482 21st Ave
4 Doelger City, 27th-39th aves
  Lawton Elementary School, 1570 31st Ave
5 Public housing, 4101 48th Ave
6 Born house, 2020 Great Highway
7 SF Zoo, Skyline at Zoo Rd
8 Lakeshore Park
  Lakeshore, Ocean & Gellert
9 Houses, Sloat to Eucalyptus
  Inverness to 21st Ave
  Central pumping station & reservoir
10 Stern Grove
  Trocadero Inn
11 Stonestown, 19th Ave & Winston
12 SF State University, 19th Ave & Holloway
13 Park Merced, 19th Ave & Crespi
14 Condos, Lake Merced Blvd & Brotherhood
15 Holy Trinity Church, 994 Brotherhood

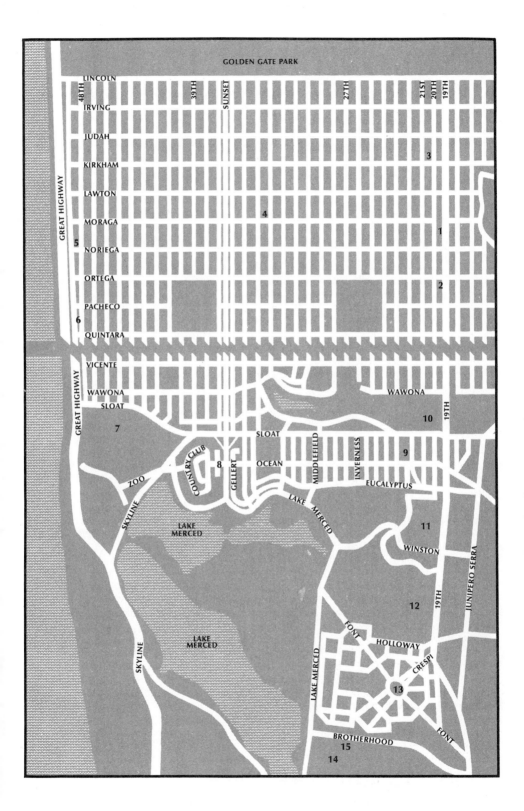

15   Outer Sunset

T he Sunset was originally part of the San Miguel Rancho, granted in 1839 to Jose Noe. In the 1850s the ranchlands lay in the path of the city's southwestern expansion. John Horner, an entrepreneurial sea captain, bought the 4,500-acre ranch in 1854, but he was mainly interested in the area now called Noe Valley. Horner lost the land to the Pioche family, from whom Aldoph Sutro acquired his estate about 1879. Sutro continued the planting of eucalyptus trees, which George M. Greene began in what is now Stern Grove in the early 1870s to ward off the invading sand dunes. The history of the Sunset, like that of the rest of the "Outside Lands," was tied to the development of transportation. Even with an acquired taste for living in the fog, the prospective buyer still looked for affordable property near transportation to downtown work places. Consequently, before the Outside Lands were tamed by municipal improvements, the sandy spaces were occupied by horse racing, farming, dairy ranching, and gunpowder production. Miles of orderly blocks of well-tended homes followed the laying of streets and tracks.

The 1851 San Miguel Ocean House and Beach Road was macadamized in the late 1860s and turned into a toll road to the popular Ocean House with its nearby racetrack. In the same decade the old Corbett Road, winding around Twin Peaks, passed by the Ocean View Riding and Driving Park. Roadhouses such as the Mountain Spring House, the Sunnyside House, the Ingleside House, and the Trocadero Inn were scattered along the route. Racing buffs not only cruised the flat, sandy no man's land, but frequented the various small racetracks of uncertain longevity.

To serve a growing tourist trade, Crocker, Huntington, and Stanford—three of the railroading Big Four—opened a steam railway service in 1879. The line ran from Haight and Stanyan to H Street, now Lincoln Way, and thence to the ocean where it terminated at 49th and Balboa. In 1883, the Park and Ocean Railroad was connected by cable cars to downtown. The line was electrified in 1898.

In 1887, Aurelius E. Buckingham christened his residential tract, laid out near the steam line, the Sunset. The plat extended for two or three blocks south from Fifth Avenue and along H Street (Lincoln Way). To aid construction, the developer hauled crushed rock from the Sutro quarry and spread a thin layer of it over the sand, which he also planted with oats, lupine, and mustard. There were hardly twenty houses between Stanyan and the ocean at the time. Nor was there any real impetus for development until the excitement of the 1894 Mid-Winter Exposition.

In 1905, William Crocker's Parkside Realty Company opened a promising tract near 21st Avenue and Taraval Street that ultimately became Parkside. Although Sutro died in 1898, his vast oceanside estate was tied up in a contested will until 1909. In 1911 the first of his Rancho San Miguel land was subdivided. The 725 acres, bought by the A.S. Baldwin Residential Development Company for $1.5 million, became Forest Hill, St. Francis Wood, Westwood Park, Balboa Terrace, and Monterey Heights. Still, the inaccessibility of these communities to the downtown business district was a problem. Though the United Railroad Company built a line out Ocean Avenue, the literal breakthrough was the Twin Peaks Tunnel, which made rapid transit available to downtown starting in 1918. Thereafter the communities west of Twin Peaks became popular for their remoteness from what many middle-class citizens regarded as urban chaos.

City Engineer Michael O'Shaughnessy, who fostered the tunnel, also blessed the area with another important umbilical chord to downtown. This was Portola Drive, a scenic route that connected St. Francis Circle to the Twin Peaks extension of Market Street. From the Circle, Sloat Boulevard, also by O'Shaughnessy, completed the scenic tour to the ocean. The major north-south arterial, 19th Avenue, was asphalted in 1924, and Sloat defined an entrance to Sigmund Stern Memorial Grove, given to the city by Mrs. Stern in 1932 as a place of natural and cultural refreshment through the medium of the summer music festival. Off the beaten path is the former Trocadero Inn, built by George M. Greene—after he planted the eucalyptuses—to accommodate the racing crowds. It is now the park headquarters.

15 Outer Sunset

As the streets and car lines multiplied, the blocks filled with houses. The major builders in these early tracts are familiar names from other parts of the city: Fernando Nelson & Sons in West Portal Park and Merced Manor; Joseph Leonard and his Urban Realty Company in Balboa and Ingleside Terrace; and Mark Daniels, who planned Forest Hill after he laid out Sea Cliff. Numerous small contractors and builders contributed to the activity by developing a lot or two at a time. But if the names change, the basic building design does not. Builders borrowed and stole from each other, keeping a weather eye out for what was selling. In the hilly areas the topography influenced house plans and orientation to some extent, but in the flatlands, despite the studied variation in facade treatment, it is architectural homogeneity that is most impressive.

Although St. Francis Wood has the most lavish plan in respect to landscaping, Forest Hill, Ingleside Terrace, and Westwood Park have formal plats that distinguish them on the map from adjacent areas. A basic component of each subdivision was the improvement club or neighborhood association, which enforced architectural standards as well as covenants restricting home ownership to Caucasians.

By far the greatest number of houses in the Sunset were built in the post-World War II decades. Most were products of the "Big Five": the Gellert Brothers, the Stoneson Brothers, the Doelgers, Chris McKeon, and Ray Galli, who began building in the 1920s and 1930s. Soon they were caught up in the boom in middle-income housing created by the lending policies of the Federal Housing Administration, established in 1934. Miles of bare land in the Sunset were carpeted with homes, some of them completed by Henry and Frank Doelger at the rate of two a day. So-called Doelger City, located roughly between 27th and 39th avenues and Kirkham and Quintara streets, suggests the magnitude of the Doelgers' operations. In fact, from 1934 to 1941 they were the largest home builders in the country.

15 Outer Sunset

Although methods of rationalizing the mass production process varied, the Doelgers' approach was similar to that of other builders. A potpourri of styles—English Cottage, French Provincial, Regency, Colonial, and International Style Modern or Modernistic— provided variations on the general theme of homes uniformly scaled and placed on 25-by-100-foot lots. Henry Doelger professed a strong commitment to building well for the average family. The Doelgers used redwood for the house frame and worked with their team to create the best possible plan for prospective buyers, who responded in droves. The last step was "putting on the architecture." Elevations of the various facades were pinned on the wall individually and shifted about until a satisfying composition resulted, which was then drawn up and built. Neighborhood planning was not left out of the process. From the beginning, the Big Five put utilities underground and located commercial strips for which they made an effort to attract merchants. After World War II, the Veterans Administration G.I. loan program created an unprecedented housing boom. The Sunset blocks developed in the post-war decades show the effect of increased costs for labor and materials. Traditional styles, still in demand, become attenuated, appearing like cardboard cut-outs compared to the earlier models. The transition to modern architecture is evident in the variations on the ranch house theme that replace some of the period revival styles.

In mapping the Sunset we considered the individual buildings to be less important than the subdivisions that contain them. Those exploring the area should not confine themselves to this list.

The first Sunset plat lies in the blocks from about Second to Fifth avenues adjacent to the park. Some wildly picturesque house rows occur in the 1200 blocks of these and higher numbered avenues—try Seventh and Fifteenth avenues, for example. A major social and physical landmark is St. Anne of the Sunset, 850 Judah, built in 1905 by E.J. Garin. This was the first major Roman Catholic parish church built to serve the area's large Italian population. Golden Gate Heights, nearby, was bequeathed to the city by restaurateur Carl G. Larsen and developed by the Doelgers.

Parnassus Heights on the slopes of Mt. Sutro is now the campus of the University of California's Medical Center. The original Toland School of Medicine was established downtown in 1864 as a private college in 1864 and became part of the University in 1873. The site, 13 acres of which were given by Adolph Sutro, was developed beginning in 1895 as the "Affiliated Colleges." There were three buildings, one of which was intended for the College of Law, which chose to remain downtown and later became Hastings College of Law. When the 1906 earthquake and fire destroyed most of the city's hospitals, portions of the Medical School Building were converted to hospital use. In 1917, the University of California Hospital was funded at its present location and designed by Lewis P. Hobart. The first master plan, drawn up in the 1920s by William Hays, strongly influenced the alignment of buildings in an unbroken line east of the hospital on the south side of Parnassus. Five acres were added to the campus in 1928; 91 acres were added in 1947. These included the Mt. Sutro holdings from the Parnassus shelf to Clarendon Avenue.

There have been two long-range development plans; one in 1964 by John Lyon Reid, and one in 1975 by Anshen & Allen. Robert Roysten has been the landscape architect since 1964.

1 Shriners Hospital
c 1920
1701 19th Ave.
Another major landmark on 19th Avenue that, through its luxurious ornamental detail and human scale, offers a thought-provoking comparison with the contemporary behemoths that hospitals have become.

2 San Francisco Conservatory of Music
1928, Louis C. Mullgardt
1201 Ortega St. at 19th Ave.
One of the city's important cultural institutions, designed by an architect of considerable reputation and talent who, alas, had few building commissions in the city. For another see 9:10.

3 Apartments
1980, Donald McDonald
1482 21st Ave.
A contemporary re-cap of the twenties International style, earlier vernacular versions of which occur throughout the Sunset.

4 Doelger City
1932-c 1945, Doelger Bros.
Ortega St. to Kirkham St.,
27th Ave. to 39th Ave.
Lawton Elementary School
1936, Dodge A. Reidy/Charles Rogers
1570 31st Ave.
Although not exclusively developed by the Doelgers, their many years of building activity in this area prompted the name Doelger City.

5 Public Housing
1981, Oakland & Imada
4101 48th Ave.

6 Born house
1951, Ernest Born
2020 Great Highway
A spartan redwood box that opens on the lee side to a sheltered garden court viewed from a two- story studio-living room.

2. SF Conservatory of Music

4. Houses, Doelger City

7 San Francisco Zoological Gardens
c 1925, Lewis Hobart
1976 Esherick, Homsey, Dodge & Davis
Sloat Blvd. and Zoo Rd.
The Mothers' Building
1925, George W. Kelham
Gorilla House, Wolf House, & Tule Elk House
1980, Esherick, Homsey, Dodge & Davis
Small Primates Complex
1983, Marquis Assoc.
In 1922 the San Francisco Park Commission, with Herbert Fleishhacker as director, passed a resolution to buy a 60-acre tract of land at the foot of Sloat Boulevard and The Great Highway for a 1,000-by-100-foot saltwater swimming pool—the world's largest—and a playing field. The proposed facilities were part of a program for the expansion and improvement of the city's park system, carried out in the twenties and thirties, intended to provide a continuous recreation zone along the western edge of the city. John

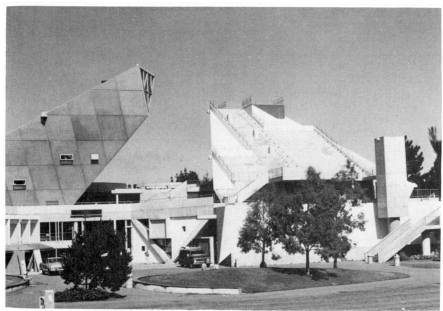

12. SF State University Student Union

McLaren prepared the plans for the construction, assisted by Engineer Earl Clements. J. Harvey Blohme of Ward & Blohme designed the landscaping. The first building in the complex was the Delia Fleishhacker Memorial Building, donated by her sons Herbert and Mortimer as a place of refreshment for mothers and small children. George W. Kelham, one of the city's most prominent architects, designed what came to be called "the Mothers' Building" as as Italian Renaissance Revival palazzo that seemed appropriately domestic and also reinforced California's similarity to the Mediterranean. The building interior was further enriched with WPA- sponsored murals by Helen K. Forbes and Dorthy W. Puchinelli. The mosaics on the exterior to either side of the loggia are by Helen, Margaret, and Esther Bruton. Some of the furniture originally designed for the building is still in use.

Fleishhacker Pool was demolished in the 1970s. Recently Esherick, Homsey, Dodge & Davis prepared a new master plan for the zoo as well as for the Gorilla House and the Wolf and Tule Elk houses.

Marquis Associates have designed the Primate Discovery Center and refurbished the 1936 WPA Lion House. This firm is also remodeling the outdoor grottos with Royston, Hanamoto, Alley & Abey, landscape architects.

8 Lakeshore Park
   1941 planned, Gellert Bros.
   9-93 Lakeshore Dr., Ocean Ave., and
   Gellert Dr.
See the introduction to this section for more information on this tract, developed by one of the "Big Five" builders.

9 Bungalow tracts
   1930s
   Sloat Blvd. to Eucalyptus Dr., Inverness Dr. to 21st Ave.
   **Central Pumping Station
   & Spring Valley Water Co.
   Reservoir Building**
   1910, Willis Polk
   22nd Ave. to 23rd Ave.,
   Ocean Ave. to Sloat Blvd.
Polk had a long association with this company, owned by one of his major patrons, William Bourn. (He also designed

the headquarters building downtown (1:22). The reservoir now serves nicely as a park for the surrounding blocks of vintage bungalows in the assorted fashionable styles of the day.

10 Sigmund Stern Grove
Trocadero Inn
19th Ave. and Sloat Blvd.
See the introduction to this section.

11 Stonestown Shopping Center
1952, Welton Beckett
19th Ave. and Winston Dr.
Apartments
1951, Angus McSweeney
An apartment complex and a related shopping center developed by the Stoneson brothers through the Stonestown Development Corporation. This was one of the first projects to use the concept of the interior mall with major department stores to anchor the ends.

12 San Francisco State University
1937-70
Office of the State Architect, master planners
New Administration Building
1977, Welton Beckett
Student Health Center
1977, Hellmuth, Obata & Kassabaum
Student Union Building
1980, Paffard Keatinge Clay
Following the acquisition of land for the campus from the Spring Valley Water Company in 1937, the State Architect's Office prepared a master plan. However, the building program did not begin until the late 1940s. The OSA was responsible for the design of the buildings erected up to 1970, when the office ceased to be the official planners.
The most architecturally notable building on campus is the 1980s Student Union, a neo-Corbusian structure dominated by two pyramidal elements, one of which serves as an outdoor amphitheater. The lobby functions as a diagonal street entered through a pivoting enameled-steel slab door, directly borrowed from Le Corbusier's Ronchamp Chapel. Though the whole may be a tad too "new space age" for some, it creates a lively scene in an otherwise bureaucratic and bland environment.

9. Bungalow tracts

15. Holy Trinity Greek Orthodox Church

13 Park Merced
1951, Angus McSweeney,
L. Schultze, Thomsen & Wilson
Main entrance 19th Ave. & Crespi Dr.
The Metropolitan Life Insurance Company built several of these residential complexes around the country, according to a prototype plan, in a very attenuated Colonial Revival style. The nearest counterpart to Park Merced is Park La Brea in Los Angeles.

14 Lake Merced Hill Condominiums
1974, Bull, Field, Volkmann & Stockwell
Lake Merced Blvd. and Brotherhood Way

15 Holy Trinity Greek Orthodox Church
1964, Reid, Rockwell, Banwell & Tarics
994 Brotherhood Way
A distinguished fusion of a traditional orthodox, cental-domed form with a contemporary concrete structure.

16
Twin Peaks West
Inner Sunset

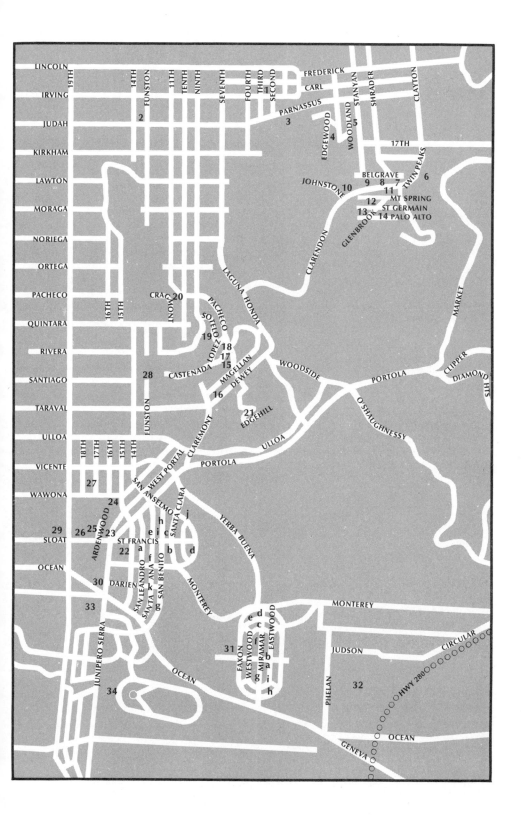

16 Twin Peaks West/Inner Sunset

1 First Sunset Plat
See introduction, p. 162.

2 St. Anne of the Sunset
See introduction, p. 162.

3 University of California Medical Center

Health Sciences Instruction and Research Units 1 & 2
1961-68, Reid, Rockwell, Banwell & Tarics
Two square, clear-span towers linked by vertical circulation. The labs have perimeter corridors; utility ducts run outside the walls.

College of Dentistry
1980, John Funk & Assoc.
A successful and well-detailed design. The building steps down the slope in terraced forms that diminish the effect of its size.

Surge Research Lab
1966, Marquis & Stoller
School of Nursing Building
1980, George Matsumoto & Assoc.
Clock tower
Stair tower of Milberry Union
1981, Hansen Assoc.
Seth Thomas Clock
(formerly in the Medical School Building)
1897-1967

Outpatients Clinic Building & Parking Structure
1972, Reid & Tarics

4 House
1911, Louis C. Mullgardt
226 Edgewood Ave.
The rear elevation, a high, battered stucco wall topped with a glass gallery facing the view, is reminiscent of Mullgardt's design for the destroyed Taylor estate in Berkeley.
House
1973, Marquis & Stoller
240 Edgewood Ave.
Edgewood Avenue itself deserves a special note. By request of the residents the street was paved in brick to preserve the red rock color of the unpaved roadbed. In the spring, purple-leafed trees with pink blossoms make the street worth a special excursion.

5 House
1936, Richard Neutra
90 Woodland Ave.
Clarendon Avenue takes its course around the base of Twin Peaks to become Twin Peaks Boulevard on the north side. Here, a set of streets not fully developed until the post-World War II period have spectacular views and houses worth glimpsing even if it is not possible to see all of them. In addition to being one of the few concentrations of Modern houses

3. UC Medical Center, College of Dentistry

4. House, 226 Edgewood

11. Moffitt house

in the city designed by prominent architects, it also has some works of note by the previous generation. The generally fine landscaping is complemented by the proximity of the Sutro Forest.

6 House
1950, Malone & Hooper
49 Twin Peaks Blvd.

7 Cottage
1917, Bernard Maybeck
196 Twin Peaks Blvd.

8 House
1955, Anshen & Allen
2 Clarendon Ave.
House
1959, Aaron Green
40 Clarendon Ave.

9 Four houses
1960-75, Lanier & Sherrill
Cor. Belgrave & Clarendon aves.

10 U.C. Med School
Married Student Housing
1959, Clark & Beuttler/George
Rockrise
Johnstone Dr. off Clarendon Ave.

11 Moffitt house
c 1920-40
30 Mountain Spring Ave.
The owner, a furniture maker and woodworker, designed and built this Craftsman-style house as a home and a workshop.

12 House
1948, John Funk
2 Glenbrook Ave.

13 House
1958, George Rockrise
150 St. Germain Ave.

14 House
1959, Campbell & Wong
175 Palo Alto Ave.
House
1959, Charles Warren Callister
176 Palo Alto Ave.

15 Forest Hill
1913, Mark Daniels, planner
Main entrance off Dewey Blvd. on Pacheco St.
As in Daniel's other subdivision, Sea Cliff (13:1), streets were laid out to follow the contours of the hill. Between the branching streets before Magellan, a triangular plot of lawn with a monumental urn suggests—but fails to carry out— a formal entrance like that of St. Francis Wood. Forest Hill is blessed with two houses by Bernard Maybeck, in addition to his vaguely Tudorish clubhouse for the Forest

17. House, 270 Castenada

18. House, 35 Lopez

Hill Association (16) at 381 Magellan Street, completed in 1919. Houses of various sizes and styles line the curving streets. Do explore and enjoy the view from the vest-pocket park at the end of Mendosa.

17 S. Erlanger house
1916, Bernard Maybeck
270 Castenada Ave. at Lopez Ave.
The clients wanted a medieval English manor house, but the product resists classification. The design reveals Maybeck's compositional skills and his ability to manipulate eclectic elements with originality.

18 House
1915, Glenn Allen
35 Lopez Ave.
A Prairie-style house with wonderful Sullivanesque ornament by an architect whose best- known work is in Stockton. Another good Prairie- style house is at 343 Montalvo.

19 E.C. Young house
1913, Bernard Maybeck
51 Sotelo Ave.
An intriguing play on the half-timber, with some features—the pulpitlike corner balcony with quatrefoils and the half-timber super graphics— that seem almost ad hoc. The gable-roofed living room, aligned with the street, is perpendicular to the rest of the long plan.

20 Arnstein house
1939, William W. Wurster
30 Cragmont Ave.
Fine vintage Wurster, also visible from below on Tenth Avenue.

21 House
1970, Backen, Arrigoni & Ross
111 Edgehill Way
A tautly stretched shingle and glass exterior wrapped around a series of wood and concrete platforms.

22 St. Francis Wood
1912-1950s, Frederick Law Olmsted, Jr./ John Galen Howard/Henry Gutterson/Louis C. Mullgardt
Entrance gates Junipero Serra Blvd.
Boundaries: Portola Dr., Santa Clara Ave., Monterey Blvd., Manor Dr., and Ocean Ave.
Laid out in 1912 as a garden suburb, St. Francis Wood was developed by the Mason McDuffie Company, a major realtor and investment company originally from the East Bay. As the most prestigious tract west of Twin Peaks, St. Francis Wood featured 50-by-100-foot lots, underground utilities, a boulevard with a landscaped median strip, and tree-lined streets separated from sidewalks by planting. Many of the trees came from the 1915 Panama-Pacific Exposition's closing sale; they

19. House, 51 Sotelo

were mature enough to give a proper garden-suburb appearance. The Olmstead Brothers laid out a central boulevarded spine punctuated midway by a circle with a fountain and terminating in another fountain and terrace at the top of the rise. The gates, terraces, and fountains were designed by John Galen Howard and Henry Gutterson and installed in 1912-13. Three model homes (h,i), designed by Louis C. Mullgardt and Henry Gutterson, were built in 1914-15 on San Benito Way. Their simplified Mediterranean styling struck a nice balance between historicism and modernism. Building proceeded slowly until the 1920s, when prosperous times and the effect of the Twin Peaks Tunnel connection to downtown brought the tract close to completion. The largely Irish population seems to have come from the Mission district and other areas of the inner city where accelerating development threatened the suburban ambience. Those who moved to the Wood were not urbanites. They enjoyed the remote, near-wilderness quality of this outer fringe area where hunting small game was still a major diversion. A strong neighborhood association controlled architectural design and enforced the racial convenants, which were not broken until the 1950s. Architecturally, St. Francis Wood is a period piece of revivalism tinged with modernism. Despite the fact that a number of notable architects contributed their talents, homogeneity of scale, color, and style—achieved through the controls—is the dominant effect. The outstanding achievement, and one that distinguishes St. Francis Wood from the rest of the

city's residential areas, is the lushness and continuity of the landscaping, which is integrated with the general plan. Following is a selection of houses that attempts to cover the range of styles and to present designs by major architects. The reader will not find it comprehensive, but will, we hope, be led on to make personal discoveries.

St. Francis Wood houses

(a) 98 St. Francis Blvd.
1917, Henry Gutterson
Rem. 1929, Masten & Hurd

(b) 435 St. Francis Blvd.
1926, Edward M. Sharpe

(c) 440 St. Francis Blvd.
1923, Henry Gutterson

(d) 30 St. Francis Blvd.
1927, Masten & Hurd

(e) 67 San Leandro Way
1921, Julia Morgan

(f) 195 San Leandro Way
1917, Julia Morgan

(g) 329 Santa Ana Ave.
1925, Harold G. Stoner

(h) 44 San Benito Way
1913, Louis C. Mullgardt

(i) 50, 58 San Benito Way
1914-15, Henry Gutterson

(j) 100 San Anselmo Ave.
1937, Angus McSweeney

(k) 345 Darien Way
1925, Harold G. Stoner

22d. House, 30 St. Francis Blvd

30. *Commodore Sloat School, Photo: Rondal Partridge*

23 Pacific Telephone Building
1980
Sloat Blvd. and West Portal Ave.
A commendable contemporary concrete building that introduces the commercial strip of the 1910s and 1920s on West Portal leading to the tunnel.

24 Arden Wood
1928-29, Henry Gutterson
Katherine Bashford, landscape architect
445 Wawona St.
A residential facility built for the Church of Christ Scientist, this monumental Chateauesque building sits in a landscaped clearing at the edge of a canyon planted with eucalyptus trees. The ground-floor public rooms, restored by Anshen & Allen, who remodeled the building for additional space in 1978-80, bring an Old World elegance to this California hybrid.

25 Ardenwood Way
1932, Gellert Bros.
The first tract developed by the Gellert Brothers, founders of the Standard Building Company, who went on to develop much of the outer Sunset in the post-World War II period. The medley of styles on this curving street is typical of the times.

26 California Scottish Rite Temple
1965, Albert Roller
NE cor. Sloat Blvd. and 19th Ave.

27 2600 blocks 16th, 17th, and 18th aves.
These blocks are lined with vintage-1930s small homes by several designers; they originally sold for about $4,000.

St. Cecilia's Roman Catholic Church
1956, Martin Rist
2555 17th Ave.
A major Irish Catholic parish church and architecturally one of the most imposing in the San Francisco Diocese. The interior is worth seeing.

28 Herbert Hoover Middle School
1953-57, Ernest J. Kump
14th Ave. and Santiago St.
Houses
1935, 1939, S.F. Johnson
2658, 2682 18th Ave.

1935, S.F. Johnson
2619 17th Ave.

1937-38, C.O. Clausen (often worked for the Doelgers)
2642, 2674 17th Ave.

1938, 1930, Charles Strothoff
1647, 2674 16th Ave.

CEMETERY — Burials in Mission Dolores Cemetery
[t]k place from the earliest days of the Mission until the
[19]0's. Originally the cemetery covered a much larger area.
[The] first grave markers were simple wooden crosses and dete-
[rior]ated completely with the passage of time. Gradually the
[cem]etery was consolidated to its present size. The unidentified
[bod]ies were reverently buried in a common grave and the
[Lou]rdes shrine built over it. Hence the dedication of the shrine
[to th]e "Forgotten Dead."

[M]ost of the extant markers designate people who died in
[the] decades following the Gold Rush, when San Francisco was
[a ra]pidly growing city which experienced much illness and
[many] early deaths. Many of those who are buried here have
[given] their names to the streets of San Francisco.

[A]mong the notable buried here are Don Luis Antonio
[Arg]ello, first governor of Alta California under Mexican rule;
[Francisco de Haro, first Alcalde (mayor) of San Francisco;
[the] victims of the Vigilantes: James P. Casey, Charles Cora,
[J]ames "Yankee" Sullivan; and a French family killed in
[the ex]plosion of the steamboat Jenny Lind.

*[We] have enjoyed having you as our guest at Mission Dolores.
[This his]toric site receives no public funds. We rely completely
[on you]r voluntary offerings to maintain, restore and beautify
[it and its buildings.*

MISSION DOLORES · SAN FRANCISCO

WELCOME TO MISSION SAN FRANCISCO DE ASIS
POPULARLY KNOWN AS MISSION DOLORES

Of the 21 California Missions this is the third most norther-
ly and the sixth to be established under the direction of Father
Junipero Serra. Lieutenant Jose Joaquin Moraga led the group
that arrived in this immediate area on June 27, 1776. A
scouting party had visited three months earlier and named a
small stream, which no longer exists, Arroyo de Nuestra Señora
de los Dolores.

Father Francisco Palou, a co-worker of Father Serra,
celebrated the first Mass in the area under a makeshift shelter
on June 29, and thus the City of Saint Francis had its official
beginning five days before the signing of the Declaration of
Independence. The formal establishment of the Mission of
Saint Francis was delayed until the arrival of the necessary
Church documents and took place on October 9, 1776.

Help keep Mission Dolores beautiful — Please Don't Litter

WITHIN THE MISSION – *This building, completed in 1791, the oldest intact building in San Francisco, is 114 feet long, 22 wide, wi thick. Masses are still celebrated here occasionally. The ceiling, although repainted, depicts original Indian designs done with vegetable statues in the altar niches came from Mexico in the early 1800's. The gold on the altars has been renewed, but they are basically the sa arrived.*

Access to the choir loft (not open to the public) was at first gained by way of an outside stairway. The present spiral staircase is a la of the mission, cast in Mexico, honor Saints Joseph, Francis and Martin. In 1868, Bret Harte wrote a poem commemorating these bells.

Immediately inside the chapel on the left wall are confessional doors. The priest would sit between the open doors. Men would sta the priest for confession, while women would go to either side and confess through the opening. Midway on the left side is the bapti baptisms take place here. The first of the more than 28,000 baptisms took place two months before the official establishment of th register is in the museum.

There are four burial places marked within the Mission walls. Beginning at the back of the chapel they are those of William businessman of the city; the Noe family; Lt. Jose Joaquin Moraga, leader of the June 1776 expedition; and Very Reverend Richard Mission Dolores after San Francisco became an archdiocese.

THE BASILICA – Exiting the chapel by the door to the right of the altar, a few steps to the right lead to the side door of the parish church. While the Mission withstood the shock of the 1906 earthquake, the parish church was not so fortunate and the present new building was completed in 1918. In 1952 Pope Pius XII designated this a basilica, an honorary church of the Holy Father himself. The partially-opened red and gold umbrella on the right of the altar and the carved coat of arms with papal insignia on the left are the marks of a basilica.

The choir window pictures Saint Francis of Assisi, patron of the Mission and the City. The lower windows depict the 21 California Missions, along with two in honor of Fathers Serra and Palou.

High above the main altar is a wood carving of Mater Dolorosa, Our Lady of Sorrows. The Seven Sorrows of Mary are depicted individually above the main door at the rear of the church and on the facades of the side balconies.

THE MUSEUM – In 1976, the bicentennial year (was completed on the restoration of this room w classroom. Artifacts, some previously displayed ir some stored away from public view, were gather but authentic museum.

Most precious among the items on display

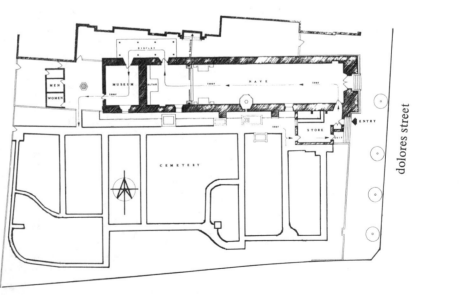

TH
toc
18:
Th
rio
cen
boc
Lot
to t

the
a r
man
give

Argu
Don
three
and
the e

lithog
Missi
and
the

We
This hi
on you
this site

rawh
stee
the
and
for
lon

29 Stern Grove
(see introduction)

30 Commodore Sloat School
1922, Angus McSweeney
Add. and rem. 1977, Marquis & Assoc.
NW cor. Ocean Ave. at Junipero Serra Blvd.

An important landmark of the area that, along with the Christian Science Church arcoss Ocean and the Moderne commercial building in the gore of Ocean and Sloat, strengthens the design of this five-point intersection. The contemporary addition is sensitive both to the older building and to its site.

31 Westwood Park
1917-27, John M. Punnett, engineer
Main entrance off Ocean Ave. at Miramar Ave.

Perhaps because of the success of Ingleside Terrace, Westwood Park was also laid out in concentric loop streets. Financed by Baldwin and Howell, the land was subdivided in 1917 into 700 lots restricted to single-family houses. A shopping district was planned to serve the residents. Largely completed by 1920, the streets, many with names ending in "wood," are lined with uniformly set-back bungalows, most of which were designed by a woman builder named Ida F. McGain. Following is a sampling of styles and designers:

Westwood Park houses
(a) 598 Miramar Ave.
1923, Charles Strothoff

(b) 600 Miramar Ave.
1922, Ida F. McGain

(c) 701 Miramar Ave.
1919, Ida F. McGain

(d) 815 Miramar Ave.
1932, G.A. Berger

(e) 889 Faxon Ave.
c 1917

(f) 162 Westwood Dr.
1919, Charles Strothoff

(g) 10 Westwood Dr.
1919, Ida F. McGain

(h) 54 Eastwood Dr.
c 1919

(i) 99 Eastwood Dr.
1927, Charles Strothoff

31a. House, 598 Miramar

31h. House, 54 Eastwood

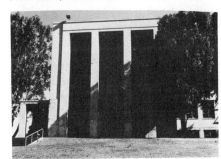
32. City College of SF, Main Building

Twin Peaks panorama

32 City College of San Francisco
1937-1978, Miller & Pflueger/Pflueger
Architects
50 Phelan Ave. at Ocean Ave.

City College occupies the site left vacant
when the county jail was moved to San
Mateo in the 1920s. In 1937, after a trip
to Italy, where he admired the new architecture erected under Mussolini, Timothy
Pflueger designed the former Main Building, which, until the 1950s, housed
nearly all the departments. A small theater building behind the Main Building
has a fine Diego Rivera mural of 1937. It
includes a portrait of the artist as well as
one of Timothy Pflueger with unfurled
plans surveying the San Francisco cityscape. From 1940 to 1976, successor
firms prepared master plans for the college. Eight buildings have been built during this period, the latest of which is
Batmale Hall, 1978.

33 Lakeside Park
1936-1950s, Harold G. Stoner
Junipero Serra Blvd., 19th Ave., and
Eucalyptus Dr.

The Stoneson brothers, who built the
Stonestown shopping Center across 19th
Avenue, laid out this picturesque residential tract with their English architect,
Harold G. Stoner, about 1936. The well-
publicized Los Angeles development of
Beverly Hills, which Ellis Stoneson and
Harold Stoner visited, was their inspiration. The north end of Lakeside Park was
built up first; the Stoneson residence was
at No. 30 Stonecrest Drive. The south
end, developed from 1947 to 1955, has a
slightly different character. Here the miniaturized homes with their picket fences
give the impression of a model village.

34 Ingleside Terrace
1911-24, Joseph Leonard, Urban Realty Co.

Stone gates on Moncada Way, Paloma Ave.,and Mercedes Way off Junipero Serra Blvd.

Stone gates at Victoria off Ocean Ave. and Urbano Dr.

Urbano Drive occupies the loop of the former Ingleside Race Track, opened in 1885. Sponsored by Claus Spreckels and other racing buffs, the track moved here after the Spring Valley Water Company closed the Ocean Beach Track. When Ingleside shut down in 1909, Joseph Leonard and his Urban Realty Company purchased 148 acres of the track property and planned a parklike subdivision with the help of engineer J.M. Morser. The company managed the track until 1924, when it was mostly built up with houses of various styles and sizes on lots that were 50 by 120 feet, twice the standard width. A special feature installed in 1915 was a large sundial that once had a reflecting pool and formal flower beds at the compass points. The dial is located at the apex of the angled Entrada Court. The earlier houses designed by Leonard such as (a) 282 and 855 Urbano Drive, 1915, and (b) 77 and 90 Cedro, 1911, are in a shingled Craftsman style. No. 140 (c), 1913, by William Curlett is an accomplished design in a mixed Mediterranean mode that was sometimes called "California." No. 149 Moncada (d) at the corner of Cedro is California mixed with Prairie, while No. 120 Moncada (e) leans toward International Style Modern. Architects and dates of the last two houses are unknown. The more conventional stripped-down Mediterranean style is represented by 20 Mercedes, designed by S. Heiman c 1920.

17
Outer Mission
Diamond Heights

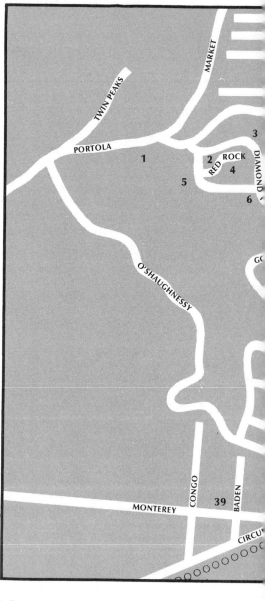

1 Eugene McAteer High Sch, O'Shaughnessy
2 Red Rock Hill town houses, Diamond Heights
3 Casa de Vida, 5157 Diamond Heights
4 Diamond Heights Village, Red Rock
5 Eichler houses, 1000 block Duncan
6 St. Nicholas Church, Diamond Heights
7 Village Square, Diamond Heights
8 St. Aidan's Church, 101 Gold Mine
9 Gold Mine Hill, Gold Mine & Ora
10 Shepherd of the Hills Lutheran Church
11 John Shelley Firehouse, 80 Digby
12 House, 1335 Douglass
13 Noe Courts, 25th St & Douglass

29 Stern Grove
(see introduction)

30 Commodore Sloat School
1922, Angus McSweeney
Add. and rem. 1977, Marquis &
Assoc.
NW cor. Ocean Ave. at Junipero
Serra Blvd.
An important landmark of the area that,
along with the Christian Science Church
arcoss Ocean and the Moderne commercial building in the gore of Ocean and
Sloat, strengthens the design of this five-
point intersection. The contemporary addition is sensitive both to the older building and to its site.

31 Westwood Park
1917-27, John M. Punnett, engineer
Main entrance off Ocean Ave. at Miramar Ave.
Perhaps because of the success of Ingleside Terrace, Westwood Park was also
laid out in concentric loop streets. Financed by Baldwin and Howell, the land
was subdivided in 1917 into 700 lots restricted to single-family houses. A shopping district was planned to serve the
residents. Largely completed by 1920,
the streets, many with names ending in
"wood," are lined with uniformly set-
back bungalows, most of which were designed by a woman builder named Ida F.
McGain. Following is a sampling of styles
and designers:

Westwood Park houses
(a) 598 Miramar Ave.
1923, Charles Strothoff

(b) 600 Miramar Ave.
1922, Ida F. McGain

(c) 701 Miramar Ave.
1919, Ida F. McGain

(d) 815 Miramar Ave.
1932, G.A. Berger

(e) 889 Faxon Ave.
c 1917

(f) 162 Westwood Dr.
1919, Charles Strothoff

(g) 10 Westwood Dr.
1919, Ida F. McGain

(h) 54 Eastwood Dr.
c 1919

(i) 99 Eastwood Dr.
1927, Charles Strothoff

31a. House, 598 Miramar

31h. House, 54 Eastwood

32. City College of SF, Main Building

Twin Peaks panorama

32 City College of San Francisco
1937-1978, Miller & Pflueger/Pflueger
Architects
50 Phelan Ave. at Ocean Ave.
City College occupies the site left vacant
when the county jail was moved to San
Mateo in the 1920s. In 1937, after a trip
to Italy, where he admired the new architecture erected under Mussolini, Timothy
Pflueger designed the former Main Building, which, until the 1950s, housed
nearly all the departments. A small theater building behind the Main Building
has a fine Diego Rivera mural of 1937. It
includes a portrait of the artist as well as
one of Timothy Pflueger with unfurled
plans surveying the San Francisco cityscape. From 1940 to 1976, successor
firms prepared master plans for the college. Eight buildings have been built during this period, the latest of which is
Batmale Hall, 1978.

33 Lakeside Park
1936-1950s, Harold G. Stoner
Junipero Serra Blvd., 19th Ave., and
Eucalyptus Dr.
The Stoneson brothers, who built the
Stonestown shopping Center across 19th
Avenue, laid out this picturesque residential tract with their English architect,
Harold G. Stoner, about 1936. The well-
publicized Los Angeles development of
Beverly Hills, which Ellis Stoneson and
Harold Stoner visited, was their inspiration. The north end of Lakeside Park was
built up first; the Stoneson residence was
at No. 30 Stonecrest Drive. The south
end, developed from 1947 to 1955, has a
slightly different character. Here the miniaturized homes with their picket fences
give the impression of a model village.

34 Ingleside Terrace

1911-24, Joseph Leonard, Urban Realty Co.

Stone gates on Moncada Way, Paloma Ave., and Mercedes Way off Junipero Serra Blvd.

Stone gates at Victoria off Ocean Ave. and Urbano Dr.

Urbano Drive occupies the loop of the former Ingleside Race Track, opened in 1885. Sponsored by Claus Spreckels and other racing buffs, the track moved here after the Spring Valley Water Company closed the Ocean Beach Track. When Ingleside shut down in 1909, Joseph Leonard and his Urban Realty Company purchased 148 acres of the track property and planned a parklike subdivision with the help of engineer J.M. Morser. The company managed the track until 1924, when it was mostly built up with houses of various styles and sizes on lots that were 50 by 120 feet, twice the standard width. A special feature installed in 1915 was a large sundial that once had a reflecting pool and formal flower beds at the compass points. The dial is located at the apex of the angled Entrada Court. The earlier houses designed by Leonard such as (a) 282 and 855 Urbano Drive, 1915, and (b) 77 and 90 Cedro, 1911, are in a shingled Craftsman style. No. 140 (c), 1913, by William Curlett is an accomplished design in a mixed Mediterranean mode that was sometimes called "California." No. 149 Moncada (d) at the corner of Cedro is California mixed with Prairie, while No. 120 Moncada (e) leans toward International Style Modern. Architects and dates of the last two houses are unknown. The more conventional stripped-down Mediterranean style is represented by 20 Mercedes, designed by S. Heiman c 1920.

17
Outer
Mission
Diamond
Heights

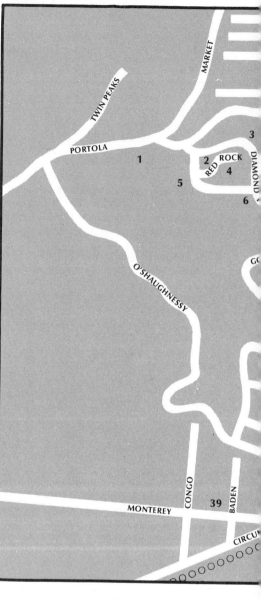

1 Eugene McAteer High Sch, O'Shaughnessy
2 Red Rock Hill town houses, Diamond
   Heights
3 Casa de Vida, 5157 Diamond Heights
4 Diamond Heights Village, Red Rock
5 Eichler houses, 1000 block Duncan
6 St. Nicholas Church, Diamond Heights
7 Village Square, Diamond Heights
8 St. Aidan's Church, 101 Gold Mine
9 Gold Mine Hill, Gold Mine & Ora
10 Shepherd of the Hills Lutheran Church
11 John Shelley Firehouse, 80 Digby
12 House, 1335 Douglass
13 Noe Courts, 25th St & Douglass

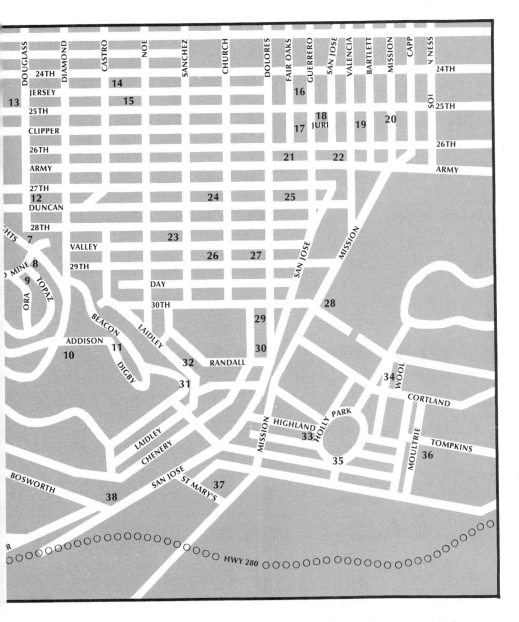

14 Flats, 1435-49 Castro
15 James Lick Middle School, 1220 Noe
16 Houses, 1200 block Guerrero
17 Holy Innocents Church & houses, Fair Oaks
18 Houses, Juri
19 Apts, 1400 block Valencia
20 Commercial-flats bldg, 25th St & Mission
21 Church of God, 3728 Army
22 Salvation Army, 1500 Valencia
23 Houses, 1514, 1566-71 Sanchez
24 Commercial-flats bldg, 1500, 1544 Church
25 Houses, 100 block Duncan
26 St. Paul's Church & School, Church

27 Reilly Funeral Service, 1598 Dolores
28 Club Elegante, etc., Mission
29 Old Fairmont School, 29 Chenery
30 Fairmont School, Chenery & Randall
31 Poole-Bell house, 196-98 Laidley
32 Houses, 123, 135 Laidley
33 Junipero Serra School, 625 Holly Park
34 House, 32 Wool
35 House, Holly Park
36 Church, Moultrie & Tompkins
37 Church of St. John, 19 St. Mary's
38 Glen Park BART Station, Bosworth & Diamond
39 Conservatory, 236 Monterey

177

17 Outer Mission/Diamond Heights

Diamond Heights is a steep and windy ridge just south of Twin Peaks. It remained undeveloped long after the rest of the city because of its austere weather and the fact that it had originally been platted in the standard gridiron plan, which here finally met its limit—many of the lots were inaccessible. For this reason it was declared a redevelopment area in the 1950s, even though it was open land. Vernon DeMars did a street plan that followed the contours, and a competition was held for the first phase of development in 1961. Of the winning design by Cohen & Leverson, which was to have high-rise towers on the hilltop and the north slopes, only one group of town houses was built. Single-family houses by Eichler and others gradually filled the western slopes; an elementary school, a shopping center, and several churches were built by the early sixties; the 1970s saw the development of the southern portion of the site with town houses and apartments. The general architectural level is undistinguished and does not compare favorably with older parts of the city.

South and west of Diamond Heights, Glen Canyon Park is a remarkably wild and secluded stretch of open space in the heart of the city.

East of Diamond Heights lies Noe Valley; its southern edge is the ridge that separates the inner and outer Mission. This area was generally built up with much smaller Victorian cottages than the northern Mission, and even today it has a more suburban flavor.

1 J. Eugene McAteer High School
1972, Reid & Tarics
O'Shaughnessy Blvd. and Portola Dr.
An exposed-concrete structure that steps down its steep site; the most recent high school to be built in the city, it was nearly declared surplus by the time it was finished.

2 Red Rock Hill Townhouses
1962, Cohen & Leverson
Diamond Heights Blvd. and Duncan St.
The only built portion of the original competition-winning scheme.

3 Casa de Vida
1981, Lanier & Sherrill
5157 Diamond Heights Blvd.
A project designed to give the handicapped the benefits of independent living on a hillside site.

4 Diamond Heights Village
1972, Gensler Assoc./Joseph Esherick & Assoc.
Red Rock Way
A well-sited Shingle group where the high-rise buildings of the original plan were supposed to go.

5 Eichler houses
1962-64, Jones & Emmons/Anshen & Allen
1000 block Duncan St.
Eichler's more-generous suburban plans were adapted here for city lots, but these are still good examples of the work of a developer who brought contemporary architect-designed houses into the Bay Area tract home market.

6 St. Nicholas Syrian Antiochian Orthodox Church
1963, William F. Hempel
Diamond Heights Blvd. and Duncan St.
A reasonably convincing contemporary concrete version of the traditional domed plan.

7 Village Square
1972, Morris & Lohrbach
East side Diamond Heights Blvd. bet. Duncan and Valley sts.
Thanks especially to its site planning and landscaping, this is one of the more attractive developments on the Heights.

8. St. Aidan's Epicopal Church

14. Flats, 1435-49 Castro

15. James Lick Middle School

8 St. Aidan's Episcopal Church
  1963, Skidmore, Owings & Merrill
  101 Gold Mine Dr.
An irregular hexagon of white stucco,
with an interior lit by a hidden clerestory
and windows in the manner of Southwest
missions. The mural painting is by Mark
Adams.

9 Gold Mine Hill
  1967, Fisher-Friedman
  Gold Mine Dr. and Ora Way
One of several groups of town houses by
this firm in the Heights. Others are on
Carnelian Way on the north slope.

**10 Shepherd of the Hills
  Lutheran Church**
  Diamond Heights Blvd. and Addison
  St.

11 John Shelley Firehouse
  1963, Rockrise & Watson
  80 Digby St.

12 House
  1942, John Funk
  Rem. 1972, Lanier & Sherrill
  1335 Douglass St.

13 Noe Courts and play structure
  1982, Albert Lanier, Synestructics Inc.
  25th and Douglass sts.

14 Flats
  c 1900
  1435-49 Castro St.
An excellent example of turn-of-the-century vernacular given new life by a sensitive paint job.

15 James Lick Middle School
  1932, Crim, Resing & McGuinness
  Reconst. 1973, city architect
  1220 Noe St.
Most of San Francisco's older schools
looked drab and undistinguished ten
years ago, but the imaginative repainting
that went along with extensive alterations
for seismic safety revived their architectural richness.

16 Houses
1200 block Guerrero St.
Guerrero is virtually lined with Victorian houses, and this block has an outstanding group. Note especially the towered mansion built by an Austrian immigrant at 1286, two double houses at 1259-65 with their original iron fences, the in- and-out facade of 1257, an elegantly consistent Stick-Eastlake at 1253, and a fine corner commercial-flats building at 1201.

17 Holy Innocents Episcopal Church and neighborhood houses
c 1900, Ernest Coxhead (church)
400 block Fair Oaks St.
In his early practice Coxhead was one of the great masters of the undulating shingled wall and here, tucked away on this quiet street, is his surviving local example. Also in this block is a wonderful collection of Victorian and Craftsman houses, and at the south end on 26th Street is a nice little Mission Revival hall.

17. Holy Innocents Episcopal Church & houses

18 Houses
1894, John Kidd
Juri St.
A small cul-de-sac off San Jose, Juri is an especially attractive street of cottages. No. 1A has a flatiron shape because of the railroad right-of-way.

19 Apartments
c 1900
1400 block Valencia St.
The shallow bow-windows of these apartment houses create the type of undulating facade that recalls the much earlier houses on Boston's Beacon Hill.

20 Commercial-flats building
c 1800
25th and Mission sts.

21 Church of God
(Iglesia de Dios Lataro)
c 1890
3728 Army St.
A brightly painted little Carpenter Gothic church. Across the street at 3763 Army is an amusing apartment house with colossal columns projecting through its stair landings.

22 Salvation Army
c 1900
1500 Valencia St.
Brickwork Gothic, appropriately fortified.

23 Houses
c 1890
1514, 1566-71 Sanchez St.
Typifying the smaller scale of housing in the outer reaches of the Mission is this brightly painted group of cottages from the 1890s.

24 Commercial-flats buildings
c 1890
1500, 1544 Church St.
Two unusually fine corner commercial-residential buildings, a type ignored by restorers until recently. Both now house antiques shops.

25 Houses
c 1885
100 block Duncan St.
More examples of small Victorians. No. 169-71 was originally a stable and still shows the old arched hayloft opening. No. 151-53A (c 1887) is an unusual Italianate with a belt cornice across the facade.

26 St. Paul's Roman Catholic Church and School
Church and Valley sts.
Built by the Jesuits, the school looks as though it was for the soldiers of Christ. The church is a rare local example of a Gothic Revival style, more common east of the Mississippi, that combined a monumental towered stone facade with an interior dimly lit by stained glass and punctuated by attenuated columns supporting plaster vaults. The whole recalls ecclesiastical engravings of the High Victorian era.

26. St. Paul's Roman Catholic Church, School

27 Reilly Funeral Service
c 1920
1598 Dolores St.
A jazzy wooden corbel table rescues this stuccoed block from banality.

28 Club Elegante, etc.
Mission St. opposite end of 30th St.
A one-story commercial group with a marvelous spikey frieze tying it all together.

27. Reilly Funeral Service

29 Old Fairmont School
c 1860
29 Chenery St.
The ancestor of the new school up the hill gives a good index of how educational styles have changed. The building's early date reflected the platting of the Fairmont Tract in 1864.

30 Fairmont School
1976-78, Wong & Brocchini
Chenery and Randall sts.
Fitting well into this hillside residential neighborhood, the new school wraps around its play area.

30. Fairmont School

31. Poole-Bell house

31 Poole-Bell house
c 1872
196-98 Laidley St.
Built by Cecil Poole, an attorney, this imposing mansard-roofed house with a phenomenal view of the city was bought around 1900 by "Mammy" Pleasant, a famous madam and a housekeeper here for Thomas Bell's widow after he died.

32 Houses
1980s, Jeremy Kotas
123, 135 Laidley St.
Two extensive contemporary remodelings of older cottages. The overhead garage doors on the second level at house No. 135 are for people, not auto, use and permit the interior to be fully opened up to the outside.

33 Junipero Serra
Elementary School
1976, Crosby, Thornton, Marshall
625 Holly Park Cir.

34 House
c 1900
32 Wool St.
An unusual formed-metal roof on a modest house.

35 House
c 1880
Richland Ave. and Murray St. on Holly Park Cir.
Holly Park dates from 1860 when two lawyers gave the land to the city. Though not so early, this miniaturized towered farmhouse recalls a rural past and appears to preserve some of its early landscaping.

36 Church
c 1890
Moultrie St. and Tompkins Ave.
The importance of towers to churches is revealed by the way this tiny structure manages to have its tower by projecting it over the sidewalk.

37 Church of St. John
the Evangelist
c 1910
19 St. Mary's Ave. at Bosworth St.
A substantial parish church that, through its formality and scale, looms over its humble neighborhood.

38 Glen Park BART Station
1972, Ernest Born
Bosworth and Diamond sts.
One of the most spatially dramatic BART stations.

39 Conservatory
c 1916, Frank Merrill
236 Monterey Blvd.
Amateur astronomer and inventor Merrill built this remarkable polygonal structure to house his exotic plants in what must have then been open country.

18
Bernal
Heights
Bayview

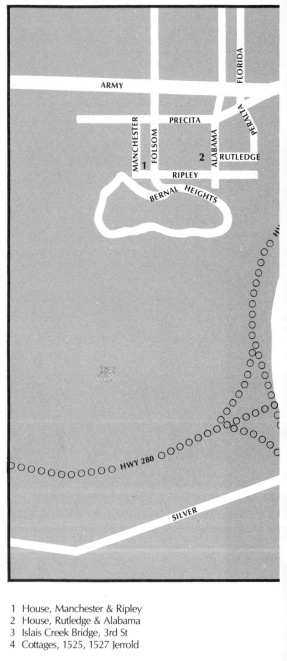

1 House, Manchester & Ripley
2 House, Rutledge & Alabama
3 Islais Creek Bridge, 3rd St
4 Cottages, 1525, 1527 Jerrold

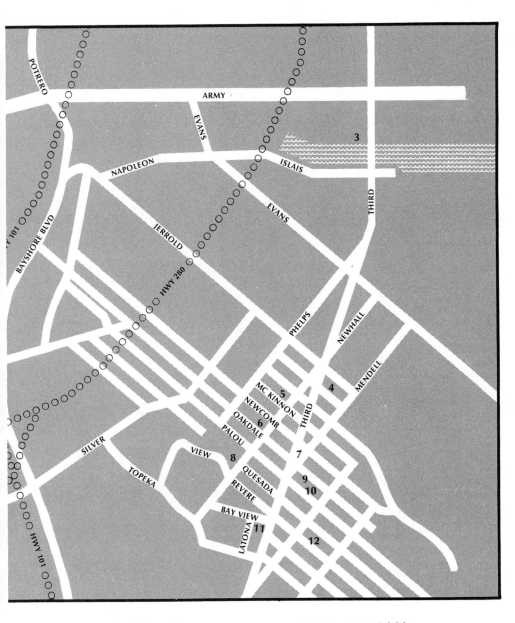

5 House, Newhall & McKinnon
6 All Hallows Church, Palou & Newhall
7 South SF Opera House, 47045 3rd St
8 House, Newhall & Quesada

9   Cottage, 1547 Oakdale
10 Cottage, 1548 Palou
11 Church, Bay View & Latona
12 Sylvester house, 1556 Revere

18 Bernal Heights/Bayview

The bayshore area of San Francisco was originally granted to Jose Bernal in 1834 as the Rancho Rincon de las Salinas y Potrero Viejo. In the 1850s the Hunter Brothers bought the hill now called Hunters Point for a town site that never developed. William Ralston, founder of the Bank of California, had a granite drydock built for the California Steam Navigation Company in the 1860s that was in use till 1916 and presaged the development of the point as a major World War II shipyard. Recreational islands such as the South San Francisco Opera House existed amidst the stockyards and shipyards, but these industries effectively prevented the growth of the area as a zone of better residence. Bayview-Hunters Point has the city's largest black population. Bayview is largely single family and a relatively stable neighborhood compared to the public housing precinct on Hunters Point. A number of early buildings are scattered throughout the Bayview area, which has a definite village quality.

1   House
c 1880
Manchester and Ripley sts.
This and the house below testify to the 19th- century development that in other parts of the city produced whole blocks of speculative houses.

2   House
c 1880
Rutledge and Alabama sts.

**3   Islais Creek Bridge
at Third St.**
c 1920
An early bridge with Art Deco ornament.

4   Cottages
c 1880
1525, 1527 Jerrold Ave.

5   House
c 1880
Newhall St. and McKinnon Ave.
An unusual brick house that retains its stable.

6   All Hallows Church
1886
Palou Ave. and Newhall St.
An outstanding Gothic Revival church that reveals the 19th-century character of the neighborhood. For another example see entry 11.

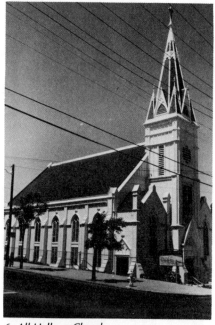

6. All Hallows Church

7. South San Francisco Opera House

8. *House, Newhall & Queseda*

12. *Sylvester house*

7 South San Francisco Opera House
1888
47045 Third St.
The area's best-known landmark, this was built by the Masonic Lodge and hosted many traveling theatrical events during its early years. It has now been renovated and is run by the Neighborhood Arts Program as a cultural center.

8 House
c 1900
Newhall St. and Quesada Ave.
A house that illustrates the old adage "a man's home is his castle."

9 Cottage
c 1870
1547 Oakdale Ave.

10 Cottage
c 1870
1548 Palou Ave.
Two cottages built back to back that stylistically look as though they were built in the 1860s, but that could have been built later from an early pattern book. Both are representative of the type of pioneer farmhouse that one sees in very early photos of Telegraph Hill.

11 Church
c 1880
Bay View and Latona sts.

12 Sylvester house
1870
1556 Revere Ave.
The scale and authority of this four-square Italianate building suggest that it was once the manor house of a considerable domain.

Glossary of Styles

GOTHIC REVIVAL
1850s-1900s

The Gothic Revival style had several phases. Buildings of the period of the 1850s and 1860s are called Carpenter Gothic because they were often built from carpenters' pattern books by "carpitects" who were not professionally trained. Such buildings were generally wooden and had a vertical emphasis, high-peaked roofs, and displayed a variety of Gothic motifs that ranged from very simple to very sophisticated, depending on the level of skill and technology.

The next phase, called High Victorian Gothic, ran from the late 1860s through the 1880s. In this phase technology advanced to the point where the wide range of Gothic styles that were admired could be copied easily or mixed together, as was often the case. In general, architects had a free-wheeling attitude about stylistic integrity. This was an architecture of imagery rather than stylistic consistency. The last of the Gothic Revival phases occurred in the decades around the turn of the century. An increasing concern for academic correctness in matters of style resulted in buildings that were either copies or careful adaptations of well-known prototypes.

In San Francisco the domestic examples of Gothic Revival vanished in the 1906 fire. Although few early examples of Gothic Revival churches survived, there are a number of wooden churches dating from the 1880s and 1890s that might be called High Victorian Carpenter Gothic. These have a rich variety of wooden decorative detail and are composed with more concern for picturesque qualities than academic correctness.

ITALIANATE
1860s-1880s

This style was originally inspired by 19th-century romantic landscape paintings of northern Italy that included towered farm houses or villas. The irregular profiles of these buildings supposedly reflected nature's informality. This image was adopted by A.J. Downing and other arbiters of taste as appropriate for the American landscape. In urban locations such as the San Francisco streetcar suburbs of the last quarter of the 19th century, the Italianate houses typically had two types of facades: the flat front and the bay windowed. Both types had parapets—called false fronts—embellished with decorative detail such as molded cornices, dentil courses, and ornamental brackets. Facades were embellished with pilasters, quoins, molded panels, decorative friezes, and a variety of ornamental frames or architraves for windows and doors. House plans were standardized to fit the 25-foot-wide lots.

Non-residential buildings were also designed "in the Italian manner." They employed the same range of Classical ornament, typically rendered in cast iron. Very few of these business or commercial blocks survived the 1906 fire, but the Italianate style prevailed in the streetcar suburbs, where a typical building type combined commerical use on the ground floor and residential above. A variant of

Gothic Revival: St. Dominic's Church

188

the residential Italianate style borrowed the mansard roof—a raised attic often with dormers—from the more imposing Second Empire style developed in France in the reign of Napoleon III, but otherwise kept the Italianate forms and decorative detail. San Francisco has very few examples of this Mansard or Second Empire style.

SAN FRANCISCO STICK
1880s

A local variant of what the architectural historian Vincent Scully defined as the American Stick style. Scully created the term to describe buildings in which the skeletal structure is expressed on the exterior. The rustic villas that fit Scully's definition were not urban types, but during the late 1870s and 1880s San Franciscans developed a town-house style that had affinities with the eastern style.

The local Stick-style facade is the Italianate facade made rectilinear by means of

Flat-front Italianates: 2115-25 Bush

squared bays and the use of angled, rather than curved, forms. In general, thin, flat wood strips expressed the structural frame of the house. Strips of wood were also used as decorative detail around windows and doors, and also for paneling. Often these pseudo-framing elements mimicked the half-timbering of a medieval or Elizabethan house. In fact, "Elizabethan" was one of the stylistic names used for these houses at the time. Ornamental detail is less naturalistic and more linear or geometric, probably in response to the increasing range of milling machinery used to produce it. Compared to the Italianate, the Stick style is more elaborate and inventive, giving the designer a greater range of possibilities for personal expression.

QUEEN ANNE
1890s

The Queen Anne style originated in England, where it described buildings that were inspired by the transitional architecture of the pre-Georgian period when Classical ornament was applied to buildings with medieval forms. The source of the style is the work of Richard Norman

San Francisco Stick: 1049 Tennessee

Glossary of Styles

Queen Anne: 1550 Page

Classic Revival: 900 Balboa

Shaw, whose domestic architecture was indirectly influential in this country during the 1870s, 1880s, and 1890s. Shaw's much-published English country houses belonged to the English "domestic revival" movement, which took medieval or Elizabethan houses as models.

The American Queen Anne style became the great picturesque style of the end of the 19th century. Gabled roofs with dormers, tall sculptural chimneys, towers, and turrets composed its irregular profile. Walls alternately bulged with bays or were hollowed out for balconies. Porches and verandas wrapped around the ground floor.

Ideally, the large Queen Anne house possessed a "living hall," a two-storied, galleried space featuring the stairway and a large fireplace alcove with seats. The urban town house or cottage lacked space

both for this amenity and for the wrap-around porch. When used, corner towers, which were very important for the castlelike silhouette, were often pulled back into the main block of the house. Exterior surfaces were covered with a variety of tactile patterns—horizontal lap siding, shaped shingles, spoolwork, and foliated plasterwork in panels and friezes. Fish-scale shingles were most popular because they mimicked the pattern made by English terra-cotta wall tiles. Stained glass or "art glass" was generously used.

ROMANESQUE REVIVAL
RICHARDSON ROMANESQUE
1880s-1890s

The Romanesque Revival style in this country received its impetus from Henry Hobson Richardson's personal version of French and Spanish Romanesque, which was first expressed in his Trinity Church in Boston (1872). This was a masonry style that differed from the Gothic chiefly in its use of the round arch.

CLASSIC REVIVAL
BEAUX-ARTS CLASSICISM
c 1890-1930

Greek and Roman architecture has been a perennial source of architectural form and detail. The pre-20th-century revival periods include the Renaissance, the Baroque, and the various Classic Revival styles of the 18th and 19th centuries—including the American neo-Georgian, Greek, and Roman Revival styles.

The basic elements of the Classical vocabulary are the "orders," which consist of the column with its capital and the structural member it supports, called the entablature. The commonly used orders are Doric, Ionic, Corinthian, Composite, and Tuscan. Other elements include the triangular pediments and cornices, which define the roofs, and the colonnades and arcades with superimposed half or quarter columns called pilasters, which articulate the walls. These were used in a theme-and-variation manner to create buildings that rarely are exactly alike, though the

Glossary of Styles

differences may be subtle. Symmetry and a hierarchy of forms and spaces are also typical of the Classic Revival styles. Ornament comprises a wide range of naturalistic and geometric forms: acanthus leaves, volutes, egg-and-dart, bead-and-reel, waves, dentils, Greek keys, swags, garlands, etc. A range of molding profiles is also an important part of the Classical vocabulary of forms.

The Paris Ecole des Beaux-Arts was the dominant influence on the Classic Revival movement that swept the country following the 1893 Columbian Exposition in Chicago. This brand of Classicism combined Roman, Renaissance, and Baroque versions of styles. Although substyles flourished, particularly in residential architecture, virtually all building types were cast in some Classical form until the immediate pre- and post-World War II decades when the Modern Movement began to influence the architectural scene. Today, the so-called post-Modern style has once again revived Classical forms. Of all the styles discussed in this glossary, the various Classic Revival styles have the best representation in San Francisco. These range from the 19th-century Italianate buildings, to the versions of Renaissance palaces which were common in the pre- and post-1906 earthquake and fire eras, to the City Beautiful Movement Classicism of the Civic Center, and finally to the stripped Classicism of the 1930s.

CHICAGO SCHOOL
c 1890-c 1915

A style associated with the city where the tall commercial building—the skyscraper—was first developed and built in significant numbers. The elevator and the steel frame, fire proofed with terra-cotta tile, were essential ingredients of the skyscraper. The building form most readily identified with the Chicago School of architects (Louis Sullivan, Daniel H. Burnham, Elihu Root, and others) relied on a clear expression of the structural frame, which generally resulted in a generous fenestration of the facade. This window-wall opened the interior to daylight and thus enhanced the marketability of offices,

Beaux-Arts Classicism: Hibernia Bank

Chicago School: Mills Building

as well as commercial and industrial spaces. San Francisco buildings influenced by the Chicago School are sometimes embellished with the luxuriant ornament typical of Louis Sullivan's work, but sometimes they are stripped of all but the most rudimentary detail, depending on the budget as well as the function of the building.

CRAFTSMAN
or ARTS AND CRAFTS
1895-1920

Almost exclusively a residential mode, the American Craftsman style evolved from the English Arts and Crafts Movement. The style was strongly associated with the graphic designs and furnishings of William Morris and the architecture of M.H. Baillie Scott and Charles F. A. Voysey. The Craftsman magazine, published from 1901 to 1917, disseminated Craftsman ideas which reflected anti- industrialism in the promotion of natural materials and hand-crafted products.

Although the bungalow was the building type identified with the Craftsman style, in San Francisco, apartment complexes— compact versions of bungalow courts—are among the most effective examples of the style. Often sited on hillsides, these apartment complexes retain the boxy forms with low-pitched roofs grouped around courtyards.

The hallmarks of the Craftsman style are expressed structural elements such as rafter and beam ends and roof braces. These elements are often overscaled. Although wood was perhaps the most favored

Craftsman: 90 Cedro

material for exterior and interior, the shingles or varieties of board siding were often combined with stucco or brick— particularly the overfired, deformed kind called clinker brick. Combinations of stucco and brick were most typical of the apartment complexes. Porches, even if minimal, were important elements in the suburban bungalow.

MISSION REVIVAL
c 1890-1912

This style originated in California and spread across the country after 1900. Identifying elements were loosely derived from the California missions. These included stepped, scalloped or curved gable ends or parapets; exposed—usually false—beam ends; arched openings and arcades; and quatrefoil windows. The light-colored walls usually were stucco over a wood frame, although reinforced concrete was also typical of industrial and commercial buildings. Elements of the Mission Revival were frequently combined with the Craftsman style; the most common transplant was the curved gable form.

SPANISH COLONIAL
MEDITERRANEAN REVIVAL
c 1915-1941

California's Spanish Colonial heritage and affinities with the Mediterranean environment have been a continuing source of architectural imagery since around the turn of the century. The Mission Revival style gave way to a variety of Hispanic styles that ranged from the formality of the neo-Plateresque and neo-Churrigueresque to the informality of Andalusian farmhouses and California's own adobe buildings. Exoticism found expression in the use of Hispano-Moresque forms. The colonial town of Monterey was particularly influential because of its stand of adobe houses. Several of these had two stories and balconies—the most famous being the Larkin house—that inspired a sub-style called Monterey Colonial. Another sub-

Glossary of Styles

Mission Revival: 12 Jordan

style with southwestern origins was the Pueblo Revival. This had a more cubistic form than the Spanish Colonial style; also, raised parapets concealed a flat roof instead of a low-pitched tiled roof. In general these largely residential Hispanic buildings have stuccoed walls, deeply recessed openings, and exposed rafter and beam ends— sometimes carved. Balconies and terraces or patios provide a close indoor-outdoor relationship where the lot size permits. Ornamental ironwork and glazed tiles may be the only decoration; or elaborate foliate and geometric motifs drawn from the Plateresque and Churrigueresque styles may be used in friezes and panels cast in terra-cotta or plaster. Tiled domes often appear on large public buildings and churches.

PERIOD REVIVAL STYLES
1900-1980s

In addition to the Hispanic-Mediterranean revival styles, there were others inspired by northern European architecture such as the English Georgian, Tudor, and Regency, and the so-called French Provincial or Norman. Although these styles peaked in popularity during the 1920s, they are still being built today.

Another enduring style, which the renewed nationalism of the 1930s Depression era made fashionable, is the American Colonial adapted from neo-Georgian and Federal buildings of the Colonial period. Although these styles span more than a half-century, each decade had a slightly different version. In general, the stylistic references have become more attentuated over time with the rising cost of craftsmanship and materials. Thus a period revival house of the 1920s is readily distinguished from one of the 1930s, 1940s, or 1970s.

ART NOUVEAU
c 1900-c 1920

Although the sinuous forms of European Art Nouveau had only ripple effects in this country, it enjoyed a vogue in post-1906 San Francisco. The slopes of Nob Hill, rebuilt with apartment houses after the fire, are a good hunting ground for local variants of this style. It was favored by a few local architects, notably Cunningham & Politeo and James F. Dunn. (The latter produced about a dozen buildings that are

Period Revival: 898 Francisco

Mediterranean Revival: 140 Cedro

remarkable for their stylistic integrity, particularly for their integration of ornament and form.) Ornamental detail featuring the whip-lash or serpentine curve enriched with varieties of foliate forms is the hallmark of Art Nouveau along with a plastic or sculptural treatment of the facade.

ART DECO
MODERNE
1925-c 1940

Whereas the Art Nouveau had a relatively small influence on local architecture, the styles called Art Deco, Moderne, and Modernistic stamped a broad range of building types from houses to skyscrapers. The labels come from the 1925 Paris *Exposition Internationale des Arts Decoratifs et Industriels Modernes*, which was organized to promote works of "new inspiration" and "originality." The Exposition consciously broke with past

Art Deco: 3565 Scott

traditions, charting the future of design as a new, radically modern course. Essentially a decorative vocabulary, Art Deco motifs were applied in all categories of design. Low-relief geometric designs—parallel lines, chevrons, zig-zags, stylized vegetation, circles and other linear motifs—may have counterparts in the Classical vocabulary of ornament, but the intent was to break with tradition and to use other cultural sources such as Egyptian, Oriental, and Meso-American. In the 1930s, the idealization of the machine and the industrial process produced a style, now called the Streamlined Moderne, that attempted to apply, perversely, the curved aerodynamic forms developed for ocean liners and airplanes to stationary buildings. The hard-edged forms of the 1920s became soft and curvaceous in the 1930s.

The term Modernistic, which appeared frequently in the magazines of the times, is admittedly vague. But it was effective in describing a transitional style that could also be termed "stripped Classic" since it retained the symmetry and massing of the Classic Revival as well as the use of arches and columns—frequently pulled into the wall plane as pilasters or shallow piers. However, the rest of the Classical vocabulary forms—entablatures and cornices, for example—as well as the common motifs were stripped away or flattened and geometrized. During the 1930s Depression, the Public Works Administration built federal buildings across the country which employed this Modernistic mode, often called P.W.A. Moderne. Other public buildings followed suit.

Art Nouveau: 1347 McAllister

Glossary of Styles

INTERNATIONAL STYLE
1935-1942

Like Art Deco, the International Style takes its name from an exhibition, this one sponsored by the Museum of Modern Art in New York City in 1932. Though the exhibition was titled simply *Modern Architecture*, its organizers, Henry Russell Hitchcock and Philip Johnson, published a slim volume the same year titled *The International Style, Architecture Since 1922*, which identified Modern architecture with the European-born style associated with Le Corbusier, Mies van der Rohe, and Walter Gropius, among others. As the catalog stated, the exhibition announced the end of the stylistic "confusion of the past 40 years." Based on contemporary structural principles and materials, the International Style also drew on painting and sculpture of the Cubist and De Stijl schools for aesthetic refinement. Essential elements of the style were planar compositions that were balanced but studiously asymmetrical modular rhythms, the rejection of decoration, and the use of banded glazed areas—ribbon windows—that wrapped around corners and turned walls into compositions of solids and voids. Although the style rarely occurs in San Francisco in its pure form, modifications abound in both residential and non-residential design of the 1930s and 1940s.

CORPORATE INTERNATIONAL
BRUTALIST
1945-1980s

The post-World War II office tower is the major building type of this style which, like the European International Style, emphasized structural expression in contemporary materials: glass, steel, and concrete. The hallmark of the office tower of the 1950s and early 1960s was the metal panel and glass skin, called the curtain wall, that was hung on the building's structural frame. Subtle variations on this rectilinear glass and metal grid created what variety there was. In the 1960s, a reaction to the thinness and insubstantiality of the curtain-walled office towers caused

a substitution of materials, mainly unfinished concrete or *brut-concret* and a shift toward plasticity. Just as the curtain wall had originated in the 1920s projects of Ludwig Mies van der Rohe, the Brutalist style, as it was called, originated in the monumental, sculptural buildings by Le Corbusier such as the Unite d'Habitation (1947-52) in Marseilles and the government buildings in Chandigarh, India. In this country the work of Louis Kahn—beginning with the Yale University Art Gallery—was influential. As far as the office building was concerned, the rectangular volumes were often clad in high-relief, pre-cast concrete panels—3-D versions of the curtain wall. The association of Brutalist buildings with unfeeling and inhuman environments, although not part of the original coining of the term, is now the basis of the popular definition.

The office tower or high rise—current label for the skyscraper—of the late 1970s and 1980s is once more being packaged in thin metal and glass panels. But the expression of the 1950s and 1960s has changed from curtain to curved or angled skin, and faceted forms have replaced the former boxed volumes.

International Style: Howard house

Glossary of Styles

BAY TRADITION
1980

Although San Francisco architecture reflects national and even international stylistic currents, the special environmental qualities of the the San Francisco Bay Area have at times modified these influences sufficiently to warrant the creation of a category we call the Bay Tradition. This is not so much a style as an attitude toward designing for this region. The traits common to this tradition are the use of wood for exterior and interior finish, an appearance of informality tinged with anti-urbanism, and a sense that the building should be part and parcel of its site. The latter trait is of course much more dominant in rural suburban settings where landscaping plays a major role. Buildings of the Bay Tradition have a modesty—even an anonymity—that sets them apart from the more formal styles such as the range of Classic Revival styles. These buildings have an affinity with structures of the Craftsman style which also emphasized man's integration with nature.

There have been three waves or periods of Bay Tradition building. The architects who contributed to the first period—A. Page Brown, Ernest Coxhead, A. C. Schweinfurth, Willis Polk, John Galen Howard, Louis C. Mullgardt, and Bernard Maybeck—came to the Bay Area from the east around the turn of the century. Their work, particularly in the residential field, produced houses in a mode that both echoed what Vincent Scully has termed "the Shingle style," and also showed the strong influence of the English Arts and Crafts movement. Although these generally restrained houses resembled the city's vernacular buildings, they also incorporated Classical detail in often perverse ways. Quite correct—or academic—door and window architraves and cornices were sparingly applied to plain wooden boxes in a shorthand manner that is even whimsical. Shifts in spatial composition are also typical of the work of these architects. By World War I, this first wave had receded.

The second wave occurred in the decades before and after World War II. With the exception of William W. Wurster, a native son, the architects who contributed most to this period also came to San Francisco from other parts of the country. Among the dozen or so firms that participated in the work of this period are Wurster, Bernardi & Emmons, Henry Hill, Gardner Dailey, Francis Joseph McCarthy, John Ekin Dinwiddie, John Funk, Joseph Esherick, Howard Friedman, Campbell & Wong, Anshen & Allen, Clark & Beuttler, Mario Corbett, Charles Warren Callister, George Rockrise, Marquis & Stoller, and Henrik Bull. Important landscape architects were: Thomas Church, Lawrence Halprin, Garret Eckbo, Robert Roysten, and Douglas Baylis.

Although the principles of the European Modern Movement were influential, the residential work produced by these Bay region architects was kin to that of the first Bay Tradition period in its emphasis on wood and juxtaposition of formal and informal elements.

While the urban suburbs did not provide large enough lots for the full-blown ranch house—California's most popular post-war house type—with its wings and courts, an urban town house evolved that, in a way, was an up-dating of the town house designed by the first wave of architects. The works of the pre-war decade show a stronger European influence in the use of light-colored, cubistic forms. Over the decades, the houses acquired more rural-suburban traits: the use of shingles and board siding and a horizontal emphasis even in a two-story house. Courts and decks—no matter how impractical in windy, foggy San Francisco—became part of the plan. The clear-cut, unadorned geometry of the houses of this period is perhaps its strongest trait.

In the 1960s and 1970s, the low horizontal volumes gave way to vertical, cut-out forms, still sheathed in shingles or stucco. A number of apartment or condominium projects have been built in this increasingly taut form. Now the pendulum has swung from the informal to the formal. A contemporary version of the 1920s International Style is merging with the 1930s Streamlined Moderne to add yet another layer of stylistic nuance.

Glossary of Styles

Corporate International:
Crown Zellerbach Building

Bay Tradition: 301 Locust

Bay Tradition: 3236–40 Fillmore

BIBLIOGRAPHY

Abeloe, William N., Hoover, Mildred B., Rensch, H. E., and Rensch, E. G. *Historic Spots in California*. Palo Alto: Stanford University Press, 1966.

Blumenson, John J. G. *Identifying American Architecture: A Pictorial Guide to Styles and Terms, 1600-1945*. Nashville: American Association for State and Local History, 1967.

Bowden, Martyn John. *The Dynamics of City Growth: An Historical Geography of the San Francisco Central District 1850-1931*. Ph.D. Dissertation, University of California, Berkeley, 1967.

Brant, Michelle. *Timeless Walks in San Francisco*. 1977.

Clary, Raymond H. *The Making of Golden Gate Park: The Early Years, 1865-1906*. San Francisco: California Living Books, 1980.

Corbett, Michael R., Ed. *Splendid Survivors: San Francisco's Downtown Architectural Heritage*. San Francisco: California Living Books, 1979.

Delehanty, Randolph. *San Francisco: Walks and Tours in the Golden Gate City*. New York: The Dial Press, 1980.

Doss, Margot Patterson. *Golden Gate Park at Your Feet*. San Francisco: Chronicle Books, 1970.

——. *San Francisco at Your Feet*. New York: Grove Press, 1964.

Gebhard, David, et al. *A Guide to Architecture in San Francisco and Northern California*. Salt Lake City: Peregrine Smith, 1973.

Olmsted, Roger, and Watkins, T. H. *Here Today: San Francisco's Architectural Heritage*. San Francisco: Chronicle Books, 1968.

Scott, Mel. *The San Francisco Bay Area: A Metropolis in Perspective*. Berkeley: University of California Press, 1959.

Watkins, T. H., and Olmsted, R. R. *Mirror of the Dream*. San Francisco: Scrimshaw Press, 1976.

Waldhorn, Judith Lynch, and Woodbridge, Sally B. *Victoria's Legacy*. San Francisco: 101 Productions, 1978.

Woodbridge, John M., and Woodbridge, Sally B. *A Guide to the Architecture of the San Francisco Bay Region*. New York: Grove Press, 1960.

Woodbridge, Sally B., Ed. *Bay Area Houses*. New York: Oxford University Press, 1976.

Index of Architects & Builders

Index